ADOLESCENCE

ADOLESCENCE
Growing Up in America Today

Joy G. Dryfoos *and* Carol Barkin

OXFORD
UNIVERSITY PRESS
2006

OXFORD
UNIVERSITY PRESS

Oxford University Press, Inc., publishes works that further
Oxford University's objective of excellence
in research, scholarship, and education.

Oxford   New York
Auckland   Cape Town   Dar es Salaam   Hong Kong   Karachi
Kuala Lumpur   Madrid   Melbourne   Mexico City   Nairobi
New Delhi   Shanghai   Taipei   Toronto

With offices in
Argentina   Austria   Brazil   Chile   Czech Republic   France   Greece
Guatemala   Hungary   Italy   Japan   Poland   Portugal   Singapore
South Korea   Switzerland   Thailand   Turkey   Ukraine   Vietnam

Published by Oxford University Press, Inc.
198 Madison Avenue, New York, New York 10016

www.oup.com

Library of Congress Cataloging-in-Publication Data
Dryfoos, Joy G.
Adolescence : growing up in America today / by Joy G. Dryfoos and Carol Barkin.
p. cm.
Includes bibliographical references and index.
ISBN-13 978-0-19-517961-3
ISBN 0-19-517961-7
1. Teenagers with social disabilities—United States.   2. Teenagers with social
disabilities—Services for—United States.   3. Teenagers—United States—Social
conditions—21st century.   I. Barkin, Carol.   II. Title
HV1431.D793   2007
362.7083'0973—dc22   2005030995

1 2 3 4 5 6 7 8 9

Printed in the United States of America
on acid-free paper

ACKNOWLEDGMENTS

This book is based on the collective work of hundreds of practitioners, researchers, policy analysts, and youth advocates from around this country and around the world. It builds upon many years of exposure to the worlds of teen life, risk prevention, youth development, educational leadership, and social policy. Obviously, I cannot name all those to whom I am indebted, although many are cited in the references.

An important member of my research team was Katie Tobin, who gathered and synthesized program information for the chapters about sex, violence, and drugs (Chapters 3–5). I also wish to acknowledge the specific contributions of Jodie Elgee, Richard Jessor, Betsey McGee, Dan Restucchio, Amy Rodgers-Dryfoos, Carol Schoen, Mark Skivorsky, Martin Sleeper, and Margot Strom, all of whom supplied important information and contacts for the work on this volume. The William T. Grant Foundation funded the first year of the research and writing.

Oxford University Press has played a major role in the production of this book. Joan Bossert, Vice-President and Associate Publisher, encouraged me from the beginning to pursue again the subject of adolescence. Jennifer Rappaport, Associate Editor, took on the task of editor and "hand-holder" through the long process of production.

The photos in this book were produced by the Photo Project, which was conducted at the Driscoll School in Brookline, Massachusetts, in 2005. In the Photo Project, 8th graders at the school were invited to participate in an after-school activity in which they would review the main points of this volume, suggest scenarios for each chapter, pose for the pictures, and take the pictures. The photographic expertise was provided by Pia Schachter, a renowned photographer and mother of one of the students, who instructed the students in photographic techniques and provided the camera and lighting for the project. The students who participated include: Chris Andrews, Taya Beattie, Dakotah Benson, Nathaniel Brown, Winston Chen, Sarah Coleman, Genevieve Greene, Samsun Knight, Nicholas McGee, Pamela Moy, Christian Nolte, Laurent Plaisimond, Julia Randle, Amy Rodgers-Dryfoos, Lucy Schachter, Eliza States, Jonathon Stevens, Rafael Toledo, Heather White, and Sarah Whitcher. The pictures were taken by Nathaniel Brown, Genevieve Greene, Pamela Moy, Christian Nolte, Lucy Schachter, and Eliza States.

Carol Schraft, principal of the Driscoll School, facilitated and supported the Photo Project's implementation and has been a source of inspiration for this effort. The Brookline Community Foundation supported the project with a grant to the Parent Teacher Organization.

My colleague and friend Carol Barkin helped me turn a messy manuscript into readable prose. Her consistent and intelligent feedback greatly enhanced the whole process.

Finally, I wish to acknowledge the strong support and loving care I have received from Cindy Rodgers-Dryfoos and Paul Dryfoos. They have enriched my life with their attention to my needs and by allowing me to participate in their lives.

This book is dedicated to Amy and Rose Rodgers-Dryfoos, my beautiful, charming, and intelligent granddaughters. Watching them navigate their way through the vagaries of early adolescence has been a rare treat and an inspiration. I know that they will grow up to be strong and responsible adults.

—Joy Dryfoos
Brookline, Massachusetts

Working on this book with Joy Dryfoos has been both inspiring and awe-inspiring. As in all of our joint projects, I have learned so much and have been energized by the give and take of the collaborative process. I hope readers will feel as invigorated and challenged as I was while working on this book.

As always, my deepest thanks go to Spike and David Barkin, whose loving support gives me strength and courage.

—Carol Barkin
Hastings-on-Hudson, New York

CONTENTS

ADOLESCENCE

CHAPTER ONE

WHY LOOK AT TEENS
IN THE 21ST CENTURY?

I (JD) was very pleased when my publisher invited me to write an update of *Adolescents at Risk: Prevalence and Prevention,* which was published in 1990. But it took me a long time to get started, and eventually I realized that I didn't really want to replicate that book. Instead, I wanted to approach the issues surrounding American adolescence from a different perspective. It seemed urgent to break out of academia and incorporate my own experience, along with that of many others, into a manifesto that would command attention and move people to change the way we deal with these critical issues.

The more I worked on this book, the madder I got. Millions of kids are in terrible trouble. Huge numbers are depressed and stressed out, and they have few sources of support and nurturing. They go to substandard schools, sit in overcrowded classes, and are taught by overworked teachers. Too many young people never graduate from high school, especially if they are African American, Hispanic, or Native American. Without a diploma, they have little access to the labor market, and many young people drift into crime and end up in jail. They also drift at early ages into casual sexual arrangements; "making out" may begin with oral sex bestowed on boys by naive girls who are seeking popularity, and too often it leads to teenage pregnancy and parenthood.

There is no point in hiding my biases. I am an unreconstructed "liberal." I believe in government intervention. I believe in taxes. I would bend over backward to protect the right to free speech. And at this moment, I live in a country in which these views are not popular with the people in power. Every day I feel as though more of our rights are threatened, including the right to a fair trial in front of an unbiased judge, the right to go bankrupt, the right to have access to abortion, the right to receive Social Security as it is now constituted, and the right of my grandchildren to learn scientific truths about evolution.

What kind of society are we creating for young people to grow up in in the years to come? Are we making choices now that will greatly affect future generations?

Obviously I believe that the quality of life now and in the future can be improved. I am not only a "liberal," I am an activist. People can effect change. In fact, the key ingredient in social change is people, the doers who are willing to commit themselves to helping others advance in the society. So in this book my intention is to document the current status of youth and to suggest improvements that can be made in both programs and policies. I also want to show the high cost of doing nothing to buck the trends and allowing millions of young people to go down the drain. If they don't succeed, neither will the society. And I won't want to live in a country that is increasingly dangerous, culturally vacuous, and segregated by social class, income, and color.

In this book I want to communicate with a broad spectrum of readers—academics and students, certainly, but also parents, politicians, media professionals, youth workers, voters, and, of course, adolescents themselves. In some places, I have written in the first person to present my thoughts, and I have incorporated the ideas of some of my most trusted advisors, including my 13- and 11-year-old granddaughters and my close friends and colleagues with whom I discuss the issues we care about so deeply.

When I completed the original *Adolescents at Risk* (*AAR*) in 1990, I was certain that we knew what to do to ensure that adolescents could grow into responsible adults. Now, my review of this field over the 15 years since the publication of *AAR* has convinced me that we haven't learned much that is new. I am troubled by the question this raises: If we already know what to do, why isn't it being done? Early intervention is a good example of what I mean. We know that young children who are talked to, played with, nurtured, read to, and otherwise stimulated enter school with a huge advantage over those who have not had these experiences. And as they mature into adolescents, they are much more likely to succeed. Yet despite all the research that proves this to be true, such rich preschool environments are not available to the children who need them most, and new efforts emerge every year to cut the funding of programs like Head Start. In so many areas we know some things that work or have promise, yet little or nothing has been done to implement them.

Perhaps even more important, we know what doesn't work. Myths, wishful thinking, and cynical slogans govern much of our approach to teenagers in the United States. For instance, it has been shown that marijuana use does not inevitably lead to addiction or to use of hard drugs, yet this myth is used to rationalize harshly punitive laws mandating jail time. Another myth, that abstinence in sexual behavior can be taught in school and that it is the only effective method of preventing teenage pregnancy, has been demonstrated to be untrue. It's easy to speculate about why adults want or need to believe such myths, but meanwhile teenagers are being deprived of the approaches that can actually make a difference.

HOW I GOT TO WHERE I AM

For those who are unfamiliar with my work on adolescents, I would like to tell you how I got to this place. For many years, I have been interested in the broad subject of adolescent development, starting with prevention of teen pregnancy and, over the years, broadening my scope to include high-risk behaviors in

general. I started my career in 1968 at the advanced age of 43 as the Director of
Research and Planning at the Alan Guttmacher Institute, a leading think tank
and advocacy group in the field of reproductive health care. Our efforts helped
launch the federal family planning program and brought attention to the issue
of teenage pregnancy. One of our most widely distributed publications was *11
Million Teenagers: What Can Be Done About the Epidemic of Adolescent Pregnancies in the United States.*[1] As we pointed out, pregnancy among teenagers in
1975 was almost as prevalent as the common cold, and, increasingly, those who
were getting pregnant were young, white, and middle class. We estimated that
1 million pregnancies were being experienced by females ages 15–19 and that 1
in 10 female adolescents were conceiving each year. More than two-thirds of
these pregnancies were unintended, and about 27% were terminated by in-
duced abortion.

The million teen pregnancies became a call to action. We urged the nation
to offer universal sex education and access to contraception for sexually active
young people, along with quality reproductive health care and availability of
safe and legal abortions.

By the early 1980s, I began to understand that the problem of teenage child-
bearing was not going to go away without new approaches that would go beyond those being offered by the reproductive health care field. Further study of
the target population convinced me that we were missing something. A strong
message was delivered to me at a conference on teen pregnancy in Florida. The
luncheon speaker was a very pregnant black 13-year-old child who described
her plight to the mostly white audience: "I was just standin' there leanin'
against a fence when he came along and stuck his thing in me . . . and later I
found out I was goin' to have a baby." How could this be? Why did this happen?
This girl's script was probably written early on—poorly educated, low expectations, and unlucky. What would it have taken to prevent this pregnancy from
occurring?

More than sex education and contraception. What she lacked was what I
called "life options." For many young people, choices are limited. They live
outside of the "opportunity structure"; they do not have parents who program
them to succeed; they do not go to schools that expect them to succeed; and
they have very low expectations for their own futures. I developed what I called
the "life options hypothesis": In order to avoid early parenthood, young people
need individual attention from caring adults, high-quality schools, and healthy

communities, in addition to access to reproductive health care. Given this conviction, it was clearly time for me to move on from the significant but narrow scope of the Alan Guttmacher Institute.

Two weeks after I left in 1981, I sat on a commuter train to New York City next to a casual acquaintance who worked at the Rockefeller Foundation. As we talked, she confided that the foundation didn't know what to do about the problem of teenage pregnancy. By the end of our brief encounter, I was assured a grant to further explore the life options hypothesis. At that time, schools did not figure as a central delivery mechanism for the kinds of programs I thought necessary, though community health clinics and community-based organizations did. However, the Rockefeller Foundation suggested that as part of my work, I investigate a new type of intervention: a school-based primary health care clinic.

The first such model I visited was in Lanier High School in Jackson, Mississippi. There I observed a fully equipped clinic staffed by a white-capped registered nurse practitioner. Students were pouring into the space and receiving primary health care, including sports examinations, pregnancy tests, asthma treatments, and whatever else they required. A room was set aside for sex education and individual counseling, and a mobile unit housing a child-care center was attached to the school for the use of teen parents. This made so much sense. The students were there. They needed help and received it with little fuss, complete confidentiality, and no bureaucracy. All the school had to do was facilitate access to the clinic.

It is interesting to note that this clinic had been initiated in 1979 by Dr. Aaron Shirley, then director of the Community Health Center in Jackson, one of the first African Americans to graduate from the University of Mississippi's medical school and a leader in the struggle for adequate medical care for impoverished families and children. He had received a grant from the Mississippi Department of Health that enabled the Community Health Center to open the clinic in the very same high school he had attended as a teenager.

Within the next year, I discovered 10 such school-based clinic programs around the country (there are more than 1,500 today). A new field was emerging, and so was I. The concept of school-based health care opened up a new possibility for comprehensive programming, and I began to see the connection between adequate health care and educational achievement. I wrote an extensive report to the Rockefeller Foundation spelling out the life options hypothesis and followed up with many published articles and presentations at conferences. In the mid-1980s, the Carnegie Corporation became interested in my work, and it supported my research and writing for the next 20 years.

As I pursued the issue of adolescent behavior, I began to focus on two overarching questions:

1. If unprotected sex among teenagers resulted from the lack of life options, was this also true of other high-risk behaviors such as substance abuse, delinquency, and school dropout?
2. If programs to prevent teen pregnancy were more successful when they were more comprehensive, was this also true of other prevention programs?

It took more than 4 years to answer these questions. I discovered a vast world of youth surveys, each covering different subjects, geographic areas, and age groups. Prevention programs were organized categorically (by problem), and the art of program evaluation was in its early stages. In 1990, all the information I had gathered was put together into *Adolescents at Risk: Prevalence and Prevention.*[2]

My major findings at that time were that a definable number of young people—7 million, or about 25% of 10- to 17-year-olds—were most at risk; that problem behaviors, no matter what they were, stemmed from similar antecedents; that successful categorical prevention programs had similar components, no matter what problem they were trying to address; and that in order for adolescents to make it, they needed powerful, sustained, comprehensive interventions.

PUTTING SCHOOLS INTO THE PICTURE

You will not be surprised to learn that schools emerged as important players in the lives of young people. But up until that point, I had perceived them as a locus for programs and not necessarily as a prevention mechanism. Around this time, I encountered a new batch of comprehensive school-based programs largely stimulated by state governments. New Jersey's Department of Welfare was way ahead of the nation with its School-Based Youth Services Program, starting in

1987. Florida launched Full Service Schools in 1991 with the goal of enhancing the capacity of comprehensive school health services to prevent teen pregnancy, AIDS, and other sexually transmitted diseases. In 1991, the California legislature came up with the large-scale Healthy Start Support Services for Children Act, which brought health and social services to hundreds of schools. These initiatives became the next stage in my research. A whole wave of support services was beginning to be provided in schools by outside providers, usually with support from state departments of welfare or health (not education).

By 1994, I had enough material to produce *Full-Service Schools: A Revolution in Health and Social Services.*[3] In collecting examples of school-based services, I came across the Children's Aid Society (CAS) community schools; in 1992, CAS had opened the first of its "settlement house in the school" models, the Salome Ureña Middle School (IS 218) in the Washington Heights area of New York City. At first I thought of it only as a good example of a full-service school and described it as such in my book, along with the Hancock Middle School in Modesto, California, a Healthy Start model. But as I observed the CAS school, I saw how the effort extended beyond the "add-on" quality of many school-based services around the country. Rather, the CAS approach was aimed at school transformation and reform, the creation of a full-fledged community school. The CAS model included a primary health clinic (where I had started on this investigation), but it had so much more.

Focusing on the Salome Ureña Middle School, I became aware of how a whole new school had been created to center around the needs of the students. The school was divided into academies, creating smaller, more cohesive learning units and encouraging intensive study in specialized areas (math and science, arts, business, and community service). What went on in the classroom was linked to after-school activities to produce a holistic experience for the children. Parents were drawn in through a resource center and exposed to their children's school experience as well. And community well-being was another value that CAS brought to the school, opening the doors of the schoolhouse to all residents and maintaining an interest in neighborhood improvement.

As my consciousness was raised about community schools being more than full-service schools, I discovered other initiatives whose intent was to transform the whole school. This exploration led to another book, *Safe Passage: Making It Through Adolescence in a Risky Society,*[4] published in 1998. Once again, I reviewed the existing practices in prevention of high-risk behaviors, but in this iteration, I focused much more on the role of schools in changing the outcomes for young people. I concluded that the fields of educational enrichment and youth development services had to be joined in marriage. For the first time, I could lay out my own vision of what I called a "Safe Passage" school, one that combined quality education with all the necessary support services to help children and families overcome the barriers to successful learning. It is important to recognize that these were not totally new ideas. A century ago, John Dewey and Jane Addams were talking about the same concepts. And in 1935, the Mott Foundation in Flint, Michigan, launched the Community Education movement, opening schoolhouses across the country to adult and community education and, later, to after-school programs.

By the time *Safe Passage* was published, a number of important "players" had come forward who shared this emerging vision of community schools. Clearly the folks from the Children's Aid Society were potential leaders, as were those from other school/community partnership models around the country; these included the University of Pennsylvania's Center for Community Partnerships (university-assisted community schools), Beacons (lighted schoolhouses), and United Way's Bridges to Success. Under the auspices of the Center for School Community Partnerships at Fordham University's School of Social Work, we organized an ad hoc gathering of community school advocates from around the country in 1998 and were pleased at the evidence of growing interest. It should be noted that most of the attendees were from fields other than education, such as social work (note the auspices), mental health, youth development, and philanthropy. We were still missing significant support from the education field.

The Institute for Educational Leadership in Washington indicated an interest in helping us organize an advocacy group. Martin Blank took on the role of executive director of what was first called the Emerging Coalition for Community Schools (CCS). By the end of 2000, "emerging" was dropped from the title, and today CCS is flourishing. More than 170 national organizations have become partners in this movement, including major educational groups such as the Council of Chief State School Officers, National Association of School Principals, National Education Association, American Federation of Teachers, and other groups representing youth and community development, family support, national and state government, local community school networks, policy and advocacy, and philanthropy.

One day I received a phone call from Sue Maguire, then principal of the

Molly Stark School in Bennington, Vermont. She said that she had just read *Safe Passage* and was "doing all of that." I visited the school and observed that she had opened it up for extended hours and brought in a wide array of services and supportive people. It was her idea to document her model and update the field in a book. Together we wrote *Inside Full-Service Community Schools*,[5] which was published in 2002. Sue provided a detailed, hands-on description of how she accumulated the components that went into her school, and I expanded on those points, bringing in the national experience. Shortly thereafter, Sue was invited to become the principal of the local high school (Mount Anthony) and is in the process of transforming it into a full-service high school.

As I became involved in analyzing community schools, I got to know Jane Quinn, Director of Community Schools at the Children's Aid Society in New York. We recently documented CAS's community school work in a coedited volume, *Community Schools in Action: Lessons From a Decade of Practice*.[6] Carol Barkin was our third partner, a writer and editor who has been an invaluable member of my team for some years. This book describes selected program components of community schools, based on the experience of the diverse people who make it happen in 10 schools in New York City. It explains how and why CAS started this initiative and how community schools are organized, integrated with the school system, sustained, and evaluated; it also presents the work of the CAS National Technical Assistance Center in hundreds of sites in the United States and around the world. Contributions from experts outside of CAS—a city superintendent, an architect, and the director of the Coalition for Community Schools—fill in the picture. Jane and I provided commentary to connect the various components and illuminate the central ideas. We put together this book for those interested in transforming their schools into effective child- and family-centered institutions and for those concerned with educational and social policy.

FINDING THE RIGHT PATH FOR ADOLESCENTS

As you can see, for the past decade, most of my own efforts have been focused on full-service community schools. As I mentioned earlier, I was surprised and delighted when Joan Bossert, vice president of Oxford University Press and my former editor, called to ask if I would be willing to update *Adolescents at Risk*. I knew that over the years, many friends and colleagues had moved ahead in working with adolescents and creating a rich new field of youth development. In a sense, they have questioned my concentration on "problem behavior," proposing that one should start with "wellness" rather than "pathology." "Problem-free is not fully prepared," a phrase coined by Karen Pittman, executive director of the Forum for Youth Investment, is the new battle cry.[7] According to Pittman and others, it is not enough to define youth outcomes as the absence of problems; one must also consider the presence of assets such as vocational readiness, social and emotional health, physical health, civic engagement, and educational attainment. In my view, in looking at the subject of youth development, we have to consider the whole society—the family, the school, the community, and the environment.

In this book, I want to set the stage for developing and implementing sound policies for American youth in the twenty-first century. It begins with basic data about drugs, sex, and violence and about health, mental health, and education. For each of these domains, I've looked at the facts and statistics we actually know, as opposed to the "accepted wisdom" and what people think they know. Working from this factual base, I've suggested the main elements of the problem that must be considered. Then, building on the labors of Katie Tobin, my research associate, I've presented brief portraits of selected programs that have been shown to be effective and analyzed the common strands that run through all of them. The last part of the book is devoted to two scenarios: first, a worst-case scenario based on our view of some negative trends in the United States; and then, a rosier picture of what life could be like for American teenagers in the future, the best case built on our knowledge of what works.

As we enter this discussion of the lives of American teenagers, a couple of essential concepts emerge. First, *diversity* must be taken seriously. We are a rapidly changing country, with increasingly different people from a vast array of backgrounds. If we are to create a healthy environment in which our young people can mature into responsible adults, we have to pay attention to the growing number of cultural, social, and language streams and view them as assets rather than liabilities. Another concept is *intensity*. If we are to have any hope of competing with the rest of the world, our young people will have to have the opportunity to study longer, harder, and better. I know that we can find the right path, but not without a lot of effort.

NOTES

1. Alan Guttmacher Institute. *11 Million Teenagers: What Can Be Done About the Epidemic of Adolescent Pregnancies in the United States* (New York: Alan Guttmacher Institute, 1976).

2. Joy Dryfoos, *Adolescents at Risk: Prevalence and Prevention* (New York: Oxford University Press, 1990).

3. Joy Dryfoos, *Full-Service Schools: A Revolution in Health and Social Services* (San Francisco: Jossey-Bass, 1994).

4. Joy Dryfoos, *Safe Passage: Making It Through Adolescence in a Risky Society* (New York: Oxford University Press, 1998).

5. Joy Dryfoos & Sue Maguire, *Inside Full-Service Community Schools* (Thousand Oaks, CA: Corwin Press, 2002).

6. Joy Dryfoos, Jane Quinn, and Carol Barkin, *Community Schools in Action: Lessons From a Decade of Practice* (New York: Oxford University Press, 2005).

7. Forum for Youth Investment, "Health and Youth Development: Connecting the Dots" *Forum Focus* 3, no. 2 (2005), http://www.forumfyi.org/files/forumfocus_may.june2005.pdf.

STATUS OF YOUTH TODAY

In the first decade of the twenty-first century, our country is in a complex transition. On the one hand, a conservative white-dominated autocracy promotes abstinence and religious observance as the teenage ideal; on the other hand, growing diversity in an articulate minority presses for nontraditional transformations of schools and social institutions. I don't really know what this looks like to the average teenager, if there is such a person. In this book I present as unbiased an account as I can of where teenagers are and how we can help them cope with the usual problems they confront. We will go beyond drugs, sex, and violence and dig into education, health and mental health, and quality of life. But before we get into those issues, we need to review some basic information about population, families, and social status.

Because we have relied on a great variety of data sources, our "facts" describe different age groups, racial breakdowns, and years. Mainly, we are interested in 10- to 17-year-olds, but few studies oblige, so sometimes we present results for ages 15–19 or for 9th through 12th grades. In tables by race and ethnicity, sometimes whites include white Hispanics, and other times they are specifically categorized as white non-Hispanics. The years range from 2000 to 2005.

Because we are interested in trends, we generally make comparisons with 1986, the year for which data were presented in *Adolescents at Risk (AAR)*.

MAJOR TRENDS

- More than 33.5 million 10- to 17-year-olds make up almost 12% of the population.
- The teen population is growing larger, fed by immigration.
- The fastest growing group is Hispanic.
- By midcentury, more than half of all teens will be nonwhite.
- Less than two-thirds of teens live with both parents.
- At least 15% of teens' families live in poverty.

POPULATION

More than 33.5 million 10- to 17-year-olds lived in the United States in 2003. This figure represents a 20% increase from almost 28 million in 1986. The younger age group, ages 10–14 (21.2 million), increased by 26%; the group ages 15–17 (12.3 million) increased by only 10%.

Much of the change in population can be attributed to immigration. The birth rate in the United States has been declining since the 1960s, reaching a new low in 2001 (the beginning of the twenty-first century) of about 14 births per 1,000 population of childbearing age. When those who were 10–17 years old in 2004 were born (1987–1994), birth rates were already coming down.

Some 16% of school-age children (ages 5–17) have immigrant mothers, so that almost 9 million students fall into the category of immigrants. The children of immigrants account for such a large percentage of the school-age population because a high proportion of immigrant women are in their child-bearing years and immigrants tend to have more children than natives. The effect of immigration on public schools will be even larger in the coming years because 18% of children approaching school age have immigrant mothers.[1]

The U.S. Census Bureau changed its methodology for defining race and ethnicity in 2000, making it a little more difficult to understand the trends. Individuals were allowed to report themselves as being of "two or more races," but we don't know what races these were. Separate tabulations were made for Hispanics or Latinos, who may be either black or white. Looking at the actual numbers reported in 2003 on Table 2.1 for 33.5 million 10- to 17-year-olds by race, 25.7 million were white, 5.3 million black, 1.2 million Asian, and 1.3 million others, including American Indians, Alaskan natives, Hawaiians, and those reporting two or more races (a growing group). Thus, 77% were white, 16% black, 4% Asian, and 4% others. About 5.6 million Hispanic teens, who may be counted as either black or white, made up about 17% of the teen population.

In light of the enormous impact of immigration, it is not surprising that the most significant population changes took place among Hispanic youths. The number of younger Hispanics doubled since 1986; in contrast, the number of white teenagers increased by 15%, and the number of black teens grew by 22%, not a huge difference.

Table 2.1 Population Ages 10–17 by Race and Hispanic Origin, 2003

Race/Origin	Number Ages 10–17 (in thousands)	Percent of Total
Total	33,519	100.0
White	25,703	76.7
Black	5,254	15.7
American Indian, Alaskan	428	1.3
Asian	1,228	3.7
Native Hawaiian, Pacific	71	0.2
Two or more races	761	2.3
Hispanic or Latino origin (may be black or white)	5,601	16.7

Source: U.S. Bureau of the Census, *Statistical Abstract of the United States 2004–2005: The National Data Book* (Washington, DC: The Bureau, 2004), Table 15.

Table 2.2 Population Projections for 14- to 17-Year-Olds by Race and Hispanic Origin (in thousands)

Year	White Non-Hispanic	Black	Hispanic	Total (not including others)	% of Total Black	% of Total Hispanic
2000	10,444	2,414	2,179	15,037	16	14
2020	9,465	2,910	3,490	15,865	18	22
2050	9,386	3,887	6,202	19,475	20	32

Source: U.S. Bureau of the Census, "Current Population Reports: Population Projections of the United States by Age, Sex, Race, and Hispanic Origin, 1995–2050," http://www.census.gov/prod/1/pop/p25-1130/p251130b.pdf.

The most dramatic change projected for the future is the further growth in the Hispanic population. By 2020, only about 15 years from the date of this writing, fully 40% of 14- to 17-year-olds will be black or Hispanic, and by 2050, more than half of all teenagers will be black or of Hispanic origin (Table 2.2). The increase among Hispanic teenagers will be much more dramatic than that among blacks; the projected growth rate between the years 2000 and 2050 is 185%, compared with a rate of 61% for blacks. Among non-Hispanic whites, the population is projected to decline by 10% by 2050, reflecting a decreasing birth rate.

Mobility

About 14% of all teenagers moved during the year 2002–2003.[2] This means that about 4.6 million young people were in different houses than they had been in the previous year and probably also in different school districts. About 40% moved to different counties.

WITH WHOM DO TEENAGERS LIVE?

Family Structure

Only two-thirds of U.S. 12- to 17-year-olds in 2002 lived in two-parent families. It is estimated that the remaining one-third (almost 11 million teenagers, or 33% of 33 million) lived in single-parent homes. Some 17% of the total lived with mothers who had been previously married, and 6% lived with mothers who had never been married.[3] Another 5% lived with their fathers, and 5% lived with neither parent. Black children were much more likely to live with their mothers only (48%) than Hispanic children (25%) or non-Hispanic white children (16%). More than 230,000 12- to 17-year-olds lived in group quarters, such as hospitals, orphan asylums, or detention facilities.

In about 69% of all married-couple families with children ages 6–17, both parents worked outside the home. In 71% of single-mother families and 85% of single-father families, the parent was working. According to one study, on the average, children were "on their own" 20–25 hours a week.[4] Another study found that 8th graders who cared for themselves 11 or more hours per week were twice as likely to use drugs as those who were always supervised.[5]

Teenagers in Foster Care

In 2001, more than half a million children were in foster care, and 45% of them (247,000) were ages 11–18.[6] Many children entering foster care have acute, chronic, disabling, or potentially life-threatening conditions. More than three-fourths of teenagers screened on foster care entry in Baltimore needed mental health referrals, and more than 12% of those entering in San Francisco tested positive for tuberculosis. Every year, large numbers of young people age 16 and over leave foster care. They often are expected to live independently; most states stop providing housing, medical care, and other services once foster care youths reach age 18.

POVERTY

In 2002, about 15% of all 10- to 17-year-olds lived in families who fell below the poverty line. This represents almost 5 million youngsters, an increase since 1986, when about 4.5 million were in poverty. Black and Hispanic young people had more than three times the poverty rate of non-Hispanic whites. For blacks the rate was 29%, for Hispanics 27%, for non-Hispanic whites about 8%, and for Asians 13%. Children living in immigrant families were much more likely to be poor than those in U.S.-born families (21% versus 14%).

Another way of viewing economic status is to measure the "net worth" of a family. This includes the values of items such as a home and car, savings accounts, and stocks, minus such debts as mortgages, loans, and credit card bills. Between 1996 and 2002, black families lost net worth and had lower levels of net worth than Hispanics. The white level was 15 times the black level and 11 times the Hispanic level. In 2002, nearly one-third of black families and 26% of Hispanics were in debt and had no assets, compared with 11% of white families. According to Robert Suro, director of the Pew Hispanic Center, "the accumulation of wealth allows low-income families to rise into the middle class . . . and to ride out the jobless recovery better."[7] White families are much more likely to own houses and to make investments.

This measure of net worth gives powerful evidence of the differential in financial support for children in nonwhite and Hispanic families. College education is unlikely for such children, as are expensive private after-school activities such as music lessons, SAT prep courses, tennis, and gymnastics.

RURAL YOUTH

Young people in rural areas are better off on some measures than their urban counterparts but worse off with regard to family economic security.[8] Higher percentages of rural adolescents are in poverty (16% urban versus 20% rural). Death rates are much higher: 87 per 100,000 15- to 19-year-olds compared with 62 per 100,000 in urban areas, a difference that is related to the higher risk of fatal car accidents on rural roads.

DISCONNECTED YOUTHS

Disconnected teens include high school dropouts, young parents, and juvenile offenders.[9] In 2003, 8% of 16- to 19-year-olds—about 1.4 million—were not in school and not holding jobs (6% of whites in this age group and 12% of both blacks and Hispanics). Among those ages 18–19, the figures are truly disturbing: 10% of whites, 23% of blacks, and 20% of Hispanics. Some of these are probably among the young people, mostly males, who hang out on street corners, often in the company of older men who are drinking and asking for handouts. Andrew Hahn, an expert on youth employment, estimated that more than 5 million 16- to 24-year-olds (15%) were disconnected from both school and work, more than half of them *permanently*.[10]

One cause of this disconnection is that more students are leaving high school after failing to pass the new high-stakes tests required for a diploma. Other causes may be teen pregnancy, with more than 850,000 teen mothers struggling to complete school, and juvenile crime, with offenders who never return to school after incarceration.

Hahn issues a call for large-scale programs, including alternative education options and special efforts for homeless teens and those aging out of foster care. He cites several examples of collaborations between schools, police, churches, and community-based organizations and "one-stop" centers that have successfully addressed the problem. But federally funded programs of this sort probably reach no more than 120,000 young people, just 4% of those who need them. And, at this time, whatever progress has been made is stalled in its tracks by budget cuts in the U.S. Department of Labor (see Chapter 8 for more on work).

WHAT ARE TEENAGERS DOING?

We know quite a lot about what adolescents are doing (or at least we think we do). We have access to significant amounts of data over an extended period of time from many different sources.

- The United States Census takes place every decade, and the Census Bureau also conducts annual surveys on population, social, and economic trends.
- The Centers for Disease Control and Prevention (CDC) has been fielding the Youth Risk Behavior Survey (YRBS) of 9th through 12th graders biannually since 1991.
- The Substance Abuse and Mental Health Services Administration (SAMHSA) sponsors an annual National Survey on Drug Use and Health that includes Americans age 12 and over.
- The National Institute on Drug Abuse supports the Monitoring the Future (MTF) study of 8th, 10th, and 12th graders, conducted annually since 1975 by the University of Michigan's Institute for Social Research.

- The National Longitudinal Survey of Adolescent Health (Add Health) was designed and fielded by Richard Udry at the University of North Carolina in the mid-1990s. In 2002 the sample was revisited.

Our knowledge of the prevalence of and trends in "high-risk behaviors" is based largely on the YRBS, a survey conducted every 2 years by the CDC of a scientifically selected sample of high school students. Data are collected for the nation, 32 states, and 28 large cities. In 2003, 15,213 questionnaires were completed by students in 9th through 12th grades. Parental permission was obtained, student participation was voluntary, and responses were anonymous.

RESEARCH HAS CHANGED

When I (JD) was writing *AAR* in the late 1980s, almost two decades ago, I did not have a computer or e-mail. With the aid of an assistant, I followed references in journals to other journals, found what I could in the local library, and typically had to contact by mail or telephone each "guru" whose program I was trying to track. Google has changed my life. I can look up phrases such as "overlap high-risk behaviors 2004" and find 46,900 references listed. For "teen violence prevention programs," there are 399,000 references, and for "teen pregnancy prevention programs," 833,000 references. The Internet provides access to thousands of articles, reports, and commentaries that I can just download with no further effort (except reading them!). However, I can waste many hours going through meaningless references and articles that are inaccurate, biased, or just not on the subject. Also, much of what is being published today is "dense"; I don't really understand the arcane statistical tests that produce obscure findings that may or may not really be significant. In this book I have tried to select meaningful and important data and present the facts so that the reader can understand them and find them useful.

DEFINING HIGH-RISK BEHAVIOR

The next three chapters look at the high-risk behavior trio—drugs, sex, and violence—to see who does what, how those actions affect them, what policies control interventions and regulations, and what programs are in place to prevent such behavior. The term "health risk behaviors" has been defined as "volitional involvement in established patterns of behavior that threaten the well-being of teens and limit their potential for achieving responsible adulthood."[11] This definition encompasses several important concepts: "volitional"—they know what they are doing; "established patterns"—certain behaviors are strongly linked; and "threaten well-being"—the behaviors are serious enough to stand in the way of successfully achieving goals. Thus, taking a few puffs of a cigarette or a sip of beer once in a while or cutting a class occasionally will not strongly affect the future of the young person, but smoking daily or drinking while driving or repeated truancy can make a significant difference in health and social outcomes.

NOTES

1. Steven A. Camarota, "Immigrants in the United States—2000: A Snapshot of America's Foreign-Born Population," Center for Immigration Studies, http://www.cis.org/articles/2001/back101.html (accessed November 13, 2004).

2. Infoplease, "Geographic Mobility by Selected Characteristics, 2002–2003," http://www.infoplease.com/ipa/A0922200.html (accessed November 12, 2004).

3. U.S. Census Bureau, "Children's Living Arrangements and Characteristics: March 2002," http://www.census.gov/population/www/socdemo/hh-fam/cps2002.html (accessed November 12, 2004).

4. Denise Gottfredson, Stephanie Gerstenblith, David Soutle, Shannon Womer, and Shaoli Lu, "Do After School Programs Reduce Delinquency?" *Prevention Science* 5, no. 4 (2004): 23.

5. Ibid.

6. The Pew Commission on Children in Foster Care, Alfred Perez, Kasia O'Neil, and Sara Gesiriech, *Demographics of Children in Foster Care*, p. 1, http://www.pewfostercare.org/research/data (accessed March 5, 2005).

7. *Boston Globe*, "Wealth gap broadened, study says," October 16, 2004.

8. Population Reference Bureau, "America's Rural Children, 2004," http://www.prb.org/rfdcenter (accessed December 17, 2004).

9. Charles Dervarics, "Minorities Overrepresented among America's 'Disconnected' Youth," Population Reference Bureau, http://www.prb.org/Template.cfm?Section=PRB&template=/ContentManagement/ContentDisplay.cfm&ContentID=11335 (accessed December 17, 2004).

10. Andrew Hahn, "Connecting Vulnerable Youth," *Youth Today*, April 2004, www.youthtoday.org/youthtoday/archives.html (accessed July 28, 2004).

11. Laura D. Lindberg, Scott Boggess, and Sean Williams, *Multiple Threats: The Co-occurrence of Teen Health Risk Behaviors*, Urban Institute Research Report, http://www.urban.org/publications/410248.html (accessed October 28, 2004).

CHAPTER THREE

SEX

At Shoemaker High School they use an abstinence-only course popular across Texas called Worth the Wait—a trademarked brand. . . .

"How are you going to keep yourself safe?" [a teacher] asked the class. "Abstinence," they chorused.

"What do you also hear will keep you safe?" she asked. "Condoms," they answered.

"Do they keep you safe?" she asked. "No," they chorused.[1]

As long as I can remember, grown-up people have been fighting about teen sex—teens shouldn't have it, they shouldn't even talk or learn about it, and they certainly shouldn't have access to condoms or other forms of protection. It is an easy target. Who among us is going to stand up and say "teens should have sex"?

Yet despite all efforts to stop it, American teenagers have initiated sex at early ages, and for many years the consequences have been very high rates of teenage pregnancy. However, all of the indicators related to sexual behavior appear to be on the downturn—early initiation of intercourse, intercourse without protection, rates of sexually transmitted diseases (STDs), pregnancy, births, and abortions. Whether we can attribute these reductions to the abstinence message, to better sex education in general, to access to contraception, to media, or to other, more subtle factors is up for discussion.

MAJOR TRENDS

- Fewer than half of all high school students have had sexual intercourse.
- Those who do have sex frequently are more likely to use contraception than in the past.
- Teen pregnancy rates are decreasing; about 8% of teen girls became pregnant in 2000, down from 11% in 1980.
- Sexually transmitted diseases are still very prevalent in this age group.
- Abstinence programs are replacing comprehensive sex education, but they have not proven to be effective at preventing pregnancy.
- The most successful pregnancy prevention programs are comprehensive, with a view toward expanding life options for young people.
- Teenagers access birth control through family planning clinics and in a few school-based clinics.

WHAT ARE THE FACTS?

Sexual Behavior

Fewer than half of all high school students have ever had sexual intercourse.

High school students reported significantly lower rates of sexual activity in 2003 (47%) than they did in 1991 (54%) when the Youth Behavior Risk Survey was launched (Table 3.1). The percentage that reported early initiation (before

Table 3.1 Sexual Behavior of 9th–12th Graders, 1991 and 2003 (by percent)

Sexual Behavior	1991	2003
Ever had intercourse	54	47
Had intercourse before age 13	10	7
Have had 4 or more partners	19	14
Intercourse within past 3 months	38	34
Among those with intercourse past 3 months, drank or used drugs	22	25
Among those with intercourse past 3 months, used condom	46	63
Been pregnant or gotten someone pregnant	6	4
Ever been taught about AIDS or HIV	83	88
Forced to have sexual intercourse	NA	9

Source: Centers for Disease Control and Prevention, "Youth Risk Behavior Surveillance, United States, 2003," *Morbidity and Mortality Weekly Report* 53, no. SS-2 (May 21, 2004): Tables 10, 42, 43, 44.

age 13) decreased from 10% to 7%, and the percentage that reported having had multiple partners decreased from 19% to 14%. The percentage having had intercourse within the preceding 3 months decreased (38% in 1991 to 34% in 2003). On the other hand, the percentage having had intercourse while drinking and/or using drugs went up a bit, from 22% to 25%.

The biggest change was among teenagers reporting condom use. The percentage rose from 46 to 63, a significant change in behavior. Self-reported pregnancy rates decreased from 6% to 4%, but that is clearly an underestimate.

The vast majority, 88%, of all students reported that they had been taught about AIDS and HIV, up from 83%. This may explain the increase in condom use.

In 2003, black students were much more likely to have had sexual intercourse: 61% of females and 74% of males (Table 3.2). Among white teenagers, females are slightly more likely to have had sexual intercourse than males, whereas among black and Hispanic students, males have much higher rates than females. The most striking difference shown in the survey is in the percentage of students having intercourse before the age of 13 (placing them at a very high risk of negative consequences). Almost one-third of black males did so, three to six times the frequency of any other group.

The 2003 survey asked students if they were ever forced to have sexual intercourse. Almost 1 in 10 reported that they had experienced forced sex: 11% of white, 13% of black, and 13% of Hispanic female students, and 4% of white, 12% of black, and 8% of Hispanic male students.

Table 3.2 9th–12th Graders Who Report Having Had Sexual Intercourse (Percentages by gender, race, and Hispanic origin)

Ever Had Sexual Intercourse	White	Black	Hispanic
Females	43	61	46
Males	41	74	57

Source: Centers for Disease Control and Prevention, "Youth Risk Behavior Surveillance, United States, 2003," *Morbidity and Mortality Weekly Report* 53, no. SS-2 (May 21, 2004): Table 41.

In the United States, young people initiate sexual intercourse at about the same age as in other Western countries, but they are more likely to have two or more sexual partners, which places them at a higher risk for becoming infected with STDs.

Why don't all U.S. teenagers have intercourse? The National Survey of Family Growth (NSFG) asked 15- to 19-year-olds, "why not?"[2] About one-third of both females and males said it was against their religion and morals. Some 25% of females and 18% of males were afraid of pregnancy, and 21% of females and 17% of males hadn't found the right person yet. Others feared STDs. White teens were much more likely to cite religion and morals than Hispanic or black teens.

About half of all teens reported that they had talked to a parent about "how to say no to sex" and methods of birth control. About 11% of males and 13% of females had taken a pledge to remain virgins until marriage. The NSFG also collected data on contraceptive use. Almost all 15- to 19-year-old sexually active females had ever used some method: 94% condoms, 61% pills, 55% withdrawal, 21% injectables, 11% abstinence, and 8% emergency contraception (morning-after pills). Hispanic females were much less likely than the others to use pills, relying heavily on withdrawal and condoms.

Oral Sex

Is it a new phenomenon among teenagers, or is it just coming out in the open? In January 2005, Katie Couric, NBC's star news reporter, conducted an hour-long special on prime time TV on the subject with a group of 20 teens and their parents, backed up with a national poll.[3] The poll elicited a variety of responses to the subject, from abstention to eager participation, and it showed that 12% of 13- to 16-year-olds engaged in oral sex, mostly to avoid intercourse or to prevent pregnancy. The prevalence of this practice was attributed to the presence of so many sexual images that young people become inured to them. Some mentioned the Clinton episode, which brought the subject of oral sex right into everyone's living room. Several girls mentioned that this was a "one-way street"—not much in it for girls except to make their boyfriends happy and be popular.

Hooking Up

"Hooking up" is a vague term in popular use among the younger set (including my 13-year-old granddaughter Amy).[4] It seems to mean anything from kissing to intercourse, including intercourse without kissing. What's different about it is its sense of anomie; you don't need to be in a relationship. "Friends with benefits" appear to be girls who perform oral sex on boys after being casually introduced or hooking up. These activities have been promulgated by certain Internet sites: hotornot.com and facethejury.com are two examples. Millions of teenagers "meet" each other through these sites and often meet in person to have a nonromantic fling.

A quick review of hotornot.com is elucidating. The subject headings for "blogs" include "alcohol," "liberal," "martial arts," "relationships," "college life," "young," "geek," "photographs," "oddities," and so forth. The 100 key words listed included *music, life, sex,* and *politics,* as well as *satire, video games,* and *fantasy.* Most of the commentaries seemed quite benign; kids were just sounding off about their lives. Facethejury.com, however, was totally committed to making sexual matches of every possible description and position.

A recent story from the prestigious Milton Academy, a prep school in Massachusetts, reveals more about what is going on. In March of 2005, a 15-year-old girl was identified who was "putting out" by giving oral sex to five members of the school hockey team on several occasions. The boys were expelled and charged by the county district attorney's office with statutory rape, the law that forbids sexual relations with anyone under the age of 16. They were required by the district attorney to apologize publicly to the girl and her family and agree to counseling, community service, and probation.

The school sent a letter home to parents, advising them to learn about "hooking up," a common practice among teenagers. It is of note that the tuition at this exclusive school is $32,000 a year, raising the question of how much parents might need to pay to make sure their children are protected from the consequences of high-risk behavior.

Gay and Lesbian Teens

We do not have an accurate count of the number of homosexuals in the United States. The most widely accepted estimate is 5–10% of the total population. The number of teenagers who would classify themselves as gay or lesbian is unknown. In one study done in Massachusetts, a question was added to the YRBS about sexual orientation; less than 1% answered "gay" or "lesbian," and 2% answered "bisexual." According to the YRBS, gay teens are much more likely to be involved in high-risk behaviors, such as smoking, using alcohol, marijuana, or cocaine, or being in fights, and to have been threatened with a weapon.

Gay teens experience feelings of loneliness and isolation and live with an undercurrent of fear of harassment and rejection. Gay and lesbian teens attempt suicide at slightly higher rates than others; this group is also more likely to use drugs and to experience early sexual activity, family problems, and a history of sexual abuse and prostitution, as well as "coming out" at an early age. Homosexually oriented male adolescents classified as "feminine" are at the highest risk for suicide attempts, drug abuse, prostitution, and arrest.

Consequences

Sexually Transmitted Diseases

Almost half of all teenagers have had intercourse. An alarming number of them acquire sexually transmitted diseases (STDs) every year, and many are undiagnosed.[5] The actual incidence of STDs is unknown, but estimates in 2000 ranged from 15 to 19 million new cases, with more than 4 million among 15- to 19-year-olds and over 6 million among 20- to 24-year-olds.[6] If this estimate is correct, then close to 5% of 15- to 19-year-olds may have had an STD, a very high percentage. In any case, many teenagers have STDs and don't know it. Yet the long-term effects can be dangerous, including infertility and, in the case of AIDS, death.

Many factors place teenagers, especially poor, runaway, and homeless females, at very high risk of STDs.[7] They have less access to health care, they endure sexual violence, and, in some cases, they are unable to protect themselves because of cultural traditions. Runaway and homeless adolescents are at very high risk because they may engage in trading sex for food or money, they may use infected needles, and they are frequent targets for assaults.

HIV An intensive study of AIDS incidence looked at teenagers ages 13–19 in 2002.[8] Of the 4,785 actual "full-blown" cases, 408 were teenagers, and of 29,945 reported HIV infections, 1,575 were in teenagers. This disease was equally represented among males and females (unlike older age groups, in which AIDS cases are predominantly male). About 47% of male teenagers with AIDS were exposed to the virus through male-to-male contact, 27% through hemophilia, 16% through injected drug use, and the rest other categories. Two-thirds of female teenagers acquired AIDS through heterosexual contact and 19% through injected drug use. Some 65% of the 2002 teenage AIDS cases were black, and 20% were Hispanic.

The estimated HIV prevalence rate in young men and women ages 15–24 in the United States is five to six times higher than the rate in Germany and three times the rate in the Netherlands.

Chlamydia Chlamydia is a bacterial disease that can be acquired through oral, vaginal, or anal sex with an infected partner. The rate for 15- to 19-year-old females was 2,536 per 100,000 women in 2001; the rate for African American female teens was seven times higher than among white teens (8,483 and 1,276 per 100,000). For male teens, the rate was 1,550 for African American teens and 128 for white teens. In special studies, chlamydia occurred among 18% of street youth and 15% of young women in juvenile detention facilities. This disease can cause infertility and can be prevented by using latex condoms.

Gonorrhea The rate for 15- to 19-year-old females, 703 per 100,000, was higher than those for other age groups; 75% of all teen gonorrhea cases were among African Americans.

The gonorrhea rate among U.S. teens is 74 times higher than in the Netherlands and France, 10 times higher than Canada, and 7 times higher than in England and Wales (all countries with public health systems).

Pregnancies

The number of pregnancies is the sum of births, abortions, and estimated miscarriages. The pregnancy rate is based on estimated pregnancies per 1,000 women.

For many years, we have talked about the million teen pregnancies in the United States. I remember the moment when that number was ascertained. In the early 1970s, when I worked at the Alan Guttmacher Institute, we wanted to communicate the "problem of teenage pregnancy" to the American public. Up until 1972, we had access to data only on the number of births by age, but a new data collection system had just been put into place to gain access to statistics on abortion for the first time. Knowing that many pregnancies end in miscarriages, we also had to adjust for that factor. A very enlightened advisory committee helped us with that problem (including Ashley Montagu, Charles Westoff, and Christopher Tietze); on the basis of existing research, we formulated the ratios of 20% miscarriages to the number of live births and 10% miscarriages to the number of abortions.

One evening when I was riding home from New York City to Hastings-on-Hudson on a train with Fred Jaffe, the president of AGI (and my boss), we applied the formula to newly available data. We knew that there were 616,000 births to teens in 1973. Now we had learned that 191,000 abortions were obtained by teens in that same year. Adding in the 142,000 estimated miscarriages (20% of births + 10% of abortions) resulted in 949,000 pregnancies. Applying this figure to the almost 10 million 15- to 19-year-olds in the country produced a pregnancy rate of 94.8 per 1,000, or more than 9%. By 1974, the total number of teen pregnancies had risen to 1,022,000, with a pregnancy rate of 99 per 1,000 (10%)! The teen pregnancy rate peaked in 1990 at about 117 pregnancies per 1,000.

But beginning in 1991, the 1 million teen pregnancy outcry of "1 in 10" was no longer true. The number began to decrease, and, by 2000, it was estimated that there were 821,810 pregnancies. The rate dropped from 117 in 1990 to 84 in 2000. Thus, almost 12% of teens experienced pregnancies in 1990, and a decade later that figure was about 8%.

In 2000, the pregnancy rate for black 15- to 19-year-olds was 151, for Hispanics it was 132, and for non-Hispanic whites it was 57.

In 1998, when the pregnancy rate was almost 89 per 1,000 15- to 19-year-olds in the United States, the comparable rates were 20 in France, 16 in Germany, and almost 5 in the Netherlands.

Births The latest year for which the number of births is available is 2003, when there were 421,626 births to women under the age of 20. Some 414,961 were to 15- to 19-year-olds and 6,665 to those 14 and under. The actual number of births to 15- to 19-year-olds peaked in 1970 with almost 650,000, so there has been a decrease of more than 35%. But the percentage of births among unmarried teens increased from 29% to 79% in the same 25-year period.

Tables 3.3 and 3.4 show the numbers and rates of births, abortions, and total pregnancies to women ages 15–19 in 1980, 1990, and 2000.

By 2003, the teenage birth rate (girls ages 15–19) was 42 per 1,000, down from 60 in 1990. (These rates can be read as percentages: for example, 42 per 1,000 = 4.2%). During the same period, birth rates for older women rose significantly (for example, for women ages 35–39, it rose from 32 to 41 per 1,000). The greatest reduction was among the younger age groups. The differential by race/ethnicity has always been large, but black teenagers experienced the largest decrease in the birth rate over that decade (see Table 3.5).

About two-thirds of all teen births are described by the mothers as "unwanted": the percentages by race/ethnicity were 47% of Hispanics, 67% of whites, and 77% of blacks.

Table 3.3 Number of Births, Abortions, and Pregnancies to Women Ages 15–19, 1980, 1990, and 2000

Year	Births	Abortions	Total Pregnancies*
1980	552,161	444,780	1,151,850
1990	521,826	350,970	1,012,260
2000	468,990	235,470	821,810

*Pregnancies include an estimate of miscarriages based on 20% of births and 10% of abortions

Source: Alan Guttmacher Institute, "U.S. Teenage Pregnancy Statistics With Comparative Statistics For Women Aged 20–24," February 19, 2004, Table 2, http://www.guttmacher.org/pubs/teen_stats.html (accessed January 9, 2005).

Table 3.4 Birth, Abortion, and Pregnancy Rates per 1,000 Women Ages 15–19, 1980, 1990, 2000

Year	Birth Rate	Abortion Rate	Pregnancy Rate*
1980	53	43	110
1990	60	41	117
2000	48	24	84

*Pregnancies include an estimate of miscarriages based on 20% of births and 10% of abortions

Source: Alan Guttmacher Institute, "U.S. Teenage Pregnancy Statistics With Comparative Statistics For Women Aged 20–24," February 19, 2004, Table 2, http://www.guttmacher.org/pubs/teen_stats.html (accessed January 9, 2005).

Table 3.5 Births to Teens Ages 15–19 by Race and Hispanic Origin (Births per 1,000 females in group)

Year	Total	White Non-Hispanic	Black	Hispanic
1990	60	43	113	100
2003	42	27	65	82

Source: Child Trends DataBank, "Teen Births," Table 1, http://www.childtrendsdatabank.org/pdf/13_PDF.pdf (accessed November 29, 2004)

In 2002, when the U.S. teen birth rate was 43 births per 1,000 15- to 19-year-old women, the comparable rates were 10 in Germany, 8 in France, and 6 in the Netherlands. Canada had half the U.S. rate (20), and the United Kingdom's rate was 31.

Abortions

The number of abortions to teenagers was 235,470 in 2000, just over half of the 1980s figure of 444,780. During the same decades, the abortion rate decreased from 43 to 24 per 1,000 women ages 15–19. In 2000, more than 19% of all abortions were obtained by women under age 20.

In 1997, when the teen abortion rate in the U.S. was 28 per 1,000 women ages 15–19, it was 10 in France and 4 in Germany and the Netherlands.

Teen Parents

About 850,000 teen women are mothers. At the time the baby is born, about 60% of the mothers are living in poverty, and within a few years, that figure goes up to 80%. About one-fourth of teen moms drop out of school; others are able to continue because of special programs that take care of the babies while the mothers are in classes. About half of teen mothers receive welfare within a few years after the birth. Teen moms are more likely to drink, smoke, and use marijuana than same-age girls who are not mothers.

Births to teenagers carry higher risk than those to older mothers because of lack of prenatal care and low birth weight. The infant mortality rate is much higher. Teen moms often lack proper nutrition during pregnancy, compounding the babies' problems.

About 21% of teenage mothers who gave birth in 2003 already had one or more children. Nearly one-quarter of teen mothers have a second baby before they reach age 20. These young women were more likely to have dropped out of school and to have low cognitive ability.[9] Lorraine Klerman, a leading expert on maternal and child health, describes the consequences of additional births to teens as "detrimental"—both to the mother's ability to complete her education and attain economic self-sufficiency and to the baby's survival and birth weight.

Predictors

Some teenagers become mothers by default. They can't see any reason not to have a baby because, as they perceive their life situations, they aren't going anywhere anyway. Many years ago, I began to formulate the "life options" hypothesis: To protect themselves from early parenthood, young people had to have a sense of the future and the assurance that there was a role for them in the society. They had to aspire to some kind of work that would be satisfying and productive. Without this kind of attachment to the society, young people would have a hard time resisting the temptations that lay before them.

The predictors of early sexual intercourse and subsequent consequences include:

1. Individual
   a. Alcohol use
   b. Smoking
   c. Drug use
   d. History of sexual abuse
2. Peer
   a. High-risk friends
3. School
   a. Low educational attainment (only 7% of those who had some college became teen mothers compared with 66% who had not finished high school)
   b. Attendance at an alternative high school (89% had engaged in sexual intercourse)[10]
4. Family
   a. Poverty
   b. Being distant from mother and/or father

Protective factors for abstaining from sex include:

1. Individual
   a. High expectations
2. Peer
   a. Low-risk friends
3. School
   a. High achievement
   b. Involvement in athletics
4. Family
   a. Living with both parents
   b. Religious involvement/attendance at services
   c. Good relationship with family
   d. Maternal pressure to abstain

Given these predictors, programs to prevent teen pregnancy should be intensive and comprehensive and should enrich educational opportunity, work with families, and give young people access to health and mental health services.

WHAT CAN BE DONE?

Policies

A common question is why adolescent sexual health outcomes are so much more positive in other Western countries such as Germany, France, and the Netherlands. One study by Advocates for Youth concluded that each of those countries has an unwritten social contract with young people: "We respect your right to act responsibly, giving you the tools you need to avoid unintended pregnancy and sexually transmitted diseases, including HIV."[11]

According to this source, "societal openness and comfort in dealing with sexuality and pragmatic governmental policies create greater, easier access to sexual health information and services for all people, including teens." Adults in other countries view young people as assets rather than problems.

Public policy in those countries on these issues is based on research rather than the influence of political or religious interest groups. Governments support massive, long-term public education campaigns that focus on safety and pleasure. Young people have access to free or low-cost contraception through national health insurance.

In this country, we have difficulty bringing diverse viewpoints together over an issue as controversial as sexual behavior among our young people. The most straightforward approach that one might suggest on the basis of the data reviewed would start with providing early sex education, open communication with supportive adults, and social skills training, as well as access to effective contraception for those young people who make the decision to engage in sexual intercourse. At the same time, we need to be sure that teenagers do have "life options" and are motivated to continue their education and move into desirable careers.

The climate in the United States in the beginning of the twenty-first century is antithetical to pregnancy prevention among teenagers. Strong forces in government and throughout the country are very well organized on every front. The only message coming through sex education is "don't do it until you are married." Access to contraception is more limited than ever. Access to abortion is being cut off through state laws that require waiting time and parental consent and forbid crossing state borders to obtain the procedure.

At the same time, the Internet plays the role of a sexual underground market. Any kid in front of a computer can find a vast cafeteria of sexual content. So young people learn about "hooking up" and can find playmates easily with just a few taps on the keyboard. This situation is problematic and difficult to control.

Access to Contraception

In 1970, Congress passed the historic Title X Public Health Service Act, which guaranteed the right to family planning for American women. Public funding for family planning is provided by Title X and administered by the Office of Population Affairs and the states. Family planning services in the United States are provided in 7,683 clinics throughout the country. Of the 6.7 million women who use these services, some 1.9 million are under the age of 20 (about 28%). Health department clinics and Planned Parenthood clinics each serve about one-third of the caseload; private doctors, community health centers, hospitals, and private agencies provide services to the remaining one-third.

In 2005, $278 million was appropriated for this program, much less than was required to serve all the women who needed medical family planning services. President Bush's 2006 budget request was for $286 million, an amount that will not allow clinics to keep up with either the heightened demand or inflation.

Although teenagers are encouraged to involve their parents, the attempt to impose a parental consent restriction on services they may use has been avoided so far. However, every year when the legislation is renewed, efforts are made to change the law. Providers believe that requiring parental consent would restrict the use of contraception significantly, especially by the highest risk teenagers, who often have difficulty communicating with their parents.

A recent survey of adolescents under the age of 18 seeking reproductive health services at family planning clinics provided evidence that parental notification would probably not curb sexual activity.[12] Some 60% of the respondents said their parents or guardians knew they were going to the clinic, and 59% said they would use the clinic for prescription contraception even if parental consent was required. Only 7% said they would stop having sex. One in five would use no contraception or would rely on withdrawal.

Other federal sources of funds for family planning clinics include Medicaid, TANF (Temporary Assistance to Needy Families), SCHIP (State Children's

Health Insurance Program), and Maternal and Child Health and Social Service block grants.

Sex Education

"Students enrolled in federally funded abstinence-only sex education programs are misinformed about science, deprived of vital health information, and exposed to gender stereotypes and religious dogma. . . ."[13]

No evidence has been generated to show that sex education "causes" teens to have sexual intercourse, nor are there evaluations that show that abstinence-only sex education programs prevent teen pregnancy. Representative Henry Waxman of California produced a report stating that 11 of the 13 most popular abstinence curricula were riddled with inaccurate medical information.[14] Here is one example from the Waxman Report:

> Curriculum: WAIT Training, by Abstinence and Relationship Training Center: Passage lists tears and sweat as "at-risk" substances for HIV transmission.
>
> Waxman Report says, "According to the CDC, 'contact with saliva, tears, or sweat has never been shown to result in transmission of HIV.'"
>
> Publisher's response: "Although the virus has been isolated in sweat, tears, and saliva, never has a reported case of HIV been transmitted through these fluids. However, one cannot say with certainty that there is NO risk when the HIV virus has been isolated in these fluids."

President Bush's proposed FY2006 budget requested $205.5 million for abstinence-only-until-marriage programs. The budget message called for programs designed to teach that "sex outside of marriage causes harmful psychological and physical effects." Faith-based organizations are permitted to apply. Up until 2005, the federal government provided funds for three different abstinence-only-until-marriage education programs. The Office of Population Affairs runs the Adolescent Family Life Program. About $36 million is allocated to demonstration projects either to promote abstinence or to work with pregnant and parenting teens (not one dollar for contraception). A federal discretionary fund through the Maternal and Child Health program, which provides Special Project of Regional and National Significance (SPRANS) grants that could be used for abstinence education, was consolidated with other programs under the auspices of the Administration for Children and Families to the tune of $186 million. In addition, welfare reform has set aside $50 million per year for 5 years for abstinence-unless-married education. Another Bush initiative involves unmarried fathers of babies on welfare: Some $50 million will go toward promoting responsible fatherhood and marriage. The Title X programs are run by the states, largely through state health departments. Many of the Adolescent Family Life projects are state administered as well.

One technique used for delaying initiation of sexual activity is the "pledge." A recent study showed that although pledgers have sex later than nonpledgers and get married earlier, most pledgers do not wait to get married before they have vaginal sex for the first time.[15] As a result, pledgers had the same rate of sexually transmitted diseases as nonpledgers, probably because they are less likely to use condoms for sexual activities. However, these findings were challenged by the Heritage Foundation, which said the earlier report "deliberately misled the press and the public."[16] After analyzing the same data set, the foundation reported that virginity pledgers were less likely to engage in any form of sexual activity and that, if they did have sex, they were less likely to engage in vaginal intercourse, oral sex, anal sex, and sex with a prostitute. Other researchers said that the foundation's unpublished paper was full of errors and underreporting.

This debate is an excellent example of how research can be used as a political tool, depending on what position the researchers take on an issue. In my view, there is no such thing as "pure" research or "absolute" truth. I believe we must all use our own judgment about the validity of what we read—does it make sense?

Access to Abortion

Since abortion became legal in 1973, repeated attempts have been made to keep teenagers from gaining access to it. Over the years, 44 states have passed laws requiring teens to notify parents or obtain consent through the courts before having an abortion. In 36 of these states, state laws have also required a 24-hour waiting period. In all but Utah, a procedure allows a minor to petition a judge for permission to have an abortion without telling her parents; in most courts, these waivers are granted routinely, but where the requests are denied, girls may opt for an abortion in a state without a parental involvement law.

In 2005, a bill called the Child Custody Protection Act was introduced to outlaw transporting a minor across state lines to obtain an abortion in order to evade parental consent or notification laws in the girl's home state. The bill's advocates evoked an image of a girl impregnated by an abusive older man who then drives her across the state border for an abortion. Opponents of the act said it would criminalize the well-meaning actions of an aunt or an older sister who might assist a girl who was terrified of being beaten or evicted from home if her parents learned of her pregnancy.[17] The bill carries a sentence of up to 1 year in prison.

Teen Mothers

Half of teen mothers rely on welfare to support their families. Recent welfare reforms have added restrictions that require teenage recipients to live with a responsible adult, usually a parent, and to attend school or work. This is supposed to reduce long-term dependence on welfare, but it may make life even more hazardous for those teenage parents who live on their own.

School systems with large numbers of teen parents can develop special programs to encourage them to stay in school. The Wilbur Cross High School in New Haven, Connecticut, hosts the Elizabeth Celetto Child Care Center, whose mission is to keep teen parents in school.[18] The center provides door-to-door transportation for teen mothers and their children. Nine day-care workers, called "teachers," supervise and play with the children, ages 6 weeks to 3 years, from 8 A.M. to 2 P.M. Each mother has a case manager who tries to connect her with community organizations for health care, housing, insurance, food, and other services. The case manager also tries to contact the fathers and help them to become part of the family; however, one-third of the fathers are incarcerated. A daily parenting class teaches the teen moms about relationships, birth control, STDs, money management, and employment opportunities.

According to the principal, Robert Canelli, "some people think it [the center] promotes our young ladies to go out and have babies."[19] But the center staff believes that the program prevents second and third pregnancies and prepares the children of teen moms to start on a stronger path toward educational achievement.

Klerman's review of programs to prevent additional births to teen mothers highlights the importance of home visiting by well-trained nurses, emphasis on family planning, and returning to school after a first child's birth.[20]

Local Issues

Although the funding for family planning comes largely through federal and state grants, operation of the clinics is local. Planned Parenthood affiliates are located in 850 clinics across the country, and they take the lead on issues related to contraceptive availability.

In the 1980s, a few health departments funded school-based clinics through which family planning services were made available in high schools. However, although the concept of locating primary health care in schools was quite acceptable, the provision of contraception was not in most places. Today there are 1,500 school-based clinics, but only 24% of those in middle schools or high schools are known to distribute condoms or prescribe contraceptive pills. On the other hand, some 60% of middle and high school clinics provide on-site treatment for STDs, 62% counsel on HIV/AIDS, and 76% do pregnancy testing.

The actual delivery of sex education is very much a local responsibility. Each school district has its standards and rules, using different curricula and different approaches to training teachers or using peer educators.

Programs

Katie Tobin, our research associate, observed:

> In the search for well-evaluated prevention programs, there appeared to be more programs aimed at preventing teenage pregnancy than were aimed at preventing other problem behaviors. As noted in this chapter, the rate of teenage childbearing has decreased over the past two decades, and youth seem to be having lower rates of sexual intercourse than most adults think. However, it is just these facts that make teenage pregnancy prevention advocates anxious about slipping off the youth development radar screen, especially in the current era of funding shortages. Effective pregnancy prevention and sex education programs are just as important as they were two decades ago. Kids are still having sex and not all of them safely.
>
> In my experience teaching and counseling in urban elementary and middle schools, younger and younger kids seem to be talking about sex. This phenomenon might not be preventable due to the media influences that penetrate the multiple environments of a child's life. However, a child's ability to make good decisions about his or her sexuality may be greatly influenced by effective pregnancy prevention and safe sex programs.[21]

All of the programs that are highlighted in this chapter have been reviewed in at least one of the following publications covering teenage pregnancy prevention:

"Science and Success," Advocates for Youth, 2003: reviews 19
  programs.[22]
*Do Abstinence-Only Programs Delay the Initiation of Sex Among Young
  People and Reduce Teen Pregnancy?* National Campaign to Prevent
  Teen Pregnancy, 2002: reviews 8 programs.[23]
No Time to Waste, National Campaign to Prevent Teen Pregnancy and
  Child Trends, 2004: reviews 13 programs.[24]
Teen Risk Taking, The Urban Institute, 2000: reviews 25 programs.[25]
Emerging Answers Summary, The National Campaign to Prevent Teen
  Pregnancy, 2001: reviews the field, selects 8 programs.[26]

The five programs presented here have all been evaluated rigorously, and three of them have been part of longitudinal evaluations. Beyond evaluation, each of the programs represents a different approach to preventing teen pregnancy or unsafe sex. The programs' foci include service learning, youth development, school-based social skills building, HIV/STD education with teenage males, and individual case management for the siblings of teen parents.

Service-Learning Approach:
Teen Outreach Program

The Teen Outreach Program (TOP) is a high school–based program that aims to prevent teen pregnancy and school dropout through both service-learning experience and curriculum materials. The program was developed in 1978 by Brenda Hostetler, then director of teen pregnancy prevention in the St. Louis schools.[27] From the beginning, this program has put much more emphasis on serving the community and promoting healthy behavior than on specific prevention of either teen pregnancy or school dropout. In fact, education about sex constitutes only about 15% of the total curriculum and is folded into the program's core curriculum of making good decisions about life options. The program evaluators pointed out that "this focus has important practical implications, because it means the program may be politically acceptable in communities where programs that explicitly focus on sexual behavior may not be feasible to implement."[28] TOP was one of three positive youth development programs recommended for widespread replication by the National Research Council in 2002.[29]

TOP targets high-risk high school students who have a history of class failure or dropping out, school suspensions, or previous involvement in a pregnancy.[30] The program has three interrelated components: supervised community service, classroom discussion of service experiences, and classroom discussion and activities related to key social and developmental tasks of adolescence. Small groups, with a facilitator or mentor, discuss values, human growth and development, relationships, dealing with family stress, and issues related to the social and emotional transition from adolescence to adulthood, while developing skills in communication and decision making. Service-learning projects take students into their communities, creating a combination of education and community service that is intended to empower young people to succeed.

A four-level, developmentally tiered curriculum called Changing Scenes[31] is taught for a minimum of 40–50 minutes per week and emphasizes cooperative learning processes (role playing, field experiences) that place the child at the center of the classroom:

> *Level 1* (for ages 12–13): Focuses on adolescent development (physical, emotional, intellectual), relationship building, and awareness of societal influence.
>
> *Level 2* (for age 14): Focuses on developing strong self-awareness, coping with divergent emotions and responsibilities, and making good decisions.
>
> *Level 3* (for ages 15–16): Focuses on promoting healthy attitudes and behavior about intimate relationships, seeking and establishing a set of values, and setting short- and long-term goals.
>
> *Level 4* (for age 17): Focuses on preparing students for the next phase of their lives that will include additional stresses and responsibilities and will require a greater level of control of one's life.

TOP requires steady funding—generally between $100 and $600 per student.[32] Merging it into an existing service-learning program can help ensure financial stability. Another necessary component is a well-trained, dedicated staff that will take a youth development approach (one that sees adolescents as assets to the community), build community partnerships, develop learner-centered classrooms, and make strong connections between the service and the learning.

Philliber Research and the University of Virginia have been involved in a joint study of TOP, one of a few programs that have been evaluated for at least 20 years using rigorous experimental techniques of comparison and control groups, both randomly and nonrandomly assigned.[33] In a study of well-run TOP programs in 24 schools, the research found:

- 33% lower rate of pregnancy than control group
- 60% lower rate of school dropout than control group
- 11% lower rate of course failure in school than control group
- 14% lower rate of school suspension than control group.[34]

In looking at this program, it is important to note the substantially higher participation level of females, even though this program is intended for all teens;[35] this imbalance makes it difficult to determine the effectiveness of the program for all teens. Another critical issue is the fact that there has been no collection of longitudinal data. Thus, although students may seem to be doing very well while participating in the program, it is impossible to know whether the program has long-term effects on risk reduction once the students have stopped their involvement in TOP.[36]

TOP exemplifies two significant approaches to behavioral change: social and emotional learning through group discussions and broadening life experience through community service.

Comprehensive Youth Development Approach: CAS Carrera Teen Pregnancy Prevention Program

Hope is a powerful contraceptive. The way that you help young people avoid pregnancy is by providing them with real evidence that good things can happen in their lives.
                                                      —Michael Carerra

The Children's Aid Society (CAS) Carrera Adolescent Pregnancy Prevention Program[37] is a sex education, pregnancy prevention, and youth development program for at-risk 13- to 15-year-olds.[38] The program was initiated in New

York City's Harlem neighborhood in 1984 by Michael Carrera, the director of the National Adolescent Sexuality Training Center.

The Carrera Program is built on a belief that the best contraceptive for young people is for them to be successful in school, to have access to quality medical care, to have meaningful jobs, and to have strong bonds with adult role models.[39] Douglas Kirby, a long-time researcher of teen pregnancy prevention, said, "Of all of the 73 studies I have looked at, the research on the Children's Aid Society Carrera Program has the strongest evidence and the only evidence that it actually reduced teen pregnancy and child-bearing for a three-year period of time."[40]

The Carrera Program, based in Harlem, has mainly served black and Hispanic young people from the inner city who are neither enrolled in an after-school program nor pregnant or parenting at the time of enrollment.[41] The program runs after school for approximately 3 hours 5 days a week. The participants are divided into groups, rotating daily between activities.[42]

The program has seven key ingredients: five are activity-based and two service-based. The activities are:

1. The job club, which offers stipends, help with bank accounts, employment experience, and career awareness
2. Academics, including individual assessment, tutoring, PSAT and SAT preparation, and assistance with applying to colleges
3. Comprehensive family life and sexuality education
4. Arts, including weekly music, dance, writing, or drama workshops
5. Individual sports activities such as squash, golf, and swimming

The two service components are (1) mental health care and (2) medical care, including reproductive health care, primary care, and dental care.

Most students participate in sports and creative activities at least once a week and receive academic assistance daily. Over the summer, program activities aim to reinforce the skills and knowledge built up during the year, give students a place to go, offer cultural trips and recreational activities, and help place participants in jobs.

In the longitudinal study completed in 2001, about 79% of the participants stayed in the program for 3 years.[43] The study compared participants in the CAS-Carrera Program with young people at six other service agencies throughout New York City; they ranged in age from 13 to 15 and were largely black or Hispanic. The knowledge base of sexual health issues rose by 22% after 3 years, compared with 11% among the control group. Moreover, various behaviors changed significantly:

- 46% of Carrera females had never had sex compared with 34% of control females.
- 75% of Carrera females had successfully resisted pressure to have sex, compared with only 36% of the control group.
- 36% of Carrera females used two methods of contraception, compared with 20% of control females.
- 74% of sexually experienced males visited the doctor for reproductive health care, compared with 46% of the control group.

Most strikingly, at third-year follow-up, the females had significantly lower rates of pregnancy and births than did control females. The evaluators said, "The study clearly documents the effectiveness among females of a comprehensive program to prevent adolescent pregnancy."

The evaluators strongly correlate the success of this program with the long-term relationships that the participants formed with the program and its staff. Furthermore, like most comprehensive programs, the Carrera Program has helped its participants in many other ways: They tend to have higher SAT scores, fewer visits to the emergency room, and more experience in the work world.

It is important to note that when this program was administered and evaluated in a midwestern city, its outcomes were minimal. Although many factors may have contributed to its lack of success in the Midwest, the experience suggests that such programs need dynamic and committed directors, such as Michael Carrera, and strong partners to help them implement their program.

School-Based Social Development Skill Building: Seattle Social Development Project

The Seattle Social Development Project (SSDP) was developed in 1981 by J. David Hawkins and the Social Development Research Group based at the University of Washington School of Social Work. The social development

model on which SSDP is based postulates that families and schools that provide positive, active opportunities for young people and that constantly encourage full participation create stronger bonds between the young people and
these institutions. These strong bonds then protect children, especially as they
grow older, against problem behavior such as early and unsafe sexual intercourse.[44] The main goal of the SSDP is to help create these bonds and to facilitate the development of strong protective factors that will reduce the onset of
problematic behavior.

Similar to the Carrera Program, SSDP is a multiyear intervention. However,
rather than targeting teens, the program targets elementary-age children
within the school setting; participants are largely urban African American and
multiethnic children.[45] Its three core components are teacher training in classroom instruction and management, child social and emotional skill development, and parent training.

The teacher training is done by professional staff from SSDP, who also conduct the parent-training component of the program. The teacher training consists of 5 full days every year focused on behavior management (such as establishing consistent classroom expectations and routines), interactive teaching
(such as modeling the skills being taught), and cooperative learning (such as
having students at different skill levels work together).[46]

The students themselves receive less direct programming than do the parents and the teachers, but there is a prescribed curriculum. Rather than focusing on specific risk issues, the curriculum centers on encouraging and supporting prosocial behavior in the first and sixth grades.[47] In first grade,
students participate in an "Interpersonal Problem Solving Curriculum" that
focuses on communication, problem solving, and decision making. The sixth-
grade curriculum is focused on developing students' refusal skills, including
recognizing negative social pressures and developing refusal capacity and alternative activities. This limited curriculum reflects SSDP's goal of redesigning
the classroom environment through teacher training and support.

The parent-training element of this project is voluntary. It aims to support
parents' behavior management skills, academic support skills, and capacity to
guide their children away from risky behavior. No measures were built into the
evaluation to look at how well the skills taught in the parent training were integrated into the home.[48] Furthermore, a study done in 1999 showed that a
somewhat low percentage of parents attended the workshops over time. These
shortcomings make it difficult to determine the relative importance of the par-

ent component. However, SSDP has been able to maintain a very high retention rate for both student and parent participants. SSDP costs about $4,355
per participant per year. One analysis showed the taxpayer and crime victim
reduction net benefit as $14,169 per year.[49]

A longitudinal study of the SSDP was initiated in 1981 when the program
began in first-grade classrooms in 18 Seattle public schools. Follow-up was
done in 1993 and 1996 with former SSDP participants who were then 18 and
21. Outcomes at age 21 included:

- 10% of the intervention group reported never having sex, compared
  with 6% of the control group.
- 32% of the intervention group reported having multiple sexual partners versus 43% of the control group.
- 50% of single African Americans reported always using a condom
  versus only 12% of the control group.
- 38% of SSDP females reported ever being pregnant, compared with
  56% of the control group females.
- 23% of SSDP females reported ever giving birth, compared with 40%
  of comparison females; the proportion of males involved in a pregnancy or birth did not differ between intervention and control
  groups.[50]

Beyond the impact on participants' sexual activity, SSDP also seemed to
make a difference in their academic achievement and school behavior. Participants seemed to do better and feel more engaged in school, to get involved in
fewer violent acts, and to drink less heavily. Furthermore, the research team
noted that the effects were greater for children in poverty and for African
Americans. These outcomes help to make the case for both early intervention
and comprehensive programs that reach children through their parents and
their teachers. (It should be noted that a project developer was involved in all
of the evaluation research.)

HIV/STD Education Focus: Safer Choices

Safer Choices is a school-based teen pregnancy and sexually transmitted disease
prevention program that largely targets sexually experienced teens in 9th and
10th grades. It was developed in the early 1990s by Karin Coyle, director of re-

search at ETR Associates and specialist in the development and evaluation of health promotion programs.[51] Coyle says, "We use a systematic approach in which we isolate behaviors of interest [such as unprotected sex or sex under the influence of drugs or alcohol], identify the antecedents of import/interest as well as their theoretical underpinnings, and develop activities to change each antecedent."[52] Coyle believes strongly that effective programs need to target both risk and protective factors; protective factors related to early and unsafe sexual behavior include creating positive peer norms, increasing self-efficacy to communicate better, and changing basic attitudes and beliefs about sexuality.

Safer Choices has been implemented in both urban and suburban areas, with white, Hispanic, African American, and Asian teenagers. It aims to increase understanding about HIV and STDs, change students' attitudes about condoms and abstinence, strengthen students' communication and refusal skills when it comes to sex, eliminate barriers to condom use, and increase students' communication with parents.[53]

The 2-year curriculum includes ten 45-minute classroom lessons each year; these include realistic activities, such as direct contact with individuals infected with HIV (both teens and adults) and lessons on how to use a condom correctly and consistently. The program also aims to reach young people through many other outlets. For example, it provides guidance and support for a school's organization of peer groups specifically centered around these issues; it also offers support for developing a school health promotion council in which parents, teachers, students, administrators, and community members can discuss and mobilize around these issues, provide training for teachers, and host parent events.

The first Safer Choices research study tracked ninth-grade students for 31 months following a baseline pretest survey.[54] Besides finding positive changes in students' knowledge about HIV and STDs and an increase in positive attitudes toward condom use, the study found that the program:

> Significantly increased the use of contraception: Sexually experienced students in intervention schools were 1.76 times more likely to use an effective pregnancy prevention method (birth control pills, birth control pills plus condoms, or condoms alone) than were students in comparison schools.
>
> Significantly increased condom use: Sexually experienced students in intervention schools were less likely to report having sex without a condom in the 3 months prior to follow-up surveys than were sexually experienced control students; intervention students who reported having

sexual intercourse during the prior 3 months were 1.68 times more likely to have used condoms than were control students.[55]

A separate study showed that bringing HIV-positive speakers into the program also produced positive outcomes, specifically for inner-city teens, including a higher perceived risk of contracting HIV and a greater likelihood of getting tested for HIV.[56] On the other hand, the evaluation showed that the program had no impact on the frequency of sexual initiation or the number of sexual partners. It also showed no impact on the use of alcohol or drugs before sexual intercourse among its participants. The evaluators believe that high school may be too late to have a meaningful impact on the initiation of sexual intercourse. Therefore, programs such as Safer Choices that are intended for high school students should focus more substantially on the use of contraceptives, including condoms, and on refusal skills rather than on abstinence.

Individual Case Management: California's Adolescent Sibling Pregnancy Prevention Program

The California Adolescent Sibling Pregnancy Prevention Program (ASPPP) was created in 1996 through a government initiative to prevent teen pregnancy that provided $3 million to the Adolescent Family Life Program (AFLP) of the Maternal, Child and Adolescent Branch of California's Department of Health Services. This money was to be spent on expanding their services to the siblings of teen parents, a group that tends to be at higher risk for teen pregnancy and involvement in early sexual activity.[57] The ultimate goal of ASPPP is to reduce teen pregnancy among adolescents by focusing on this high-risk group.

Since 1996, ASPPP has served approximately 1,500 eleven- to eighteen-year-olds, all siblings of clients in the AFLP.[58] The program, funded by Title XIX (Medicaid) and state general funds, operates at 44 nonprofit social service agencies, community-based organizations, schools, hospitals, and health departments in California. The services provided at each site often include individual case management, home visits, guidance for academics, job placement, sex education (including information on abstinence and contraception), and social skills development.

The most important component of the program is the one-on-one contact between the site agency staff and the participants. In fact, participants who received more hours of direct case management had a lower likelihood of pregnancy and used more effective methods of birth control.[59]

In the evaluation of the program, carried out between 1997 and 1999, 1,176 eleven- to seventeen-year-olds who had at least one sibling who was a parent were both interviewed and given a questionnaire before and after participation in the program. Of this group, 60% were female and 70% were Hispanic.[60] The evaluation produced the following statistics:

- 4% of participants became pregnant, compared with 7% of controls.
- 7% of participants initiated sexual activity, compared with 16% of controls.

Furthermore, participants had "significantly more definitive intentions of remaining abstinent at posttest." In addition, unlike other teen pregnancy prevention programs, ASPPP had an impact on male participants' use of contraception, which rose for participants but actually decreased for controls. Like SSDP and the Carrera Program, ASPPP showed an impact on other aspects of its participants' lifestyles, such as truancy.

Implementation of specifically targeted programs such as this one can be challenging. However, they certainly can have a great impact on lowering teenage pregnancy and births for those young people considered most at risk. This program is also a testament to the capacity of a state government to effect teen pregnancy reduction. It demonstrates the importance of intensive individual attention through case management, a significant lesson that should be applied across behavioral domains.

CONCLUSION: WHAT WORKS?

Most of the characteristics of the effective programs essentially involve good pedagogy, good teaching practices. They actively involve youth. They got youth to think about things and personalize behavior. They gave them knowledge, but they did not just give them knowledge. They taught them skills, they tried to change their norms, they had a very clear goal from the beginning. . . .

—Doug Kirby

Problems like teen pregnancy and sexually transmitted diseases don't exist because there is information out there that teens don't hear about; those problems are symptoms. They are the yield of poverty, lack of health care and more. We do not prevent teen pregnancy. They do.

—Michael Carrera

Summary of Programs

The five programs presented here are a good sample of what's out there. Most of them are targeted on high-risk adolescents, and most are very intensive. The Carrera model is the most comprehensive and includes a whole array of activities to strengthen the young person's ability to succeed in school and in life. In addition, participants learn why and how to use contraceptives. The Teen Outreach Program uses community service experience to teach about life and to open up discussion about social and emotional issues, including sexuality issues. The Seattle Social Development model digs into both the classroom and the home, stressing healthy youth development throughout. Safer Choices also seems to use social and emotional learning principles on top of a traditional sex education program. The Sibling Program is both targeted and intensive, with case managers assigned to each participant, a strong intervention that is very successful in helping young people succeed. The concept that young people need to form attachments to responsible adults is implemented in these efforts; so is the idea that teenagers can learn skills that will help them make informed and responsible decisions.

None of these exemplary programs is free. The range of cost is significant, from $100 per participant to more than $4,000. The amount of time the intervention takes and the kind of staff required vary as well.

Comment

No single approach is going to ensure that teenagers do not get pregnant. Certainly they need access to knowledge about their sexuality and access to contraceptives when they become sexually active. More important, though, is the difficult truth that many young people are not currently motivated to take precautions. They do not particularly want babies, but they do not perceive that it will negatively affect their lives if they become mothers at early ages (and they may be right about that).

Pregnancy prevention has to be comprehensive. It has to offer the young person an alternate route to adulthood. Programs such as the Children's Aid Society Carrera Teen Pregnancy Prevention Program and the Teen Outreach Program recognize this need by encouraging community service and exposing young people to broader opportunities.

Teen childbearing is a product of social class differences. Children from upper-class families rarely become teen mothers. If they get pregnant, they can be quickly whisked off for an abortion. Lower-class families are less likely to take this route. Thus, in suburban high schools, there are virtually no teen moms or dads, but in inner-city high schools, and even middle schools, there are special classes for teen parents and nurseries that provide day care for the babies.

Of course, issues surrounding sexuality extend much further than pregnancy prevention. Children must be able to communicate with their parents about reproduction and sexual behavior right from the beginning. They need to be told the facts; even more, they need to be instructed in a rational value system that allows them to make good decisions for themselves at appropriate ages. It is difficult to say what the "right" age is to initiate sexual relations, but clearly, when it does happen, the young person should be ready to shoulder the responsibility and handle the consequences. Teenagers have to be prepared to deal with the current, self-contradictory climate of overt sexuality in the media and repressed sexuality in the body politic, which definitely creates a challenging setting in which to come into maturity.

NOTES

1. Joanna Walters, "No Sex Is Safe Sex for Teens in America," *The Observer*, January 2, 2005, http://observer.guardian.co.uk/international/ story/0,6903,1382117,00.html (accessed January 9, 2005).

2. J. Abma, G. Martinez, W. Mosher, and B. Dawson, "Teenagers in the United States: Sexual Activity, Contraceptive Use, and Childbearing," *Vital Health Statistics* 23, no. 24 (2004).

3. *The Katie Couric Special: The 411: Teens and Sex.* Broadcast January 29, 2005, by NBC.

4. Benoit Denizet-Lewis, "Friends, Friends with Benefits and the Benefits of the Local Mall," *New York Times Magazine,* May 30, 2004, http://www.nytimes.com/2004/05/30/magazine/30NONDATING.html?ex=1401249600&en=b8ab7c02ae2d206b&ei=5007&partner=USERLAND.

5. Hillard Weinstock, Stuart Bernam, and Willard Cates Jr. "Sexually Transmitted Diseases Among American Youth: Incidence and Prevalence Estimates, 2000," *Perspectives on Sexual and Reproductive Health*, 36, no. 1 (2004): 6–10.

6. Sue Alford, "Adolescents: At Risk of Sexually Transmitted Infections" (fact sheet), Advocates for Youth, January 2003, http://www.advocatesforyouth.org/publications/factsheet/fssti.htm.

7. Ibid.

8. Centers for Disease Control and Prevention, *HIV/AIDS Surveillance Report,* 14 (2002), http://www.cdc.gov/hiv/stats/hasr1402/2002SurveillanceReport.pdf (accessed November 12, 2004).

9. Lorraine Klerman, *Another Chance: Preventing Additional Births to Teen Mothers* (Washington, DC: National Campaign to Prevent Teen Pregnancy, 2004).

10. Lydia Shrier and Richard Crosby, "Correlates of Sexual Experience Among a Nationally Representative Sample of Alternative High School Students," *Journal of School Health* 73, no. 5 (2003).

11. A. N. Feijoo, "Adolescent Sexual Health in Europe and the US: Why the Difference?" (fact sheet), Advocates for Youth, http://www.advocatesforyouth.org/publications/factsheet/fsest.htm (accessed January 9, 2005).

12. Rachel Jones, Alison Purcell, Susheela Singh, and Lawrence Finer, "Adolescents' Reports of Parental Knowledge of Adolescents' Use of Sexual Health Services and Their Reactions to Mandated Parental Notification for Prescription Contraception," *Journal of the American Medical Association* 293, no. 3 (2005), 340–348.

13. National Coalition against Censorship, "Abstinence-Only: Short on Facts, Long on Fancy," *Censorship News* 96 (Winter 2004–2005).

14. John Kelly, "In Abstinence Curricula, Where Does the Truth Lie?" *Youth Today,* February 2005, 7.

15. Vaishali Honawar, "Study: Pledgers of Sex Abstinence Still At Risk of STDs," *Education Week,* March 30, 2005, 20.

16. Lawrence K. Altman, "Studies Rebut Earlier Report on Pledges of Virginity," *New York Times,* June 15, 2005, http://www.nytimes.com/2005/06/15/health/15pledge.html (accessed October 5, 5005).

17. David Crary, "Passage of Teen Abortion Bill Called Likely," *Boston Globe,* January 31, 2005, A10.

18. Gillian Gillers, "Teenage Mothers Strive for Balance," *Yale Daily News Forum,* February 4, 2005.

19. Ibid.

20. Klerman, *Another Chance.*

21. Katie Tobin, research associate, interview with Joy Dryfoos, March 12, 2005.

22. Sue Alford, "Science and Success: Sex Education and Other Programs That Work to Prevent Teen Pregnancy, HIV, and Sexually Transmitted Infections," Advocates for Youth, 2003, http://www.advocatesforyouth.org/publications/sciencesuccess.pdf (accessed April 15, 2005).

23. Douglas Kirby, *Do Abstinence-Only Programs Delay the Initiation of Sex Among Young People and Reduce Teen Pregnancy?* (Washington, DC: National Campaign to Prevent Teen Pregnancy, October 2002).

24. Jennifer Manlove, Kerry Franzetta, Krystal McKinney, Angela Papillo, Elizabeth Terry-Humen, *No Time to Waste: Programs to Reduce Teen Pregnancy Among Middle School-Aged Youth* (Washington, DC: National Campaign to Prevent Teen Pregnancy and Child Trends, February 2004).

25. M. Eisen, C. Pallitto, C. Brodner, and N. Bodshun, *Teen Risk Taking: Promising Prevention Programs and Approaches* (Washington, D.C.: Urban Institute Research Report, 2000).

26. D. Kirby, *Emerging Answers: Research Findings on Programs to Reduce Teen Pregnancy* (Washington, DC: Campaign to Prevent Teen Pregnancy, 2001).

27. TOP, originally distributed by Cornerstone Consulting, now available from Wyman Institute for Youth Development, http://www.wymancenter.org (accessed January 31, 2006).

28. J. P. Allen, S. Philliber, S. Herrling, and G. P. Kuperminc, "Preventing Teen Pregnancy and Academic Failure: Experimental Evaluation of a Developmentally Based Approach," *Child Development* 64 (1997): 729–742.

29. National Research Council and Institute of Medicine, *Community Programs to Promote Youth Development,* ed. J. Eccles and J. A. Gootman (Washington, DC: National Academy Press, 2002): 307.

30. Alford, "Science and Success."

31. Promising Practices Network, http://www. promisingpractices.net/program.asp? programid=14 (accessed March 9, 2005).

32. Ibid.

33. Allen et al., "Preventing Teen Pregnancy and Academic Failure."

34. Ibid.

35. Promising Practices Network, http://www.promisingpractices.net/program.asp? programid=14#issuestoconsider (accessed March 9, 2005).

36. Ibid.

37. Children's Aid Society Carrera Adolescent Pregnancy Prevention Program, http://www.stopteenpregnancy.com (accessed January 26, 2005).

38. Alford, "Science and Success."

39. Children's Aid Society Carrera Adolescent Pregnancy Prevention Program, http://www.stopteenpregnancy.com (accessed January 25, 2005).

40. Kirby, *Emerging Answers.*

41. Alford, "Science and Success."

42. S. Philliber, K. J. Williams, S. Herrling, and E. West, "Preventing Pregnancy and Improving Health Care Access Among Teenagers: An Evaluation of the Children's Aid Society—Carrera Program," *Perspectives on Sexual and Reproductive Health* 34 (2002): 244–251.

43. Ibid.

44. H. S. Lonczak, R. D. Abbott, J. D. Hawkins, R. Kosterman, and R. F. Catalano, "Effects of the Seattle Social Development Project on Sexual Behavior, Pregnancy, Birth, and Sexually Transmitted Disease Outcomes by Age 21 Years," *Archives of Pediatrics and Adolescent Medicine* 156 (2002): 438–447.

45. Alford, "Science and Success," http://www.advocatesforyouth.org/programsthat work/17seattle.htm (accessed January 25, 2005).

46. Richard F. Catalano, "Developmental Prevention in Schools: Seattle Social Development and Raising Healthy Children Projects," http://depts.washington.edu/sdrg/DevPrev.pdf (accessed January 26, 2005).

47. Promising Practices Network, "Seattle Social Development Project," http://www.promisingpractices.net/program.asp?programid=64&benchmarkid=4#programoverview (accessed on March 9, 2005).

48. Ibid.

49. S. Aos, P. Phipps, R. Barnowski, and R. Lieb, "The Comparative Costs and Benefits of Programs to Reduce Crime," Washington State Institute for Public Policy, http://www.wsipp.wa.gov/pub.asp?docid=01-05-1201 (accessed March 9, 2005).

50. Alford. "Science and Success."

51. ETR Associates, ReCAPP, "Evidence Based Programs," http://www.etr.org/recapp/programs/saferchoices.htm (accessed March 5, 2005).

52. ETR Associates, ReCAPP, "Forums," http://www.etr.org/recapp/forum/forumsummary200309.htm (accessed March 5, 2005).

53. K. Coyle, K. Basen-Engquist, D. Kirby, G. Parcel, S. Banspach, R. B. Harrist, E. R. Baumler, and M. L. Weil, "Short-Term Impact of Safer Choices: A Multicomponent, School-Based HIV, Other STD, and Pregnancy Prevention Program," *Journal of School Health* 69 (1999): 181–188.

54. Alford, "Science and Success," http://www.advocatesforyouth.org/programsthatwork/4saferchoices.htm (accessed February 28, 2005).

55. K. Coyle, K. Basen-Engquist, D. Kirby, G. Parcel, S. Banspach, S. Collins, J. Baumler, S. Carvajal, and R. Harrist, "Safer Choices: Reducing Teen Pregnancy, HIV, and STDs," *Public Health Reports* 116 (2001, Suppl. no. 1): 82–93.

56. C. Markham, E. Baumler, R. Richesson, G. Parcel, K. Basen-Enquist, G. Kok, and D. Wilkerson, "Impact of HIV-Positive Speakers in a Multicomponent, School-Based HIV/STD Prevention Program for Inner-City Adolescents," *AIDS Education and Prevention* 12 (2000): 442–454.

57. P. East and E. Kiernan, *California's Adolescent Sibling Pregnancy Prevention Program: Evaluating the Impact of Pregnancy Prevention Services to the Siblings of Pregnant and Parenting Teens* (Final report), California Department of Health Services Maternal and Child Health Branch, March 2001.

58. ASPPP Homepage, http://www.mch.dhs.ca.gov/programs/asppp/aspppfacts.htm (accessed January 26, 2005).

59. P. East, E. Kiernan, and G. Chavez, "An Evaluation of the California Adolescent Sibling Pregnancy Prevention Program," *Perspectives on Sexual and Reproductive Health* 35, no. 2 (2003).

60. East and Kiernan, *California's Adolescent Sibling Pregnancy Prevention Program.*

CHAPTER FOUR

VIOLENCE AND DELINQUENCY

Stories of violence by and against youth explode from the news like gun-shots from a passing car. It would seem that America is under attack by armed teenagers. During the early 1980s, about a thousand murders were committed by teens in the United States each year. By the middle of the 1990s, that had grown to over three thousand per year, or almost 10 percent of all murders. Numbers like that make it sound like teen vio-lence is a growing epidemic, an impression given further validity by the Centers for Disease Control and Prevention, which now identify teen violence as a major public health problem.

Talking about teen violence in terms of murder is the obvious thing to do because of the dramatic finality and loss that death brings, but the epidemic—if that is actually what it is—encompasses much more than murder. The statistics for armed robbery, assault, rape, and carjackings by juveniles in the United States are higher than in any other country in the world. The teenage perpetrators and victims come from every walk of life and every ethnic background. People of all ages are shocked, saddened, and frightened by this news, but no one is more immediately affected by the epidemic of teen violence than teenagers themselves.[1]

This is scary stuff, and certainly the vision of a society "under attack by armed teenagers" is a threatening one. But it's not really new. Adult society has long been afraid of teenagers to a greater or lesser degree. It's traditional for the older generation to bemoan its children's and grandchildren's lack of morals; this has been going on at least since the ancient Greeks and probably since the dawn of civilization. People have always thought that society was in worse shape than when they were young and that "kids today" have no respect or decency or ambition or—fill in the blank. This rosy picture of the past combines with media hype about teen violence and personal apprehension about young people's perceived lack of inhibition and control to create a very real fear of teenagers.

Is America under attack by teenagers? Are we threatened by marauding gangs of thugs and bands of purse snatchers? Does Columbine, where two boys opened fire in a high school, killing 15 people, injuring 23 others, and finally killing themselves, represent a pattern of behavior for social rejects? Are innocent young people afraid to go to school?

MAJOR TRENDS

- Most adolescents are not engaged in violent behaviors.
- 17% of high school students carry a weapon, 6% a gun.
- Some teenagers are involved in many high-risk behaviors: gang warfare, bullying, gambling.
- More than 1.6 million young people committed offenses in 2002, and many of them went to prison.
- More than 400,000 teenagers reported that they were victims of violence in one recent year.

WHAT ARE THE FACTS?

"Alarmist rhetoric about a new generation of juvenile 'superpredators' and a 'ticking time bomb' of juvenile crime pervaded the public consciousness during the 1990s and diverted political leaders' attention from the crucial task of investing in what works. This rhetoric is unfounded."[2]

In actuality, at least 75% of all 10- to 17-year-olds have experienced little or no violent behavior. They do not carry weapons, rarely get in fights, are not bullied, and do not bully others. They are good, peaceful young people trying to succeed in a sometimes violent society. The fact is that a very small group is responsible for most of the teenage violence. About 5% of 15- to 19-year-olds were adjudicated as juvenile offenders in 2003, and it is estimated that 15–20% of all teenagers commit 80% of all crimes attributed to their age group.

It is true that teen violence rates are higher in the United States than in any other Western country. We have more shootings, more fights, more sexual violence, and more Columbine-like high school attacks than any comparable society. However, the rates for all of the various situations in which young people act out violently have decreased in recent years. The number of juvenile arrests peaked in 1995, a decade ago, for almost all categories except possession of marijuana and dangerous nonnarcotic drugs such as amphetamines and barbiturates.

Using self-reported data from several different surveys, we can examine the current incidence of behaviors that fall under the broadly defined category of violence and delinquency. Weapon carrying, including guns and knives, and fighting are significant indicators of the violent environment in which some young people live. Bullying is a negative behavior that is often a marker of deeper trouble within. Gambling is not physically threatening but is an example of an illegal activity that flourishes without much attention from law enforcement.

Delinquency arrest and case rates derive from official crime statistics reports, which provide an annual measure of the degree to which young people are in trouble with the law. The number of teenagers who resort to killing others with guns (firearm mortality) is a significant indicator of a violent society. Finally, information about victims helps show which young people are getting hurt, either by their peers or by adults.

Our purpose is to determine not only who does what but also how best to prevent destructive behaviors and encourage positive ones.

Self-Reports of Weapon Carrying

It is true that quite a few high school students apparently fear violence and want to be ready when it comes. We know that about one in six students in 9th–12th grades walk around with a gun, a knife, or a club and that 6% (or slightly more than one-third of this weapon-carrying group) report that they carry guns (Table 4.1).[3] In 2003, about 17% of 9th–12th graders had carried a weapon within the preceding month; this was a significant decrease from the 1991 report of 26%. Male students are much more likely to carry weapons than females, and there are few differences by race.

Gun-carrying rates dispel the myth that only minority teens have access to weapons. Table 4.1 shows that 10% of white males, 11% of black males, and 8% of Hispanic males reported having carried a gun within the preceding month. A few female high school students also reported carrying guns, including almost 3% of Hispanic girls, 2% of black girls, and 1% of white girls in 9th–12th grades. The differences by race are insignificant. Rates of gun carrying did not differ by grade: 9th graders had similar rates to 12th graders.

Gun-carrying rates were higher in certain parts of the country, such as Detroit, Dallas, and Houston (among the local cities with surveys) and in the southern and western states (for example, 10% in Wyoming vs. 3% in Massachusetts).

Reports also showed a marked decrease in fighting; during 2003, one-third

Table 4.1 Percent of High School Students Who Carried a Gun or Other Weapon, by Gender, Race, and Grade, 2003

	Weapon			Gun		
	Total	*Male*	*Female*	*Total*	*Male*	*Female*
Total	17	27	7	6	10	2
White	17	27	6	6	10	2
Black	17	25	10	6	11	1
Hispanic	17	24	9	5	8	3
9th grade	18	27	9	6	9	2
12th grade	16	25	5	6	10	1

Source: Centers for Disease Control and Prevention, "Youth Risk Behavior Surveillance, United States, 2003," *Morbidity and Mortality Weekly Report* 53, no. SS-2 (May 21, 2004): Table 6.

of high school students had been in a fight, compared with 43% in 1991. Male students are more likely to have been in a fight (38% white, 46% black, and 43% Hispanic), but female students also have high rates (22, 34, and 30%, respectively). About 4% of all high school students reported that they had been injured in a physical fight. Despite these lowered rates of fighting, more than 5% of all high school students said they had stayed away from school because of safety concerns on at least one day of the preceding month.

Bullying

Bullying is a behavior with mostly minor short-term consequences but serious long-term sequelae. It is considered an "early warning": Those who are victimized can explode later on, and those who do the victimizing are often on a path toward more violent acts.

About 15% of all students are either bullied regularly or bully other children.[4] Such behaviors as teasing, taunting, threatening, hitting, and stealing are generally initiated by one or two students against a victim. Boys are more frequently involved in direct bullying; girls tend to use more subtle, indirect strategies such as socially isolating other girls. Children who were bullied frequently in school often are depressed as adults.[5]

The most serious bullies were seven times more likely to carry a weapon to school than those who were neither bullied nor bullies. By age 24, 60% of boys classified as bullies in grades 6–9 had been convicted of a least one crime, and 40% had three or more convictions (compared with 10% of those who were not bullies).

Illegal Gambling

Gambling is a new addition to the list of illegal high-risk behaviors. It is of interest here because it shows how the adult world turns a blind eye to illegal teenage activities. A unique survey, the Annenberg National Survey of Youth (2003), found that 45% of 14- to 17-year-olds had gambled within the previous month.[6] More than 1 in 10 teens had purchased lottery tickets, bet on horses, gambled on the Internet, or played slot machines, all clearly illegal activities for minors. About one-fourth had bet on sports.

States are supposed to regulate these practices and prohibit sales or participation at prescribed age limits. According to Durand Jacobs, an expert on gaming, teen gambling spikes significantly in states that launch lotteries. "State-run gaming lends an air of credibility to behavior that might otherwise be considered risky."[7] Jacobs found that most children gamble first with parents or family. Adolescents are five times more likely to have gambling problems than are adults.

A study in Indiana found that 60% of adolescents there had played instant lottery games. Observers have found that the major problem with vending machine sales is the difficulty of enforcing the legal age requirement. When school lets out, local convenience stores are packed with children rushing to buy lottery tickets. Surveys in various states show that a high percentage of underage adolescents play the lottery: 32% in Louisiana, 34% in Texas, 35% in Connecticut, and 75% in Massachusetts. Lottery retailers in many other states are lax in enforcing age regulations. An experimental survey found that a 16-year-old girl succeeded in purchasing lottery tickets from 49 of 50 central Illinois lottery retailers.

Gangs

Gangs are often organized in the inner city as protection against other groups and appear to be structured along racial/ethnic lines.[8] Gang members are usually between 14 and 20, but some are recruited as young as age 9, especially if they come from a gang background. Once gang membership is established, it is hard to convince a young person to break away from the camaraderie and protection offered by the group.

Hmongs are people from southeast Asia who came to the United States after the Vietnam War. The Cobras were the first such gang in Minnesota among young Hmong boys. A group of friends who played on a soccer team banded together to protect themselves and other Hmong youth from the racism they encountered at school, in their housing projects, and in their neighborhoods. This led to criminal behavior, including auto theft and aggravated assault. When some 10- and 11-year-old Hmong boys were turned down for membership, they started their own gang, White Tigers, and broke into gun stores to steal weapons. In 1999, within a 6-week period, at least 22 shootings with 2 deaths and 14 injuries were attributed to rival Hmong gangs in the St. Paul area. The easy availability of guns made this violence possible.

—Richard Straka, "The Violence of Hmong Gangs and the Crime of Rape," *FBI Law Enforcement Bulletin*, February 2003, 12–15.

In 2002, a survey of youth gangs produced the estimate that there were about 21,500 gangs in the United States, with about 731,500 members. Some 39% of gang members were 17 or under, 46% were 18–24, and 14% were older. Eight percent were females. One-third of the gang members were black, almost half were Hispanic, 12% were white, and 8% Asian and others.[9] However, gang membership is on the wane, along with all the other indicators of teen violence except drug-related violations.

In Denver, the 14% of teens who were in gangs committed 89% of violent acts by teens. Gang members lead hazardous lives; they are 60% more likely than non–gang members to be killed, especially in recent years, as gangs have begun to use more lethal weapons and have more frequently used cars in drive-by shootings.

According to Michael Carlie,

> There are many kinds of gangs in the United States and elsewhere. They may be categorized in several ways: by their degree of organization (from loosely organized street gangs to highly organized crime units such as the Mexican Mafia and Sicilian Mafia); location (i.e., street gangs, prison gangs); nation (i.e., Bloods and Crips, Gangster Disciples, People, Folk, and Mexican Mafia); mode of transportation (i.e., car clubs, biker gangs); or longevity (i.e., generational); to name a few.[10]

Understanding diverse cultures is essential in order to address the complex issues that underlie the creation of gangs.

Delinquency Cases

Delinquency figures are difficult to sort out. The National Center for Juvenile Justice reports estimates of the number of arrests of juveniles under 18 in one source document and numbers of delinquency cases disposed of by juvenile courts in another. In 2002, law enforcement agencies estimated that 2,261,000 arrests were made of young people under the age of 18.[11] Table 4.2 shows the total number of arrests, listed from most serious to least serious offense. The most prevalent offense was larceny-theft, followed by assaults, disorderly conduct, drug abuse violations, liquor-law violations, curfew violation and loitering, running away, and vandalism.

Table 4.2 Number of Juvenile Arrests in 2002

Offense	Estimated Number of Arrests
Total	2,261,000
Violent crime total	92,000
Murder	1,360
Forcible rape	4,270
Robbery	24,470
Aggravated assault	61,610
Property crime total	481,600
Burglary	86,500
Larceny-theft	341,700
Motor vehicle theft	45,200
Arson	6,200
Nonindex crimes total	1,832,000
Other assaults	236,300
Stolen property	26,100
Vandalism	105,900
Weapons possession	35,100
Sex offense	20,900
Drug abuse violations	186,600
Driving under the influence	21,800
Liquor law violations	149,400
Drunkenness	18,700
Disorderly conduct	192,900
Curfew and loitering	141,300
Runaways	125,700
All other offenses	429,000

Source: U.S. Department of Justice, Federal Bureau of Investigation, *Crime in the United States 2002* (Washington, DC: U.S. Government Printing Office, 2003), Tables 29, 32, 34, 36, and 40. Arrest estimates developed by the National Center for Juvenile Justice.

For uniformity of reporting information, arrests for eight offenses (murder, rape, robbery, aggravated assault, burglary, larceny, motor vehicle theft, and arson) are reported by law enforcement agencies nationwide. These offenses are referred to as index crimes and, based on their seriousness, a change in frequency of their occurrence is an indication of national trends in crime. Other offenses are called nonindex crimes, and together the index and nonindex crime rates add up to the total crime rate.

The number of delinquency cases disposed of in 2000 (the most recent data available) was reported as 1,612,000, compared with 2,261,000 juvenile arrests in 2002. Why is there so much difference? The reason is that the larger figure includes multiple arrests (offenses) of the same individual in one year, whereas the lower figure counts individuals (juveniles) who were arrested at least once and brought to juvenile court. These data are gathered by the National Center for Juvenile Justice from courts with juvenile jurisdiction in participating states.

A delinquency offense is an act committed by a juvenile for which an adult could be prosecuted in a criminal court. Disposition of a case involves taking a definite action, such as waiving the case to criminal court, dismissing the case, placing the youth on probation, placing the youth in a facility for delinquents, or imposing a fine or requiring restitution or community service. The FBI requires law enforcement agencies to classify an arrest by the most serious offense charged in that arrest. For example, the arrest of a youth charged with aggravated assault and possession of a controlled substance would be reported to the FBI as an arrest for aggravated assault. Thus, an unknown number of arrests included a drug charge as a lesser offense, which makes the statistics less reliable as indicators of total numbers of various offenses.

The number of delinquency cases increased by 22% from 1.3 million in 1990 to 1.6 million in 2000. However, because of the growth in population, the case rate increased only from 51 to 52 per 1,000 ten- to seventeen-year-olds, indicating that about 5% of the youth population was in trouble with the law. There was little change in the number of violent offenses and property offenses during this decade, but a sizable increase took place in lesser crimes (delinquency offenses) such as assault, drug-law violations, and minor violations such as trespassing and disorderly conduct. The case rates (per 1,000) were higher among males (77) than females (26) and higher among black teenagers (92) than white (46); however, the black rate actually went down from 112 in 1992, while the white rate stayed the same. More than 50% of the juvenile cases of murder, robbery, prostitution, and gambling were attributed to blacks. Very few black teenagers were arrested for drunkenness, driving under the influence, or disobeying liquor laws. Three-fourths of the drug violations were committed by white teenagers, a percentage that is close to their representation in the population.

According to the Center on Juvenile and Criminal Justice, African Americans represent 15% of the population, 26% of juvenile arrests, 44% of teens who are detained, 46% of those who are judicially waived to criminal court, and 58% of those admitted to state prisons.[12]

Arrests for Drug Abuse

Table 4.3 presents a compilation of 133,557 juvenile drug arrests in 2002, according to the specific charge (the figure in Table 4.2 for drug abuse violations is larger, for reasons not explained in the source documents). Most of the arrests were for possession of drugs: Close to 86,000 young people were arrested for marijuana possession, a huge number of cases.

Table4.3 Number of Juvenile Arrests for Drug Abuse, 2002

Offense	Number of Arrests
Total	133,557
Sale and manufacturing	
Total	22,086
Heroin/cocaine	8,832
Marijuana	9,962
Synthetic narcotics	974
Dangerous nonnarcotic drugs (e.g., amphetamines, barbiturates)	2,318
Possession	
Total	111,471
Heroin/cocaine	10,969
Marijuana	85,769
Synthetic narcotics	2,805
Dangerous nonnarcotic drugs	11,928

Source: U. S. Department of Justice, Federal Bureau of Investigation, *Crime in the United States Annual* (Washington, DC: U.S. Government Printing Office, 2003), Table 312.

Homicide

The number of juvenile arrests for homicide declined dramatically from 1993, when there were 3,284, to 2002, when there were 1,360. This decline has been attributed to a better economic situation, improvements in law enforcement (such as community policing and restrictions on gun access for young people), and after-school programs that keep young people off the street.

Looking at data by state, Murman and colleagues found that firearm prevalence was the single significant independent variable; it predicted 47% of the state-to-state variation in child and adolescent firearm mortality.[13] The more guns in a state, the more they were used by teenagers.

School Violence

Students ages 12–18 reported almost 2 million crimes that occurred at school or going to or from school in 2000, a rate of 72 per 1,000 students (around 7%).[14] Those with the highest rates were males and younger teenagers (12–14). About 64% of the crimes were theft, and 7% were serious violent crimes (rape, sexual assault, robbery, and aggravated assault). The rest were nonserious violent crimes (fighting).

The U.S. Secret Service and the U.S. Department of Education joined forces to examine school violence after the devastating Columbine incident.[15] They organized the Safe School Initiative, an intensive study of 37 incidents involving 41 attackers in targeted school violence that had taken place between 1974 and 2000. In most of these incidents, the attacker shot one or more students or faculty in the school.

Attackers—students who engaged in targeted school violence—did not fit any profile. They were all boys, mostly between 13 and 18, mostly white (12% African American, 5% Hispanic, 5% other), and from a variety of family settings. They were doing reasonably well in school, and two-thirds had never been in trouble in school. Only about one-fourth associated with known "fringe" or unpopular groups. More than half of the attackers were involved with some form of violence-related media (Internet, movies, books).

What distinguished these boys from others is their sense of being bullied, persecuted, or injured by others prior to the attack. Although they did not have a history of mental health diagnoses (only one-third had ever had a mental health evaluation), most seemed to be extremely depressed or desperate. Almost all had experienced a significant loss, such as a loved one, illness, or failure, and had had difficulty coping with it.

Most had no history of prior violent or criminal behavior, although one-quarter had a prior history of arrest. Almost all these boys had caused others to be concerned and had indicated a need for help. At least 59% had access to guns, and 15% had prior experience with bombs or explosives.

These findings suggest that potential attackers might be identified through more thorough mental health evaluations, particularly focusing on young men who are depressed and grieving.

After an Arrest

What happens to the juvenile delinquency cases that reach juvenile court? Various outcomes may ensue. A case disposed means that a definite action has been taken as a result of a referral to juvenile court. Of the 1.6 million cases that reached juvenile court in one year (2000), about two-thirds were adjudicated as delinquent. Of those adjudicated delinquent, the majority (63%) were placed on probation; 24% were placed out of home; 10% were disposed of through fines, restitution, community service, and referrals outside the court; and almost 3% were dismissed. About half of the nonadjudicated cases were dismissed, a quarter placed on probation, and the rest disposed of through fines and other means.

Another window on the juvenile justice system comes from reports from local police departments. In 2002, these reports listed 737,282 juveniles taken into custody (not including traffic and neglect cases). Of these, 73% were referred to juvenile court, 18% were handled within the department and released, 7% were referred to criminal or adult court, and the remaining 2% were referred to welfare or other police agencies.

It is difficult to find out exactly how many young people are incarcerated. More than 110,000 juveniles were in public or private residential facilities in 2000.[16] In 2004, it was reported that there were about 2,500 youths under 18 in state prisons and about 7,000 in local jails. These figures were lower than earlier ones.[17]

Victims

Direct exposure to violence has been associated with anxiety and depression and with later violent behavior on the part of the victim. More research has been done on the effects on actual victims than on those who simply witnessed violence (indirect exposure).

Child Abuse and Neglect

A very large number of teenagers are victims of child abuse and neglect every year. In 2002, there were almost 325,000 reports of child abuse and neglect for 10- to 17-year-olds, a 35% increase from 239,000 in 1990. (These are individual reports, and the same child might be reported repeatedly in the same year.)[18]

Juvenile Victims

Almost 400,000 teenagers reported that they had been victims of violence in 2000. This produces a rate of 16 per 1,000 twelve- to seventeen-year-olds, or 1.6% of this age group. The rates are higher among older teens and much higher among males (23) than females (9).

In 2003, 1,333 murder victims were under the age of 18; this was 54% lower than the peak year of 1993, when an estimated 2,880 juveniles were murdered. Almost half of the juvenile victims were killed with a firearm and almost one-fourth by physical assaults (hands, fists, etc.). The younger the child, the more likely he or she was to die from physical assault.

Victims of Dating Violence

About 10% of all high school students report that they have been hit, slapped, or physically hurt on purpose by their girlfriends or boyfriends one or more times within the preceding year. For this factor, few differences were apparent between genders and racial groups. However, 10% of females, compared with 5% of males, said that they had been forced to have sexual intercourse.

Predictors

As we have seen, about one in six teenagers carries a weapon, and about one-third of those weapons are guns. One in 20 teenagers becomes a delinquency case in a given year, about the same proportion as those who carry guns.

Many studies have been conducted on risk and protective factors related to youth violence. The Office of Juvenile Justice and Delinquency Prevention brought together 22 researchers to examine current research through a meta-analysis of existing data sets.[19] This analysis, published in 2000, identified a number of significant factors that lead to violent behavior and ranked them according to the strength of the correlation between the predictor and the outcome. We have indicated those predictors that were most relevant at earlier ages (6–11) as E and at later ages (12–14) as L; we have indicated with an asterisk those predictors with the strongest correlations (more than .15).

1. Individual factors
   a. *Male (E) (L)
   b. *Early aggressiveness (E) (L)
   c. Hyperactivity and concentration problems (attention deficit) (L)
   d. Involvement in other high-risk behaviors such as smoking, early sexual intercourse, using or selling drugs (E) (L)
2. Family factors
   a. *Low socioeconomic status (E)
   b. Lack of involvement in child's life
   c. Parent criminality; fathers had committed crime/been arrested (E)
   d. Child physical abuse or neglect
   e. Poor family management practices: lack of monitoring and supervision, inconsistent discipline (L)
   f. Overly strict, authoritarian parents
   g. Parent-child separation; single-parent family
   h. Exposure to violence and family conflict
   i. Lack of emotional attachment to parents or caretakers
3. School factors
   a. Academic failure (L)
   b. Being held back in school
   c. Low attachment and commitment to school

    d. High truancy rate

    e. Attending a school with high delinquency rate

    f. Behavior problems in school

4. Peer-related factors

    a. Delinquent siblings

    b. Delinquent peers (L)

    c. Gang membership

    d. Social rejection by peers

5. Community and neighborhood factors

    a. Poverty

    b. Community disorganization: crime, gangs, poor housing, drugs

    c. Exposure to violence and racial prejudice

    d. Lack of economic opportunity

    e. Transience

Most of the significant relationships between these factors and violent outcomes were found among young males but not females.

There is no big news in these data. Children who exhibit aggressive behavior at early ages are at high risk of behaving aggressively as they grow older unless some intensive intervention takes place with them and their families. Young people who "hang with" others who are acting out in gangs or small groups are likely to get in trouble. Children doing poorly in school are at high risk of unacceptable behaviors, including carrying weapons to school, bullying others, giving teachers a hard time, and even plotting against the school. Although being depressed or "stressed out" does not appear on the experts' list, these conditions are often precursors of violent behavior, as evidenced among the Columbine-type teenagers.

A State-of-the-Science Conference on preventing violence, convened by the National Institutes of Health in 2004, reached conclusions similar to those of the Office of Juvenile Justice and Delinquency Prevention researchers:

> There is evidence suggesting that violence develops along distinct trajectories, each with different natural histories and sets of risk and protective factors . . . there appears to be an early-onset form of violence that seems to persist into adulthood as well as a later-onset and limited-duration form of adolescent violence . . . in early childhood [risk factors] are children's involvement in fighting, crimes or status offenses,

victimization, or substance abuse in childhood. At the family level, risk factors include inconsistent or hard parenting and family conflict. Poor peer relations, involvement in gangs, lack of connection to school, and living in a violent neighborhood appear to be more important risk factors in adolescence.[20]

One study reported that the percentage of young people convicted for violent crimes increased from 3% for those with no risk factors to 31% for those with four risk factors (low family income, large family size, low nonverbal IQ at ages 8–19, and poor parental child-rearing behavior).[21] The study group concluded, "The larger the number of risk factors to which an individual is exposed, the greater the probability that the individual will engage in violent behavior. Multicomponent targeting identification of shared predictors and constellations of risk factors may be more effective in preventing violence than those that target single risk factors." We certainly agree with this conclusion.

WHAT CAN BE DONE?

As we have seen, violence comes in many forms, from little children teasing one another to adolescents carrying guns to school and even using them to kill other teenagers or adults. All of this activity is taking place in a society that fosters violence at many levels. As a nation, we have been quick to invade other countries and use our weapons not only to kill the "enemy" but also to wipe out large numbers of innocent civilians. Children grow up seeing destructive behaviors on the television news. This is reinforced by the media with violent crime shows and movies, computer games, and comic books.

Policies

Most of the laws that govern the issues relating to violence—and most particularly gun control—emanate from state governments. Gun control programs have proven their effectiveness in lowering homicide rates: the tighter the regulations, the lower the juvenile homicide rate. (Tight regulation has not had the same effect on juvenile drug arrests, at least for marijuana and nonnarcotic drug possession.) Police efforts to work in the community in positive ways have contributed to the decline in gang membership. And because most teenagers are in school, at least initially, increased attention is being given to school-based prevention programs.

Gun Control

"Consider: a 12-year-old in North Carolina needs parental permission to play Little League Baseball but not to possess a rifle or shotgun. In Texas and five other states, there is no minimum legal age requirement for gun possession."[22]

The first major gun control initiative, enacted by Congress in 1934, regulated the sale of fully automatic weapons such as machine guns.[23] In 1938, further legislation required gun sellers to be licensed, and persons with felony records were prohibited from purchasing guns. Forty years later, in 1968, the Gun Control Act was passed; it regulated imported guns and prohibited minors, mental incompetents, and users of illegal drugs from purchasing guns. By 1986, mandatory penalties were established for using guns in commission of a federal crime, and in 1990, legislation was passed that banned the manufacture or importation of semiautomatic assault weapons.

The Brady Bill in 1994 imposed a 5-day waiting period for purchasers of handguns and required local authorities to conduct background checks on all purchasers. However, the Supreme Court ruled that the background check was unconstitutional because it infringed on states' rights. The law was revised so that a background check could be made instantly through a national computer system. In 1994, Congress passed a ban on certain types of assault weapons; it expired in 2004, and the newly elected Congress did not renew the legislation, not surprising given that of the 251 candidates endorsed by the National Rifle Association, 241 won seats in the House that year. Gun Owners of America has published a list of gun control laws that they would like to see repealed, including the ban on machine guns, the Brady background check, prohibitions on firearms within 1,000 feet of school property, and a Washington, D.C., gun ban.

It is currently possible to buy guns at gun shows and flea markets. About 10% of guns used in crimes by juveniles were sold in these locations, mostly by unlicensed sellers. No background checks are required. The guns used by the boys in the Columbine incident were purchased at a local gun show.

Every state has its own set of laws, a situation that creates confusing discrepancies. For example, federal law prohibits the sale of handguns to those under 21, but it makes possession of a gun unlawful only for persons under the age of 18.[24] Therefore, unless prohibited by state law, sales to persons 18–21 can take place in the secondary or private (resale) market. In 2004, only 12 states and Washington, D.C., prohibited sales in the private market to those under 21, and 6 others regulated all sales. In the other 32 states, there were no restrictions, and a background check was not required in private gun sales to persons 18–21.

Deborah Prothrow-Stith and Howard Spivak point out how deeply ingrained gun ownership is in the culture of this nation.[25] Estimates of the number of guns currently in circulation range from 80 million handguns to 192 million firearms, including rifles and shotguns.

The failure of the United States to deal effectively with the regulation of handguns is perplexing in light of international comparisons. For example, the United Kingdom, after a single school shooting episode, passed one of the strictest gun regulation laws in the world; there you cannot even transport a handgun from a gun club to your home. But although there is strong support in the United States for regulation of guns, so far the opposition is too well organized to overcome.

Therefore, it makes sense to look at other ways of trying to keep guns out of teenagers' hands. A strategy that may be more successful than gun control is product liability lawsuits; gun manufacturers can be sued for deaths of individuals murdered with guns. In addition, states have passed various laws to regulate guns, including making it a crime to leave a loaded weapon within easy access of minors and prohibiting concealed weapons.

From Washington
House Votes to Repeal District Gun Restriction

The U.S. House of Representatives voted overwhelmingly yesterday to repeal one of the District's gun restrictions, prohibiting the city from spending funds to enforce a law that requires any firearms kept at home to be unloaded and disassembled or bound by a trigger lock.

The vote of 259 to 161 marked the third time since 1999 that the House has targeted the city's gun laws, which are among the most stringent in the nation. A broader repeal passed the House by a slightly narrower margin last fall but died in the Senate.

Gun rights groups said this measure's chances of clearing the Senate are greater because it is attached to a spending bill that Congress must pass to avoid a government shutdown.

Opponents of the repeal said they still have a good chance of stopping it. The Senate has yet to act on the spending bill, and differences between the House and Senate versions will be resolved by conference committee members who traditionally dislike unrelated amendments, opponents said.

Rep. Mark Edward Souder (R-Ind.), the measure's sponsor, said it marked "an extremely simple, common-sense . . . first step" toward freer gun ownership, allowing residents to keep loaded, assembled and unlocked weapons in their homes, just as D.C. business owners are allowed to do at workplaces.

Under D.C. law, residents can keep rifles and shotguns in their homes, as well as handguns owned and registered by Feb. 22, 1977, but only if they are stored in a nonoperating condition. The House amendment would prevent the city from enforcing that restriction. Unlike the bill passed by the House last year, it would not alter the city's ban on handguns, Souder said.

"This amendment does not legalize anything that can't be legally owned now. No machine guns, sawed-off shotguns, AK-47s or Uzis," he said. "All it does is . . . [it] gives D.C. citizens the same rights at home that they have at work."

Del. [non-voting delegate to the House of Representatives] Eleanor Holmes Norton (D-D.C.), Mayor Anthony A. Williams (D) and Police Chief Charles H. Ramsey condemned the House action, calling it a subversion of democracy for 550,000 District residents who are denied a vote in Congress and who have long battled gun-related killings, robberies and assaults common to large cities. Washington area House members also criticized the measure, noting that Chicago and New York have restrictive gun laws but are not singled out by Congress under pressure from interest groups.

D.C. officials said the measure, although narrowly drawn, could have broader impact. Norton, a Georgetown University law professor, said she believed the language could undo the District's limits on gun possession, enabling residents to openly carry rifles and shotguns in public. Ramsey said the measure would take away the ability of police to charge negligent gun owners with gun safety violations, such as when their weapons are fired in accidental shootings involving children.

"It's discouraging when members of Congress who don't represent our city try to shove their laws down our throats," Williams said in a statement. "The entire community in the District is working hard to keep handgun violence down, and this effort led by Republicans in Congress would take us in the wrong direction."

—Spencer Hsu, "House Votes to Repeal District Gun Restriction," July 1, 2005, www.washingtonpost.com/wp-dyn/content/articles/ 2005/06/30/AR2005063001793.html (accessed July 18, 2005).

Improving the Justice System

"Children in adult institutions are five times as likely to be sexually assaulted, twice as likely to be beaten by staff, 50 percent more likely to be attacked with a weapon, and eight times as likely to commit suicide as children confined in juvenile facilities."[26]

The American Youth Policy Forum has raised a number of issues at the state and local levels that pertain to reducing juvenile crime.[27] State policies that need to be changed include the trial in adult criminal courts of young people who are not chronic or violent offenders. Locking up juvenile offenders in adult jails and prisons subjects them to sexual assaults, physical beatings, and close contact with career criminals. They are much more likely to be rearrested after release and to commit more serious new offenses. States should facilitate their entry into effective prevention programs rather than incarcerating them.

Creating an Integrated Local Response to the Issue of Delinquency

Multnomah County (Portland), Oregon, has a plan for decreasing juvenile arrests developed by its Juvenile Justice and Delinquency Prevention Strategic Planning Committee, which was appointed by the Department of Community Justice.[28] This document appears to cover the major points that should be addressed at the local level to prevent violence and promote prosocial behavior among young people.

1. Support at-risk youth in completing high school and engaging in structured activities after school. Encourage at-risk students to participate in shaping their own school experience and school decision making. Help parents become more involved in school, and keep schools open after school, weekends, and summers. Place juvenile court case counselors in schools to increase contact with parents and teachers.

2. Prevent and intervene early in delinquency. Ensure that high-risk young people have regular contact with adult role models. Support neighborhood-based community courts. Establish a Teen Court, community service projects, and a receiving center for homeless teens and other status offenders for referral to appropriate resources.

3. Improve the juvenile justice system. Develop a case classification system and improve the functioning of the juvenile court case counselors. Provide access to alcohol and drug counseling, mental health programs, and other needed services and expand access to Multisystemic Family Therapy. Develop alternatives to detention for low-risk and first-time offenders.

4. Direct specialized resources toward the highest-risk young people. Track youth gangs and violence incidents, especially in "hot spots." Disrupt the flow of illegal guns to juveniles.

The American Youth Policy Forum would add to this list:[29]

- Offer intensive, family-focused counseling by trained therapists employed by local juvenile justice agencies.
- Provide close supervision and effective counseling and support services after completion of incarceration.
- Provide innovative services, such as youth aid panels, family group conferencing, drug courts, and teen courts, that hold young people accountable while connecting them to positive resources in the community.
- Ensure that probation officers have no more than 30 cases to supervise at any one time.
- Support early intervention with infants and families.
- Provide coordinated high-quality child welfare, mental health, special education, and juvenile justice services for high-risk teens.
- Provide high-quality after-school programs and other positive youth development opportunities, particularly in less advantaged neighborhoods.
- Collect data on critical risk factors and develop comprehensive plans to reduce juvenile crime rates.

School Safety

"'Zero tolerance' policies are a reflection of our nation's zeal to 'get tough on crime,' and are a misguided reaction to violent tragedies such as the shooting at Columbine High School. These policies have increased schools' use of their harshest tools for controlling student behavior—barring students from school, either temporarily or permanently."[30]

There is little agreement about how schools should be made safer or whether it is even necessary.[31] The hard line calls for metal detectors, security personnel, and zero tolerance for weapons possession. (In a recent year, Baltimore schools suspended 14,356 students, 16% of the entire student body.) Others favor counseling, conflict resolution programs, and better communication between school and home. The National Education Association believes we should follow both approaches by expanding access to counseling, anger management, and peer mediation; by attaching students to adult role models in after-school education and recreation programs; and by encouraging communication between students and adults about rumors and threats. Obviously, schools that pay attention to the needs of high-risk children and that have adequate resources for smaller class sizes and well-qualified teachers are an important component of violence prevention.

Schools should start with a comprehensive violence prevention and response plan. The National Mental Health and Education Center calls for multidisciplinary mental health teams that offer specific programs for social skills training, individual and group counseling, and consultations with school staff and parents.

Programs

Our review of the predictors or antecedents of violence-related behaviors sets the stage for an appraisal of prevention programs. Given what we know about young people at risk for violent acts and about factors that help protect against violent behaviors, we would look for early intervention, intense and sustained individual attention from a caring adult, outreach to families, and strong efforts to ensure effective educational experiences.

Much research has been done on programs that aim to prevent youth violence. These efforts are summarized in three significant reports:

- *The Best Practices Sourcebook,* compiled by the Centers for Disease Control and Prevention, outlines approximately 70 effective programs that are broken down into four domains of intervention: family, home-visiting, social-cognitive strategy, and mentoring.[32]

- *Youth Violence,* the Surgeon General's Report, for which Delbert Eliott, an expert on violence prevention, was the senior consultant, outlines 27 programs categorized into risk prevention and violence prevention.[33]
- *Blueprints for Violence Prevention,* completed at the University of Colorado at Boulder in collaboration with the Office of Juvenile Justice and Prevention, is probably the most extensive search, reviewing more than 600 violence prevention programs and ultimately selecting 11 model programs and 21 promising programs.[34] The Blueprints initiative has also made a commitment to support superior programs and to fund the replication of eight of these programs nationwide.

When reviewing these sources, it is important to note that although the publications are current, the evaluations of the programs were conducted some years ago under different circumstances.

Each of the five prevention programs described here displays at least one strong outcome that either directly shows a reduction in youth violence (such as lower delinquency rates) or directly correlates with future reduction of aggressive or violent behavior (such as a significant increase in socially acceptable behavior). In addition, these five programs focus on different domains of children's lives: individual, family, school, and community.

Early Intervention: The Incredible Years Training Series

The goal of the Incredible Years Training Series (IYS) is "to prevent and reduce the occurrence of aggressive and oppositional behavior in children (aged 3–10), thus reducing the chance of developing later delinquent behavior."[35] IYS was developed in the 1980s by Dr. Carolyn Webster-Stratton, professor and director of the Parenting Clinic at the University of Washington.[36]

IYS's theoretical framework is rooted in Gerald R. Patterson's social learning model, which holds that a child's socialization or behavioral problems exist, in part, because of constant negative reinforcement from adults. Patterson postulates that if parents and teachers can learn and model positive discipline strategies and problem-solving techniques, children will develop stronger social competencies, such as sharing, making friends, or resolving conflicts well, and their aggressive tendencies will be reduced.[37] Because young children who display high levels of aggressive behavior may be at greater risk than others for developing violent tendencies in adolescence, Webster-Stratton believes that prevention is most effective in the early, preadolescent years.

IYS's three components are parent training, teacher training, and child training. Therapists generally run the parenting programs and are encouraged to build strong, intimate, and friendly relationships with the parents they serve.[38] The three parent-training curricula (basic parenting skills, parental communication and anger management, and parental promotion of children's academic skills) are taught weekly for 12–14 weeks.[39] Videotaped vignettes lead to discussion of important parenting skills, such as setting up a positive playtime, praising their children, providing meaningful incentives and consequences, setting limits, using time-outs, and learning to monitor their own reactions and manage their own stress.[40] As the parents move through the three curricula, they tend to discuss broader issues that may affect parents of children with conduct problems, such as depression, lack of support or resources, and poor coping skills. The goals of the parenting program include strengthening parental competence, guiding parents to nonviolent discipline practices, supporting every family, and connecting families to the community.

The parent training component is at the core of IYS; in fact, at some sites it may be the only training element used. However, there is substantial evidence that adding the teacher and child training components greatly enhances the parent training. The teacher training revolves around developing positive classroom management techniques, which help free teachers to concentrate on the emotional, social, and academic development of their students. The child training, which can be done in either small-group or whole-class settings, works to build children's emotional language and problem-solving capacities and helps children develop positive peer relationships. It consists of 60 lesson plans that can be taught one to three times per week in 45-minute time blocks.[41]

IYS is a relatively expensive program. In 2004, the cost of the complete curriculum materials was $5,295.[42] Having an IYS trainer come to a school site cost $1,500 per day, plus transportation and room and board.

Two randomized control studies of the child component of IYS have demonstrated a strong increase in appropriate problem-solving strategies, social competence, and play skills, as well as a reduction in conduct problems at home and at school.[43] Another study showed that at least 66% of children who had been diagnosed with oppositional defiant disorder/conduct disorder and whose parents had participated in the parenting program were in the normal range at 1- and 3-year follow-up.

IYS is part of the growing body of evidence that working consistently with young children and their families is a powerful way to reduce aggressive tendencies in children as they mature. It has been recognized as a model program by many organizations and reports, including the Office of Juvenile Justice and Delinquency Prevention, the Substance Abuse and Mental Health Services Administration (SAMHSA), the U.S. Department of Health and Human Services, the Colorado Blueprints, and the Surgeon General's Report on Youth Violence. In 2004, it was in use in the United States and around the world in elementary schools and preschool programs, including Head Start.

Family Support and Outreach: Functional Family Therapy

Functional family therapy (FFT), an intensive, family-based therapeutic program for adolescents, was created in 1969 by James Alexander and Bruce Parsons, then researchers at the University of Utah's Psychology Department Family Clinic.[44] One of their initial goals was to develop an accountable and well-articulated model for how a family therapy program should work.[45] To this end, they have always stressed early outcomes and early process research. They were also interested in providing therapeutic family treatment to populations that lacked resources and were often perceived as not motivated to change. FFT can be seen as both a treatment program and a prevention program, helping families learn to communicate better and helping to steer at-risk young people away from involvement in the juvenile justice system.

Children ages 11–18 and their siblings are typically referred to FFT through probation officers, schools, mental health clinics, substance abuse programs, and child welfare entities. FFT targets a range of teenagers, from at-risk preadolescents to those with very serious problems such as conduct disorder, violent acting out, and substance abuse.[46]

The program is short term but intensive. The family is always seen together, for 8 to 12 sessions for typical cases and up to 30 sessions for more serious cases. Sessions are most often held in the families' homes, though they can be held in an office, by therapists who typically have master's degrees in marriage and family therapy, counseling, psychology, or social work. The multiyear FFT training includes ongoing supervision, clinical training, observations, and continuous assessment.[47]

FFT encompasses three phases of intervention: engaging and motivating the family, changing the behavior of the family, and generalizing the changes so that the family can achieve greater stability. In the early phase of the program, the therapist focuses on developing an alliance with the family through building up trusting relationships; at the same time, he or she aims to reduce negative communication between family members and to alleviate feelings of hopelessness by helping the family focus on a goal. In the second phase of intervention, the clinician begins to create individualized plans for change; the goal is to have the family members carry out a specific plan for how they will relate to each other and deal with their problems. In the final phase of the FFT intervention, the therapist strives to connect the family to useful community resources; at the same time, he or she also focuses on maintaining the plan for change and doing any necessary relapse prevention.[48]

In comparison with other programs that target similar populations, FFT has proven 25 to 60% more effective. In addition, though the delivery of FFT seems expensive, the cost benefit for the family and for society is great, especially when compared with that of traditional punitive approaches. For example, in 2004, 30 days of detention cost approximately $6,000, and 90 days of residential treatment cost around $13,000; in contrast, 12 sessions of FFT cost about $1,000 in a home-based setting and even less in a clinic setting.[49] A recent statewide evaluation done at Washington State University calculated FFT's actual long-term savings to taxpayers at $10 for every $1 invested in FFT. Cost savings calculations are based on decreased crime victim and criminal justice costs through reductions in felony recidivism for high-risk juvenile offenders.[50] Furthermore, the positive outcomes of FFT remain relatively stable at follow-up as much as 5 years later, and the positive impact also affects siblings of the identified adolescents.[51] Programs similar to FFT, such as Multisystemic Family Therapy, have been equally successful. In 2004, FFT was being used in about 150 sites in 26 states,[52] in statewide programs in New York, Washington, California, and Pennsylvania, and in five sites in the Netherlands.[53]

FFT clearly demonstrates the value of intensity in addressing complex problems. Working consistently with the family is an important route to the improved well-being of the young person.

School Achievement: Project ACHIEVE

Project ACHIEVE is a multitiered school reform program developed in 1990 by Howard Knoff,[54] a school psychologist and then the director of the school psychology program at the University of Southern Florida.[55] Project ACHIEVE aims to greatly reduce violent and aggressive behavior, as measured by the number of discipline referrals, suspensions, and expulsions; at the same time, it aims to promote healthy, positive behavior in teachers and students and ultimately to increase the academic achievement of every student.

The program began as a district-wide professional development initiative for school psychologists, social workers, and guidance counselors in Florida. Since then, it has evolved into a whole-school professional development program whose goal is to foster a healthy school climate at every level.[56]

Project ACHIEVE can be implemented with the staff and resources available in most schools, especially when there are a large number of special education or Title I students referred to or already in an existing program. It is recommended that school districts employ a project coordinator for every three to five schools involved.

Project ACHIEVE includes seven critical components:

- Generating a large-scale plan to promote a positive school climate and reduce aggressive behavior
- Consultation that focuses on linking assessment and intervention
- Classroom teacher and staff development
- Instructional consultation
- Behavior management consultations and social skills interventions
- Parent training and tutoring
- Research and accountability

All of the training is facilitated by pupil services personnel, such as school counselors, school psychologists, parent/community educators, speech/language therapists, and school nurses.[57] This team trains everyone within the school: the teachers, administrators, paraprofessionals, lunch aides, janitors, and so forth. The team's services are further extended to parents and to community organizations that may run after-school programs.

Project ACHIEVE implements a social skills program, a problem-solving process, parent and community school safety outreach and involvement activities, and curriculum-based assessments. Its "Training for Trainers" approach helps spread the training quickly throughout a district.

Project ACHIEVE functions through strengthening the many relationships that exist within a school, and the effectiveness of this approach is demonstrated in the program's outcomes. Longitudinal studies were done in three middle schools in Florida and Texas. All three sites showed substantial reduction in aggression and violence; for example, school-wide discipline referrals decreased by 80%, and classroom-based discipline referrals decreased by 86% in the Dallas school.[58] In other schools, fighting, disruptive behavior, and suspensions dropped significantly. Interestingly, in some sites special education testing referrals decreased by as much as 75%.

In 2004, Project ACHIEVE had been shown to have substantially reduced aggressive and violent behavior in more than 1,500 sites in more than 40 states. The adaptability of Project ACHIEVE allows it to be replicated in urban, rural, and suburban areas, though most of the evaluations have been done in schools with high levels of poverty. Project ACHIEVE has been recognized as a model prevention program by many organizations, including the Office of Juvenile Justice and Delinquency Prevention.[59]

This approach shows how to combine many essential program components into a strong, comprehensive intervention in a school setting.

Bullying Prevention: Olweus Bullying Program

In 1983, after the suicides of three adolescent boys who had been bullied, Norway's Ministry of Education asked Dan Olweus, a professor at the University of Bergen, to conduct a large-scale research and intervention project on bullies and their victims. The Olweus Bullying Prevention Program aims to greatly decrease bullying in elementary and middle schools by reorganizing the school climate and reducing opportunities for bullying to occur. This program was created to protect not only the bullied but also the bullies themselves, who may be at risk for developing more severe aggressive behavior as they grow older.[60]

Olweus intervenes at three levels: whole-school, classroom, and individual. Because the program is largely implemented by school staff, it demands a high level of commitment from the administration, teachers, and other staff members. Everyone is required to attend a half-day training before the program is implemented, and members of the coordinating committee must attend a 2-day training, which in 2004 cost $3,000 to $5,000, depending on the size of the school.[61] During the first year of implementation, the staff is expected to participate in regular teacher discussion groups. Depending on the size of the school, a part- or full-time coordinator is required.

Typically, staff training takes place during the summer, followed by a school-wide kickoff in the fall. Once a coordinating committee has been formed and the teachers have been trained, school-wide rules against bullying are established by all the stakeholders and a rigorous schedule is drawn up for supervision of students during break times. The main element of the classroom intervention is weekly 20- to 40-minute classroom meetings about bullying and peer issues; there is an effort to include parents in these classroom meetings. Finally, students who chronically bully or are bullied meet individually with the coordinator or school counselor.[62]

The Olweus Bullying Prevention Program has shown a 30–70% reduction in student reports of being bullied and bullying others; in addition, there have been significant reductions in truancy, vandalism, and fighting. During the 1990s, Dan Olweus began implementing the program in the United States in collaboration with Sue Limber and Gary Melton, both at Clemson University.

Judging from this experience, combining group discussion and individual treatment can produce significant changes in high-risk students.

Individual Attention: Operation Eiger

Violence in the community has been identified as a risk factor for aggressive and violent behavior among children. The need for prevention programs in communities that have historically struggled with violent crime led to the development in 1997 of Operation Eiger in North Baton Rouge, Louisiana (Eiger is the name of a challenging mountain in Switzerland). Operation Eiger aims to reduce gun violence and to increase safety in the community; it specifically targets repeat youth offenders.[63] The program is an integral part of the Baton Rouge Partnership for the Prevention of Juvenile Gun Violence, a multipronged collaboration among law enforcement agencies, city officials, community agencies, and grassroots volunteers.

The problem was clear: Between 1992 and 1997, juvenile arrests in Baton Rouge increased by 71%, and the statistics on guns in the schools had become staggering. An initial task force began researching the issues, involving organizations from all sectors of the community. The task force developed a mission statement and a set of realistic goals, which included enforcing laws and holding juveniles accountable, developing interventions to address risk factors, breaking the cycle of delinquency through preventive education and providing positive opportunities, and involving the entire community in mobilization toward sustainability.

Operation Eiger began with its first "Eigers": 311 at-risk youths who had committed violent crimes, been caught carrying or using firearms, or committed drug offenses.[64] Every Eiger is given an individual service plan (ISP) to ensure focus and effectiveness. A three-member police/probation pilot team makes regular and intensive contacts with Eigers and their parents to ensure that the elements of the ISP are enforced.[65] A first-year Eiger typically receives the following intervention services: substance abuse evaluations and treatment, a chemical awareness clinic, an anger management clinic, a crime prevention clinic, psychological evaluations and counseling, family counseling, a mentor, preemployment job skills training, and job training and placement. At the same time, efforts are made to improve the home environment, including working on parenting skills and providing access to appropriate community resources and services. In addition, Operation Eiger teams contact an identified group of non-Eiger young people who are at risk of becoming repeat offenders because of the severity of their acts, their relationships to gang activity, or their sibling relationship with an Eiger. Meanwhile, law enforcement agencies take charge of enforcing gun laws, tracing guns, and holding juveniles accountable for their actions.

Since the program began in 1997, Operation Eiger's partnership activities have grown from 44 to more than 200,[66] illustrating a capacity to positively penetrate the community. Outcomes have been impressive. When the program started, almost 45% of its participants had probation violations; as of December 2003, that figure had been reduced to 21%. Furthermore, whereas 72% of the control group committed new offenses, 43% of the Eigers did so.[67] Operation Eiger's dramatic effect on recidivism rates among its participants led to its being one of only two programs nationwide that were named as Exceptional Juvenile Gun Crime Reduction Programs by the U.S. Department of Justice in 2004.

It is important to recognize that Operation Eiger could not stand alone. It is a part of a complex, intensive community-wide initiative that has created a web of interventions that interact with and depend on one another for their effectiveness. Quick fixes or short-term programs have not been successful in communities like Baton Rouge, where youth violence is widespread. Operation Eiger exemplifies the concept of saturating whole communities with interventions that have a common goal.

CONCLUSION: WHAT WORKS?

Summary of Programs

Certain core threads run through these five highly successful programs. First, whether a program works with an individual child or an entire community, communication is essential. This is easy to say but not at all easy to do; communication takes time, energy, and the hard work of collaboration. None of these programs would be as successful as they are without first carefully assessing the needs of the child, the family, the school, or the community and then collaborating to construct a comprehensive plan that is achievable; this can't be done without frequent and open communication.

The selected programs each exemplify a particular approach, reflecting the needs of those at risk for violent behavior: early intervention, family support and outreach, individual attention, attention to bullying, and school success. However, they all spill over into one another in various ways. For example, both IYS and FFT have recognized the importance of working with teachers and schools, not just families; Operation Eiger is constantly trying to find innovative ways to mobilize the community. This leads to another important thread: empowering the people. Whether they work with a family in need of a vision for the future or a community riddled with violence, each one of these programs moves beyond just stopping bad behaviors. Rather, they motivate their "clients" to change by helping them find and enhance their strengths. As you can see, although these programs have been labeled categorical, they are all comprehensive; they just start from different places and are configured in different ways. What are some specific elements that make these programs successful?

- Dedicated founders and directors
- Dedicated staff
- Stable funding sources
- Strong research base
- Involvement of key stakeholders
- Comprehensive and accurate needs assessment as a component of strategic planning
- Replication of programs with a high level of fidelity
- Systematic and collaborative program planning, training, implementation, and operation
- Intensity
- Individual attention

Comment

Deborah Prothrow-Stith and Howard Spivak, in their study of prevention of teenage violence, sum up many of the issues relating to the problem.[68] They warn us to beware of quick fixes. Building on their recommendations and those above, we would suggest:

- Using innovative approaches to gun control, such as liability suits and confiscation
- Changing the juvenile justice system to keep young people out of adult prisons
- Identifying high-risk children at early ages, giving them adequate individual attention, and working with their families
- Building a broad-based coalition of support, including community and school leaders and political leaders where possible
- Improving police-community relationships
- Turning schools into community centers, implementing social skills programs, and getting rid of "zero tolerance" attitudes toward youth

- Controlling the content of violent media.
- Involving teenagers themselves in the programs in various ways, from naming the program to developing the curriculum

Ridding a violent nation of violence is a challenge. Many public and private interests must join together to find ways to implement these recommendations. As Richard Mendel told the American Youth Policy Forum, "America has the knowledge to reduce adolescent crime and violence without a substantial long-term increase in spending. Yet the policy and program reforms necessary to win the battle against juvenile crime are not being enacted."

When teenagers commit crimes or are threatening to the public, a kind of hysteria often arises in the local community. In one such case in Marshfield, Massachusetts, first one student and then another were turned in to the police by fellow students because they had plans to harm the school and the people in it. In the home of one of the students, detectives found evidence of a successfully exploded device and hand-drawn plans of the high school, as well as information on the computer about weapons dealers and bombs. The second student was known as a tough guy whose father was the head of the police union in a nearby city. They were put in jail for several weeks and finally let out on bail awaiting trial. Postings on an Internet chat room revealed how at least one local citizen felt.[69]

> . . . they both deserve to be hanged. Excuse the violence but I've known both of them for a while. (xxx) used to give my relative a hard time in school and (yyy) used to threaten my best friends daily. They were really going somewhere in life . . . sitting under a bridge getting high all [the] time knowing people in high places. They will both get off unscratched because the state is gonna let this one fade. (yyy's) police force papa is gonna be his get out of jail free card. . . . American justice at its finest, ladies and gents.

Of course, the Internet is an invitation to anonymous and extreme sounding off, but many adults believe that teenage perpetrators should be disposed of by the law enforcement and justice systems as rapidly as possible. Yet there are other, less harsh courses of action. We have looked at several programs that appear to work and examined some of the legal and policy issues that might make a difference.

Like so many of the issues we have raised in this book, our views of violence prevention are shaped by our values. I personally believe in using the strong arm of the law to protect our children, particularly in terms of guns. Why should the interests of the National Rifle Association take precedence over the interests of our children? Where are the voices calling for the restoration of the Federal Assault Weapons Ban?[70] Parents, teachers, youth workers, community leaders, and, most important, the young people themselves have to join together and demand a healthier environment in which children are assured the right to grow up.

NOTES

1. William Goodwin, *Teen Issues: Teen Violence* (San Diego, CA: Lucent Books, 1998), http://www.enotes/com/teen-violence (accessed January 3, 2005).

2. Richard Mendel, *Less Hype, More Help: Reducing Juvenile Crime, What Works— and What Doesn't* (Washington, DC: American Youth Policy Forum, 2000), 2.

3. "Youth Risk Behavior Surveillance–United States, 2003," *Morbidity and Mortality Weekly Report* 53, no. SS-2, Table 6, May 21, 2004, http://www.cdc.gov/mmwr/PDF/SS/SS5302.pdf.

4. Ron Banks, "Bullying in Schools," *Eric Digest,* April 1997, http://www.ericdigests.org/1997-4/bullying.htm (accessed November 2, 2004).

5. Fight Crime: Invest in Kids, *Bullying Prevention Is Crime Prevention* (Washington, DC: Fight Crime: Invest in Kids, 2003).

6. Dan Romer, Research Director, Adolescent Risk Communication Institute, personal communication, November 7, 2004.

7. Chad Hills and Ronald Reno, *Lotteries in the United States: An Overview,* http://www.family.org/cforum/fosi/gambling/lottery/a0026821.cfm (accessed January 8, 2005).

8. National Youth Violence Prevention Resource Center, "Gangs Fact Sheet," http://www.safeyouth.org/scripts/facts/gangs.asp (accessed July 20, 2005).

9. Michael Carlie, "The Number of Gangs and Gang Members," http://www.faculty.missouristate.edu/m/mKc096F/what_I_learned_about_GANGS/demographics_number.htm (accessed March 3, 2005).

10. Ibid.

11. U.S. Department of Justice, Federal Bureau of Investigation, *Crime in the United States 2002* (Washington, DC: U.S. Government Printing Office, 2003), Tables 29, 32, 34, 36, and 40.

12. Center on Juvenile and Criminal Justice, "Race and the Juvenile Justice System," Center on Juvenile and Criminal Justice, http://www.cjcj.org/jjc/race_jj.php (accessed January 12, 2005).

13. Judy Murman, Joseph Dake, and James Price, "Association of Selected Risk Fac-

tors with Variation in Child and Adolescent Firearm Mortality by State," *Journal of School Health* 74, no. 8 (2004): 335–340.

14. U.S. Census Bureau, *Statistical Abstract of the United States: 2003* (Washington, DC: U.S. Government Printing Office, 2004), 156, Table 232.

15. B. Vossekull, R. Fein, M. Reddy, R. Borum, and W. Modzeleski, *The Final Report of Findings of the Safe School Initiative* (Washington, DC: Department of Education, May 2002).

16. Office of Justice Programs, Office of Juvenile Justice and Delinquency Prevention, National Report Series, Bulletin: "Juveniles in Corrections," June 2004, http://www.ncjrs.gov/html/ojjdp/202885/contents.html.

17. U.S. Department of Justice, Federal Bureau of Investigation, *Crime in the United States* (Washington, DC: U.S. Government Printing Office, 2003).

18. U.S. Department of Health and Human Services, Administration on Children, Youth, and Families, *Child Maltreatment, 2001* (Washington, DC: U.S. Government Printing Office, 2003).

19. J. David Hawkins, T. Herrenkohl, D. P. Farrington, D. Brewer, R. F. Catalano, T. W. Harachi, and L. Cothern, "Predictors of Youth Violence," *Juvenile Justice Bulletin*, NCJ 179065, April 2000.

20. Preventing Violence and Related Health-Risking Social Behavior in Adolescents, draft statement presented at the State-of-the-Science Conference, National Institutes of Health, October 13–15, 2004.

21. D. P. Farrington, "Early Prediction of Violent and Nonviolent Youthful Offending," *European Journal of Criminal Policy and Research* 5 (1997): 51–56.

22. *Gun Control in the United States* (New York: Open Society Institute, 2000): 1.

23. News Batch, "Gun Control Policy Issues," http://www.newsbatch.com/guncontrol.htm (accessed January 6, 2005).

24. Brady Campaign to Prevent Gun Violence, "Juvenile Possession Laws by State," http://www.bradycampaign.org/facts/issues/?pages=juvposs (accessed January 6, 2005).

25. Deborah Prothrow-Stith and Howard Spivak, *Murder is No Accident: Understanding and Preventing Youth Violence in America.* (San Francisco: Jossey-Bass, 2004).

26. Building Blocks for Youth, "Children in Adult Jails," http://www.buildingblocksforyouth.org/issues/adultjails (accessed February 5, 2005).

27. American Youth Policy Forum, "Reducing Juvenile Crime: What Works—and What Doesn't," Aforum, July 14, 2000, http://www.aypf.org/forumbriefs/2000/fb071400 (accessed January 12, 2005).

28. Priorities and Strategies for Juvenile Justice and Delinquency Prevention, Coordinated Plan for Children, Families, and Community, Multnomah County, January 2002, http://www.orucommission.org/pdf/stateplanpdfs/psjuv.pdf (accessed May 21, 2005).

29. American Youth Policy Forum, "Reducing Juvenile Crime."

30. Jane Sundius and Aurie Hall, "Op-Ed: Locked Out of Learning," *Baltimore Sun*, January 20, 2004.

31. National Education Association, "School Safety," http://www.nea.org/schoolsafety/index.html (accessed June 15, 2005).

32. T. Thornton, C. Craft, L. Dahlberg, B. Lynch, and K. Baer, *Best Practices of Youth*

Violence Prevention: A Sourcebook for Community Action (Atlanta, GA: Centers for Disease Control and Prevention, 2002).

33. *Youth Violence: A Report of the Surgeon General,* http://www.surgeongeneral. gov/library/youthviolence (accessed May 20, 2005).

34. D. Ballard, D. Elliott, A. Fagan, K. Irwin, and S. Mihalic, *Blueprints for Violence Prevention* (Boulder: University of Colorado, Center for the Study and Prevention of Violence, and Washington, DC: U.S. Department of Justice, Office of Juvenile Justice and Delinquency Prevention, 2004), Report No. NCJ204274

35. Substance Abuse and Mental Health Services Administration, "The Incredible Years Training Series," http://modelprograms.samhsa.gov/pdfs/FactSheets/IncYears.pdf (accessed February 7, 2005).

36. Lisa St. George (administrative director, The Incredible Years), personal communication, February 16, 2005.

37. The Incredible Years, Research History, http://www.incredibleyears.com (accessed February 8, 2005).

38. J. Pearce, "Personal Profile: Carolyn Webster-Stratton: Just an Ordinary Person?" *Child and Adolescent Mental Health* 9, no. 1 (2004): 36–37.

39. National Center on Addiction and Substance Abuse, *Criminal Neglect: Substance Abuse, Juvenile Justice and the Children Left Behind* (New York: Columbia University, 2004).

40. C. Webster-Stratton and L. Hancock, *Training for Parents of Younger Children with Conduct Problems: Content, Methods, and Therapeutic Process,* in *The Handbook of Parent Training,* ed. C. E. Schaefer & J. M. Briesmeister (New York: Wiley, 1998).

41. The Incredible Years, Programs, http://www.incredibleyears.com (accessed February 8, 2005).

42. C. Webster-Stratton, S. Mihalic, A. Fagan, D. Arnold, T. Taylor, and C. Tingley, "Blueprints for Violence Prevention," http://www.colorado.edu/cspv/blueprints/model/ programs/IYS.html (accessed February 8, 2005).

43. SAMHSA, "The Incredible Years Training Series."

44. T. Sexton and J. Alexander, "Functional Family Therapy," *Juvenile Justice Bulletin,* December 2000.

45. James Alexander, personal communication, February 8, 2005.

46. T. Sexton and J. Alexander, *Functional Family Therapy: Principles of Clinical Intervention, Assessment, and Implementation,* FFT, LLC, 2002, http://www.cipohio.org/ pfd/functional%20Family %20Therapy%20Principles.pdf (accessed February 2, 2006).

47. Ibid.

48. Ibid.

49. Ibid.

50. Sexton and Alexander, "Functional Family Therapy," 2000.

51. T. Sexton, G. Weeks, and M. Robbins, eds., *The New Handbook of Marriage and Family Therapy* (New York: Brunner-Routledge, 2003).

52. Douglas Kopp, personal communication, November 23, 2004.

53. Sexton and Alexander, *Functional Family Therapy,* 2002.

54. H. Knoff, *Project ACHIEVE: Building Strong Schools to Strengthen Student Outcomes* (Little Rock: Arkansas Department of Education, Special Education Unit, 2003).

55. Center for Effective Collaboration and Practice, Presentations, Howard Knoff, http://www.cecp.air.org/resources/nasp/knoff.htm (accessed February 2, 2006).

56. H. Knoff, "Project ACHIEVE: Project Overview and Focus on Creating a Building-Based Social Skills, Discipline/Behavior Management, and School Safety System," http://cecp.air.org/teams/greenhouses/projach.pdf (accessed February 1, 2005).

57. Knoff, *Project ACHIEVE*, 2003.

58. Substance Abuse and Mental Health Services Administration, "Project ACHIEVE," SAMHSA Model Programs, July 1, 2003, 7–8, http://www.modelprograms.samhsa.gov.pdfs/Details/ProjectAcheive.pdf (accessed February 2, 2006).

59. Ibid.

60. Substance Abuse and Mental Health Services Administration, "Olweus Bullying Prevention Program," http://modelprograms.samhsa.gov/pdfs/Details/Olweus%20Bully.pdf (accessed February 16, 2005).

61. Olweus Bullying Prevention Program, http://www.clemson.edu/olweus/program.html (accessed February 16, 2005).

62. Ibid.

63. Office of Juvenile Justice and Delinquency Prevention, "Operation Eiger: Baton Rouge Partnership for the Prevention of Juvenile Gun Violence," http://ojjdp.ncjrs.org/pubs/gun_violence/profile32.html (accessed February 16, 2005).

64. Ibid.

65. Office of Juvenile Justice and Delinquency Prevention, "Promising Strategies to Reduce Gun Violence," http://ojjdp.ncjrs.org/pubs/gun_violence/173950.pdf (accessed February 16, 2005).

66. John Jay Cosmos, in discussion with the author, February 15, 2003.

67. Caught in the Crossfire: Arresting Gang Violence by Investing in Kids (Washington, DC: Fight Crime: Invest in Kids, 2004), http://www.fightcrime.org/Resources/Reorts (accessed February 2, 2006).

68. Prothrow-Stith and Spivak, *Murder Is No Accident.*

69. Associated Press, "Columbine-Style Murder Plot Uncovered in Marshfield," *Boston Globe*, October 6, 2004.

70. Brady Campaign to Prevent Gun Violence, www.bradycampaign.org (accessed February 2, 2006).

CHAPTER FIVE

DRUGS

The notion that we have the power to deter our children from experimentation with drugs is ludicrous. Most of us were teenagers in the 1960s and 70s and many of us including our President and Vice President tried marijuana. Although the vast majority of us no longer use drugs, those who did know that with moderate use marijuana remains the most benign substance on the drug scene, safer not only than cocaine or heroin but alcohol, pharmaceuticals, and certainly cigarettes.[1]

MAJOR TRENDS

- About 22% of teenagers smoke cigarettes regularly, down from 28% in 1991.
- Some 45% of teenagers occasionally drink alcohol, also a decrease; but 28% are binge drinkers (five or more drinks at a time).
- Marijuana is used by 22% of high school students, up from 15% in 1991.
- Hard drugs (cocaine, heroin, etc.) are used by a small number of teens, but the number is increasing slightly. Steroid use may have leveled off or decreased slightly in recent years.
- Many of these substances appear to be easier to obtain than they were in the past.

WHAT ARE THE FACTS?

Most teenagers have tried smoking cigarettes or drinking a beer at some point in their tender years. A much smaller number drink to excess or have tried hard drugs. Substance use follows distinct trends, with certain substances moving up the charts (marijuana) while others almost disappear (heroin). Marijuana use has been more common over the years than the use of other illicit drugs. All of these substances are subject to supply and demand, as well as to regulation and law enforcement.

We start with smoking and alcohol use and then move on to harder or illegal drugs. The data for 9th–12th grade high school students come from the Youth Risk Behavior Survey (YRBS).[2]

Tobacco Use

Cigarette use among adolescents has clearly declined on every measure, even the percentage who have ever tried cigarettes (Table 5.1). In 2003, 58% reported having even one or two puffs, down from 70% in 1991. Fewer high school students reported early initiation: 18%, down from 24%, started before age 13. Only 16% were daily smokers by 2003, compared with 21% in 1991, and only 3% were heavy smokers, down from 5%.

Table 5.1 Cigarette Use Among 9th–12th Graders by Percentage, 1991 and 2003

Tobacco Use	1991	2003
Ever tried	70	58
Smoked before age 13	24	18
Smoked within past month	28	22
Heavy smoker	5	3
Smoked daily past month	21	16

Source: Centers for Disease Control and Prevention, "Youth Risk Behavior Surveillance System, Data & Statistics, Youth Online Comprehensive Results," http://apps.nccd.cdc.gov/yrbss (accessed September 6, 2004).

Still, each day more than 4,000 young people ages 12–17 try a cigarette for the first time, and one-third to one-half of them will go on to become daily smokers.

Which adolescents are most likely to smoke now? Almost 27% of white females are current smokers (smoked on one or more days in the month preceding the survey), compared with 11% of black and 18% of Hispanic females. Some 23% of white male students smoke, as do 19% of both black and Hispanic males. As would be expected, the rates go up with grade level, from 17% of 9th graders to 26% of 12th graders.

Alcohol Use

Alcohol use, according to the YRBS, has also declined somewhat over the past decade (Table 5.2). Still, in 2003, 75% of all high school students had tried drinking (down from 82% in 1991), and 45% had had a drink within the preceding month (down from 51%). Binge drinking (consuming five or more drinks within a couple of hours) was reported by 28% in 2003, not a significant reduction from 31% in 1991. The same percentage (28%) started drinking before age 13, suggesting that more than one-fourth of all teens are at very high risk of negative outcomes from drinking.

Among female students, whites and Hispanics are more likely to use alcohol than blacks (48% vs. 37%). Males have slightly lower rates: 46% of white, 43% of Hispanic, and 38% of black males reported drinking on occasion. White

Table 5.2 Alcohol Use Among 9th–12th Graders by
Percentage, 1991 and 2003

Alcohol Use	1991	2003
Ever tried	82	75
First drink before 13	33	28
Drank within past month	51	45
Binge (5+ drinks) within past month	31	28

Source: Centers for Disease Control and Prevention, "Youth Risk
Behavior Surveillance System, Data & Statistics, Youth Online
Comprehensive Results," http://apps.nccd.cdc.gov/yrbss
(accessed September 6, 2004).

students (32% of both males and females) were more likely to drink heavily (5
or more drinks in a row), compared with 15% of black students and 30% of
Hispanics.

The press is full of stories about alcohol abuse among teenagers. In one
community, parents allowed high school students to entertain their friends
with a keg of beer. When the party got wild and the neighbors complained, the
police raided the house and confiscated the keg. The parents defended their actions by saying that because all teens drink, it was better for them to drink at
home and not get into cars after bingeing. Here's the news from a suburban
high school:

> The chaos that descended on a . . . High School dance began with
> large numbers of students drinking at a series of unchaperoned house
> parties, a weekend practice that students described as commonplace. In-
> toxicated students vomited in the bathroom and on the dance floor . . .
> and at least one student's stomach was pumped after ambulances arrived
> at the school. . . . [O]ther students had trouble walking or speaking
> and one girl passed out. . . . [M]ore than a dozen of the 450 students
> were found to be under the influence of alcohol or other substances, in-
> cluding 6 students who were rushed to the hospital. . . . The students
> said that before the dance many had been downing vodka shots.[3]

One student summed up the situation: "People are going to drink whether
or not there's a dance . . . [this town] is really boring, so we just drink to
have fun."

Table 5.3 Drug Use Among 9th–12th Graders by
Percentage, 1991 and 2003

Drug Use	1991	2003
Marijuana ever tried	31	40
Marijuana tried before age 13	7	10
Marijuana used during past month	15	22
Cocaine ever tried	6	9
Cocaine used during past month	2	4
Steroid pills ever tried	3	6
Ecstasy ever tried		11
Heroin ever tried		3
Methamphetamine ever tried		8

Source: Centers for Disease Control and Prevention, "Youth Risk
Behavior Surveillance System, Data & Statistics, Youth Online
Comprehensive Results," http://apps.nccd.cdc.gov/yrbss
(accessed September 6, 2004).

Drug Use

Though cigarette and alcohol use have declined during the past decade, the use
of some drugs, most notably marijuana, has increased significantly (Table 5.3).
By 2003, fully 40% of all students had tried it, and 22% had used it during the
preceding month.

In 2003, 37–39% of all female students and 40% of white males had used
marijuana. However, black and Hispanic males had much higher rates, 49%
and 47%, respectively. Thus, more than one-third of all female high school students have tried marijuana, as have almost half of all male high school students. Current use (within the preceding 30 days) of marijuana follows a similar pattern, with 18–20% of females and 23% of white, 30% of black, and 27%
of Hispanic males reporting such use.

The percentage currently using cocaine in 2003 was low (4%), but among
Hispanic students, this very risky and illegal behavior was reported by 6%. Almost no black females and 3% of black males reported cocaine use. Among
white students, about 4% were cocaine users.

In the 2003 survey, students were asked if they had ever used Ecstasy. White
(11%) and Hispanic (13%) teens had higher rates than blacks (6%). Hispanic
males had very high rates (14%) and black females very low (4%).

The Monitoring the Future study provides further information on illicit drug use (not including alcohol or tobacco) among teenagers.[4] The 2004 study showed that just about half of all young people (8th, 10th, and 12th graders) had ever used any illicit drug, but just under half of those had used only marijuana. Looking at current use of any illicit drug (within the preceding 30 days), the range is from 8% of 8th graders to 23% of 12th graders. Heroin use was minimal (below 1%), and use of cocaine ranged from 1% to 2%. This study found that about 2–5% used amphetamines.

Prescription and Over-the-Counter Medications

The Partnership for a Drug-Free America reported that in their 2004 study, one in five teens had ever abused a prescription painkiller to get high, and one in 11 abused over-the-counter (OTC) products, such as cough medicine. According to Roy Bostock, chairman of the Partnership, "A new category of substance abuse is emerging in America, teenagers are getting high through the intentional abuse of medications. . . . Generation Rx has arrived."[5]

About 18% of all teenagers reported ever using Vicodin and 10% OxyContin, both prescription painkillers. Some 10% had tried prescription stimulants such as Ritalin or Adderall without a doctor's order. Teenagers believe that it is much safer to get high on painkillers than on street drugs. They describe easy access to these pills through parents' or friends' medicine cabinets.

Steroids

Anabolic steroids are synthetic derivatives of the male sex hormone testosterone. They promote muscle growth and increased strength, and they also foster the development of male sexual characteristics. Steroids have been very much in the news in recent years because of their use by athletes. The percentage of teenagers who reported ever using steroids doubled from 3% to 6% since 1991; but in recent years it has shown a decrease. One estimate is that about 300,000 teenagers abuse steroids every year, almost half for cosmetic reasons. Side effects include gonad shrinkage, acne, aggressiveness, and unwanted hair and breast growth. Withdrawal from steroids can cause such problems as depression and suicidal ideation, as well as headaches and muscle pain. Many teenagers access steroids without prescription over the Internet, in Mexico, or through local dealers.

Consequences

As with most high-risk behaviors, a small group of young people are in the most trouble. Binge drinkers are actually teenage alcoholics; their functioning is often limited by their drinking behavior, so that they cannot succeed in school and are in physical danger, especially if they drive. In 2002, 25% of 15- to 20-year-old passenger vehicle drivers who were fatally injured in crashes had high blood alcohol concentrations.

A few young people are drug addicts and require intensive and often long-term treatment. It is not clear whether moderate users of marijuana suffer any physical or emotional consequences from their behavior, but they are at high risk of being arrested. As can be seen in the delinquency data (Chapter 4, Table 4.3), 85,000 juveniles were picked up by the police in one year for possession of marijuana. This may lead to incarceration and a criminal record, which can have severely adverse consequences for the future.

Much has been written about marijuana as a "stepping stone" to hard drug use. An intensive study in Amsterdam during a period from 1987 to 1994, when cannabis (as it is called in Europe) use went from being highly suppressed to "hassle-free" (illegal but without consequences), provides interesting insights.[6] In a large survey, it was determined that among those who used cannabis, 75% did not consume any other drugs. A very small group went on to frequent hard drug use. Among those who never used cannabis, most never used any other drugs. Among hard drug users, most had used cannabis at some point in time. The research concluded, "Apparently in Amsterdam, where use was made possible due to hassle-free availability, cannabis satisfies almost all curiosity." In other words, drug use typically stops with marijuana smoking.

The Institute of Medicine studied the use of marijuana for medical purposes and concluded that it does not lead to harder drugs, that its addiction potential is not very serious, and that its side effects are within the range tolerated for other legal medicines.[7]

Predictors

According to Joseph Califano, president of the National Center on Addiction and Substance Abuse, "The thunder of sexual activity and dating behavior may signal the lightning of substance abuse."[8]

Predictors for Substance Abuse

- Aggressiveness in early childhood
- Rebelliousness
- Unconventionality
- High-risk friends
- Parents who have problems or use drugs

Predictors for Alcohol Abuse

- Alcoholic parent(s)
- Restless, impulsive, aggressive behavior in early childhood
- Conduct disorder
- Depression
- Peers who drink
- Lack of parental monitoring, support, and supervision

Protectors

- Parents who talk to their teens, set expectations, and enforce consequences; close family ties
- Adult role models
- Participation in religious and other activities
- Positive attitudes toward school, achievement

Given the circumstances surrounding substance abuse, prevention efforts should focus on early intervention, social skills, and providing reliable information about potential damage, particularly from cigarette smoking and binge drinking. For those very high-risk adolescents who use heavy drugs, treatment is necessary.

WHAT CAN BE DONE?

Policies

Smoking

The U.S. Task Force on Community Preventive Services strongly recommends using the following four population-based interventions to reduce tobacco-related illness and death:

- Banning or restricting smoking in public places
- Increasing the unit price for tobacco products
- Conducting mass media campaigns combined with other interventions
- Offering telephone support to those who are trying to stop (quitlines)

Others believe that teen smoking cessation programs and community interventions are also viable prevention approaches. However, the amount of money states spent on tobacco control dropped by 28% in the 2 years between 2003 and 2005. Spending is down to $541.1 million—less than 3% of the potentially available $19 billion that the states received in 2003 from tobacco excise taxes and tobacco settlement money.

Advocates for smoking reduction maintain that the various antismoking media campaigns have had an effect. The American Legacy Foundation launched a national youth smoking prevention campaign in 2000, funded by the National Public Education Fund established with the tobacco settlement money. This effort reached teens through print, radio, the Internet, and television, especially on youth-oriented outlets. The campaign exposed the tactics of the tobacco industry and presented the truth about addiction, health effects, and social consequences of smoking, allowing teens to make informed choices about tobacco use by giving them the facts about the industry and its products. Later evaluation found that teens who were exposed to a greater number of truth advertisements were less likely to smoke.

Smoking cigarettes is not the "thing to do" among the current crop of early adolescents. The message has reached many of them that smoking causes cancer, and they take that threat seriously. The financing of these messages can largely be attributed to the availability of "tobacco money" in certain states (before the funds were slashed).

Strict enforcement of laws that prohibit the sale of cigarettes to minors might make a difference. Higher prices might also act as a deterrent to youth smoking. If the prices went up significantly, say by $1.00 a pack, the impact might be greater.

A review of smoking prevention by a group called MASCOT (Multicultural Advocates for Social Change on Tobacco) came to the following conclusion: "Adolescent smoking prevention efforts have had mixed results. No one approach is likely to reverse that finding. . . . [T]here are few new revelations about the effectiveness of these programs. . . ."[9] Although it seems logical from the standpoint of youth advocates (such as myself) that the focus of public policy should be on reducing teenage smoking initiation rates, those with a public health orientation feel that it might be more fruitful to promote cessation among adult habitual smokers.

Alcohol Use

It has been estimated that this country experiences a $53 billion a year loss from traffic deaths, violent crime, and other destructive behavior related to underage drinking. The adoption of the National Minimum Drinking Age Act of 1984 required all states to raise their minimum age for purchase and public possession of alcohol to 21. It is believed that this led to some decrease in automobile crashes. States that did not comply faced a reduction in highway funds under the Federal Highway Aid Act. The law prohibits purchase and possession, but it does not prohibit persons under 21 from drinking. Actually, 19 states do not specifically prohibit the consumption of alcohol by minors.

Law enforcement may partially explain the slight reduction in heavy drinking (the rates have not come down as dramatically as they have for smoking). All states have also established lower thresholds for blood alcohol for younger drivers. Mothers Against Drunk Driving (MADD), the leading activist organization, calls for additional measures such as increased enforcement of the law through highly publicized sobriety checkpoints, enforcement of seat belt laws, tougher sanctions against repeat offenders, increased excise taxes on alcoholic beverages, and fixing the shortcomings in the judicial system to produce higher conviction rates and stiffer sentences.[10]

Serious "carding" takes place in bars across America. Young people have to show their IDs to prove that they are old enough to drink legally. However, the use of false IDs is endemic. One study of students under 21 showed that 59% of college students and 28% of high school students in New York and 37% of college students and 14% of high school students in Pennsylvania had used false IDs to obtain alcohol.[11]

The United States has the world's highest minimum drinking age. Many countries have no minimum (such as China, Poland, and Sweden), most set the limit at age 16–18, and only South Korea, Japan, Iceland, and New Zealand are at age 19–20. In addition, we know that teens in other parts of the world must be older to obtain drivers' licenses than young people in the United States and that they are more inclined to use public transportation. American teenagers probably have much greater access to cars and greater numbers of subsequent car crashes.

Another issue in prevention of underage drinking is the restriction of television ads for alcoholic beverages.[12] Apparently, some years ago, the industry accepted the concept of a "30% reform"; companies pledged not to place commercials for alcoholic products on shows for which 30% or more of the audience is younger than 21. However, this clearly did not happen. In 2003, 90% of young people ages 12–20 saw an average of 284 alcohol ads, and the one-third with the highest TV viewing rates saw an average of 780 alcohol ads. Some 69,000 ads were actually more likely to have been seen by adolescents than by older people. Altogether, there were almost 300,000 alcohol ads, mostly for beer, for which the industry paid $879,000,000.

In addition to the ads, many TV shows in 2005 portrayed alcohol use in a positive way. In four consecutive episodes of the 20 most popular TV shows among teens, alcohol was mentioned in 73% and consumed by major characters in more than half of the shows. Alcohol use is also common in rental videos, with negative consequences only rarely depicted for the user. Many popular songs, especially rap, feature drinking as an acceptable pastime.

Journalists regularly write about teenage drinking that is condoned or abetted by parents; indeed, beer is bought by many parents for teens' parties. Some parents see this as a safety measure ("they'll drink anyway, and at home they won't drive or get into trouble"), but others have a different perspective. They say, with a rueful smile, that "boys will be boys," and they also feel that if they drank a beer or several without ill effects when they were teenagers, why shouldn't their own children do the same? Still another variation on parental permissiveness toward teenage drinking is the belief that having a glass of wine or beer with parents at dinner helps to take the illicit thrill out of the concept of drinking for teens. What effect these various parental actions and attitudes have on teenage drinking is extremely difficult to measure.

Marijuana

Increases in marijuana use have been attributed to cultural influences that minimize the danger or promote the attractiveness of drug use. In one study, 43% of teens and 53% of their parents say that American culture glamorizes the use of illegal drugs.[13] Some 65% of baby boomer parents who had used marijuana regularly expected their own children to use it, compared with 29% of baby boomer parents who had never used marijuana. Thus, parental attitudes and expectations regarding risk are important factors. So is popular culture. Marijuana is the most frequently mentioned drug in teens' favorite movies and songs.

In a study conducted by the Hazelden Foundation, 98% of parents said they would be upset if they discovered that their teens were using marijuana, yet only 40% talked to their children about the practice.[14] And many people with whom I discussed these questions say that, although they themselves smoked pot with few side effects and no lasting harm, they would not like their children to smoke marijuana for fear that it would lead to use of harder drugs. Such inconsistency can look like hypocrisy to teenagers and can make them doubt the truth of their parents' warnings. It also contrasts with the comment made by many parents that a beer or two won't do a kid any harm—"it certainly didn't hurt me!" Teenagers may well wonder why a beer is winked at and tacitly approved but a joint is forbidden.

A poll conducted by the AARP, the largest advocacy group for seniors, showed that almost three-fourths of the respondents agree that adults should be allowed to use marijuana for medical purposes if recommended by a physician.[15] However, only half thought that marijuana had medical benefits.

The use of marijuana for medical reasons is growing, with several states passing laws to permit it. However, the Bush administration, as of 2005, had taken the position that allowing marijuana for medical purposes undermines federal drug control programs and that pot grown for medical use might be used for illegal purposes and cross state lines.

Steroids

Nutrition stores may legally sell hormonally active pills. More than 40% of teens say that steroids are easily accessible, more so than any other illicit drugs. But intensive coverage of steroid use in major league baseball in 2004–2005 increased awareness of its dangers. High school coaches and athletic team leaders can be trained to educate team members about the effects of steroid use and about alternative training techniques for improving performance without steroids.

Programs

Federal programs that deal with these issues include the Center for Substance Abuse in the Substance Abuse Mental Health Services Administration (SAMHSA), the Centers for Disease Control and Prevention, the National Institute on Drug Abuse, and the National Institute on Alcohol Abuse and Alcoholism. It is estimated that about $700 million is spent on school-based prevention programs every year.

SAMHSA supports a National Family Partnership that organizes Red Ribbon Week to draw awareness to the problems of substance abuse. Family-centered activities include contests, workshops, rallies, media events, theatrical performances, and educational programs. Everyone is encouraged to wear a red ribbon and to plant red tulips. The goal is to help children embrace a healthy drug-free lifestyle with zero tolerance for use of substances of any kind.

The overlap between programs that aim to prevent drug and alcohol abuse among youth and programs that aim to prevent teen pregnancy or violence is quite evident. Many of these programs share similar approaches to prevention, such as teaching life skills that will enable young people to confidently refuse and resist risky behavior such as drinking or taking drugs. Within this life skills training (which one of the programs that follows is called), there is a heavy emphasis on communication skills, general social skills, and cultivating proficiency in control and self-management. These all seem to make good sense: If young people are able to communicate effectively and to resist negative influences from their peers, then they should be able to steer clear of involvement in alcohol and drugs. Unfortunately, it is not that simple. Many programs that aim to teach these skills have failed in their prevention mission.

Besides the dearth of solid recent evaluations, much of the research on this area of prevention is disheartening, especially concerning school-based drug prevention programs. "They are not extensive or consistent enough to do much good," according to a 5-year Department of Education commissioned study. "Most schools don't have the time, resources, or leadership to effectively run such programs."[16] Certainly some programs have succeeded in reducing alcohol and drug use among their participants, but these require training and additional staff, all of which cost money. In fact, a lot of money is being spent on ineffective programs that were created a long time ago. For example, DARE, a program that has been proven completely ineffective in preventing drug use among this nation's youth, continues to be the most widely used drug prevention program in many states.[17] The bottom line is, "the list of exemplary [drug prevention] programs is short, static and politically controversial."[18]

On the other hand, with the exception of the first program we discuss (DARE to Be You, which is not to be confused with DARE), all of the programs reviewed here have shown a direct impact on reducing drug and alcohol use among their participants. Furthermore, they have been mentioned or reviewed by more than one reputable source, including SAMHSA,[19] the U.S. Department of Education, Safe and Drug-Free Schools Program's Expert Panel,[20] the Promising Practices Network (operated by the RAND Corporation and founded by four state-level intermediary organizations),[21] the Center for Substance Abuse Prevention, and the Centers for Disease Control. Also, some of the important resources mentioned in the violence prevention section, such as the Colorado Blueprints and the Office of Juvenile Justice and Delinquency Prevention, include programs that cross over to substance abuse prevention and, in fact, show strong outcomes for preventing substance abuse among youths.

Individual/Early Childhood Prevention: DARE to Be You (DTBY)

The DARE to Be You (DTBY) program was established in 1979 at Colorado State University by Jan Miller-Heyl, who had obtained a research grant from the Centers for Disease Control to create a community-based system that would help reduce alcohol and tobacco use in 8- to 12-year-olds. DTBY is a multilevel primary prevention program for children 2–5 years old and their families. Its goal is to lower the risk of future substance abuse and other risky behaviors such as violence or sexual promiscuity by dramatically improving child-parent relations through building stronger communication and problem-solving strategies and fostering higher levels of parental competence.[22]

Although DTBY has a K–12 curriculum, a special program for teen parents, and a training program for child-care providers and social service agencies, our focus is on the core early childhood program. It is the component that has been the most rigorously evaluated, and it makes the case for strong early intervention programs for at-risk children and their families. Participants include 2- to

5-year-old children who are considered at risk—those in foster care, with a history of abuse or neglect, with parents who have dropped out of school, or with a family history of substance abuse or mental illness—and their parents.[23]

Typically, the parent/child program comprises 10 to 12 two-hour sessions for 10 to 25 families at a time. Every session begins with a joint activity for the parents and their children (the parents may bring all of their children, not just their 2- to 5-year-olds, and infant child care is provided). The parents then go to another area to focus on building parental communication and decision-making skills, feelings of competency, understanding of their children's development, and strategies for dealing with high levels of stress.[24] The children work on similar skills and on strengthening peer relationships. After completing the program, families are offered annual workshops.

According to many of the family service agency staff workers who have been involved in this program, the curriculum is its strongest feature.[25] They also felt that such components as good child care and booster sessions were important. Little was said about the strength of the staff. The program was initially funded by the Center for Substance Abuse Prevention, of the U.S. Department of Health and Human Services; now costs vary according to community site and use of existing social service agencies.[26]

The evaluation of this program included 827 adult participants and their 2- to 5-year-old children from various economic, social, and cultural backgrounds in the state of Colorado; for the four initial evaluation sites, the parents were given a cash incentive for finishing the program. One- and two-year follow-ups were done, although there was an attrition rate of 29% between years 1 and 2.[27] The evaluation showed the following outcomes for parent participants:

- Significantly increased feelings of parental confidence
- Better reasoning skills and less blame placed on the self or the child
- Increased awareness of social support networks in the community
- Better communication skills and appropriate discipline strategies (better use of limits, less use of harsh punishment)

Furthermore, the parents seemed to understand their children's behavior better, and children seemed to exhibit less oppositional behavior than reported by the control group parents.

Compared with the other substance abuse prevention programs discussed in this chapter, this program has the weakest evaluation in terms of measuring outcomes directly related to substance abuse. However, it is a good example of a program specifically intended to prevent substance abuse, starting from the bottom at early childhood and adding components over time that reach children and families throughout development. A longitudinal study including 10- to 14-year-olds who participated in the program as toddlers, as well as evaluations of other elements of the DTBY program, such as the K-12 curriculum and teacher training, was taking place in 2005. It would be interesting to see how communities that have been saturated with DTBY services (including parent-child training, K-12 curriculum, programs for teen parents, and training of social service agencies) compare with communities that receive few or no DTBY services.

Family-Based/Parenting Intervention: Guiding Good Choices (GGC)

Guiding Good Choices (GGC), which used to be known as Preparing for the Drug-Free Years, is designed to teach parents of 9- to 14-year-old children skills to help prevent drug and alcohol use in their families.[28] Developed by David Hawkins and Richard Catalano, both professors at the University of Washington, Seattle, School of Social Work and co-directors of the Social Development Research Group, the program design was inspired by the social development model. This theory postulates that strong bonds with a positive influence, such as a parent or mentor, help reduce problem behaviors such as experimental drug and alcohol use. GGC has been labeled a model program by SAMHSA and an exemplary program by the Office of Juvenile Justice and Delinquency Prevention.

GGC works specifically on mitigating the following risk factors for families: poor communication, lack of warmth or affection, undefined expectations, harsh or inconsistent discipline, and high levels of conflict. A strength of this program is the fact that it was field-tested in 10 Seattle public schools in the early 1980s.[29] By 1987, GGC had evolved into a video-assisted program that could be replicated in various parts of the country. It has since been implemented in 30 states and in Canada and has trained more than 120,000 families.

GGC strives to foster stronger bonds between parents and children between the ages of 9 and 14, a time in childhood development when the number of external risk factors is increasing. This is done through a series of parent sessions (two 5-hour sessions or ten 1-hour sessions), typically facilitated by two trained community volunteers:[30]

- "Getting Started: How to Prevent Drug Abuse in Your Family" includes information on why the bonds between parents and their children are so important in reducing the risk of drug abuse.
- "Setting Clear Family Expectations on Drugs and Alcohol" focuses on parenting skills and how to hold productive family meetings.
- "Avoiding Trouble," attended by parents and children, deals with the reality of peer and social pressures and helps teach "refusal skills."
- "Managing Family Conflict" helps parents learn how to properly control and express their anger and reduce negative interaction between family members.
- "Strengthening Family Bonds" shows parents ways to increase family involvement.

The program costs approximately $730 (in 2003 dollars) per participant. A cost-benefit analysis estimated that there is a $5.85 benefit for every dollar spent on GGC.[31]

Two intensive evaluations of the program, in 1997 and 2000, included pretests and posttests after 1 year, 2 years, and $3^1/_2$ years; 70% of the initial participants completed the 3-year follow-up evaluation. The results of these studies include the following:

- The GGC youths were less likely to use alcohol; after $3^1/_2$ years, 52% of GGC participants reported using alcohol, compared with 65% of the control group.
- After the same length of time, 24% of GGC participants reported using alcohol in the preceding month, compared with 40% of the control group.
- 32% of GGC participants reported ever being drunk, compared with 42% of the control group.[32]

The program has had important effects on families, including an increase in proactive communication skills and a decrease in negative interaction between children and parents. Moreover, the program has an impact even when parents do not attend every available session.

Two important issues arise concerning this program and its evaluation. First, although the evaluation was comprehensive, only 57% and 48% of participants, respectively, agreed to take part in the two evaluations. Second, as in many other "rigorously evaluated programs," the evaluation team included a developer of the program.[33]

GGC is a good example of a curriculum-based parent education program that not only helps the parent strengthen important skills but also influences child behavior.

Classroom-Based Prevention: LifeSkills Training (LST)

LifeSkills Training (LST) was developed in the late 1970s by Gilbert Botvin, a faculty member of Weill Medical College at Cornell University. Botvin is also the director of Cornell's Institute of Prevention Research, the founding editor of *Prevention Science,* and president of the Society for Prevention Research.[34] LST's goal is to prevent substance use in teens before it begins by influencing known risk factors through classroom-based curricula for elementary, middle, and junior high schools.

The curricula are based on the belief that if children develop in three domains—drug resistance skills, personal self-management skills, and general social interaction skills—they will be less likely to experiment with alcohol and drugs. A unique element of LST, and a probable cause of its effectiveness, is the implementation of the curricula over a 3-year period. In middle or junior high school, the curriculum is taught for 15 class periods of 45 minutes the first year, 10 class periods the second year, and 5 the third year. The elementary school model runs for 8 sessions each program year, for a total of 24. There is also flexibility in the intensity of the program delivery. For example, the program can be taught three to four times a week or once a week for a longer period of time; these options have been shown to be equally effective.

The program sessions use lectures, discussions, coaching, and practice to work on a variety of skills. To develop drug resistance skills, the focus is on empowering students to recognize common misperceptions about substance use and to combat peer pressure to engage in experimental substance use. The program also helps students look more closely at how they see themselves, set realistic goals, and make thoughtful decisions.

Classroom teachers typically implement the LST program after a 2-day training workshop.[35] The cost of the training is $100 per day; the 3-year curriculum package costs $625.

In contrast to many other drug prevention programs, LST has been evaluated rigorously and by multiple parties. In 20 studies of LST since 1980, impact immediately following the program was evaluated, and some studies have followed the participants for up to 6 years. As the program has evolved over time, so have the studies; for example, seven of the studies looked only at cigarette use, one looked solely at alcohol use, and five looked at various combinations of cigarette, alcohol, and marijuana use. The studies have been completed in diverse neighborhoods—rural, urban, and suburban. The outcomes are wide ranging:

- Four of the studies show that LST effectively reduces smoking.
- Nine studies showed a significant impact on the prevention of alcohol use: Many students who did not drink did not begin; many students who did drink reduced their frequency and had lower rates of drunkenness; and binge drinking was reduced.
- Of the seven studies analyzing the effects of LST on students' marijuana use, many showed at least some effectiveness in reducing the use of this drug.

Although some of the studies that measured cigarette and alcohol use showed a significant decrease, a few showed little to no impact on either. Peer-led groups often showed a more significant decrease in cigarette smoking than teacher-led groups.

LST demonstrates the importance of frequent and consistent exposure to concepts relating to behavioral risk, particularly resistance to peer pressure.

School-Based Prevention: Keepin' It R.E.A.L.

The Keepin' It R.E.A.L. (Refuse, Explain, Avoid, Leave) program, like LST, is a school-based prevention program that helps young people develop the skills to refuse and avoid drug and alcohol use in ways they can feel good about. The greatest difference between LST and Keepin' It R.E.A.L. is the latter's foundation in cultural relevance; it draws from diverse adolescent stories that highlight the unique strengths of different ethnic groups.

The program was developed in 1988 at Arizona State University by Michael Hecht and Flavio Francisco Marsiglia, who were studying adolescent perceptions of drug resistance strategies. In their research, they looked at different situations for which refusal or resistance strategies were either effective or ineffective, the importance of continued resistance, the role of peer pressure, and the importance of communication skills. They were convinced that involvement with drugs begins before high school for many teenagers; the goal of Keepin' It R.E.A.L. is to increase communication capacity and enhance general life skills among middle-school students.[36]

In a pilot study in 35 middle schools in Phoenix, Arizona, groups of students created videos dealing with issues of drug and alcohol resistance. These videos, which present everyday scenarios of Mexican American, African American, and white adolescents of the Southwest, were then incorporated into the program.

The curriculum is designed to be taught in ten 45–60 minute sessions. Four strategies that can help students resist drug use without becoming socially isolated are presented:

- Refuse—saying no without an explanation
- Explain—saying no with an explanation
- Avoid—avoiding situations in which alcohol or drugs may be present
- Leave—leaving situations in which alcohol or drugs may be present

The curriculum is available in three different versions: Mexican American, which is focused on Latino values such as family, respect, and kindness; non-Latino, which focuses more on goals and individualism; and multicultural, which combines the first two. The multicultural curriculum is the most popular and tends to be the most effective. Lessons encourage student participation and include role playing, pair discussions, group brainstorming, and activities. Student-created videos and follow-up activities are used throughout the sessions.

The Keepin' It R.E.A.L. evaluation was done over 48 months and included a preservice questionnaire for all schools and two postservice questionnaires.[37] The evaluation showed that substance use, especially of alcohol, was reduced among program participants. After the multicultural curriculum (which had the strongest impact):

- 2% of the R.E.A.L. participants smoked marijuana, compared with 7% of the control group.
- 1.4% of the R.E.A.L. participants smoked cigarettes, compared with 3% of the control group.
- 4% of the R.E.A.L. participants drank alcohol, compared with 12% of the control group.

Besides the reduction of substance use, R.E.A.L. participants tended to have better behavioral and psychological outcomes, including strong resistance capacities in regard to substance use. They also tended to develop unfavorable attitudes toward peers who used substances.

This evaluation was short term; we do not know what happened to these students a year or two after they participated in the R.E.A.L. program. In addition, the developers of the program were part of the evaluation team, potentially creating a bias in the results. However, this program's strong emphasis on cultural diversity and the different ways that young people react to the pressures of substance use is a conscious effort to reach adolescents "where they are" in terms of cultural and moral development. The videotapes of and by students are another important element of this program; adolescents often listen with keener ears to the voices of their peers.

Community Program: CASASTART

CASASTART (Striving Together to Achieve Rewarding Tomorrows), a neighborhood-based, school-centered substance abuse and delinquency prevention program, was developed in the early 1990s at the National Center on Addiction and Substance Abuse (CASA) at Columbia University in New York City.[38] CASASTART was based on the belief that, although experimentation with drugs happens for similar reasons for all adolescents, those who lack access to community resources and support are at higher risk of continuing substance use into adulthood. CASASTART was first implemented as the "Children At Risk Program" from 1992 to 1995 in six cities; in 2005 it operated in 43 schools in 16 cities and counties.[39]

One of CASASTART's main objectives is to reduce the level of crime and illegal drug use in the neighborhoods where so many adolescents live. A complementary goal is to provide the services and access to resources necessary for adolescents to become healthy members of society. In order to accomplish these goals, CASASTART brings together key members of the communities in which it is being implemented, including families, schools, community mental health and social service agencies, and law enforcement agencies.[40] CASA-START has been designated a model program by the U.S. Department of Health and Human Services Center for Substance Abuse Prevention and the U.S. Department of Justice Office of Juvenile Justice and Delinquency Prevention Program; it has been labeled promising by both the Surgeon General's Report and the Colorado Blueprints.

CASASTART targets 8- to 13-year-olds who display at least four of the following risk factors: poor academics; in-school behavioral problems; truancy; family violence or family involvement in drugs, gangs, or criminal convictions; poverty; personal involvement in drugs or drug sales; gang membership; possession of weapons; teen pregnancy; or the mere state of living in a dangerous neighborhood. CASASTART's prevention approach is intensive case management; each case manager, who coordinates a comprehensive menu of services for each child, serves 15 children and their families.[41]

Because CASASTART operates in diverse settings, each site determines its own approach to designing and delivering services. However, the services provided are consistent across sites; they include social support, family services, educational services, after-school and summer activities, and mentoring. Participants who have gotten in trouble with the law also receive juvenile justice services. Biweekly case review meetings and quarterly administrative meetings ensure that all of the partners are on the same page in terms of the program, as well as the individual cases.

As with most comprehensive, community-oriented programs, CASASTART requires a slow immersion into each community. This time of relationship building and goal setting generally takes 6 to 8 months. Once the groundwork has been laid, including securing stable funding, the staff can be hired and the delivery of services commenced. At each new site, CASA staff provides 6 days of initial training and 6 additional days of on-site assistance. The cost of CASASTART training in 2005 was $1,300 per day.[42]

The evaluation of CASASTART included three groups: a treatment group that received CASASTART services; a control group that received no services; and a quasi-treatment group that received no direct CASASTART services but resided in the same neighborhoods as the treatment group, thus potentially benefiting from broader aspects of the program, such as greater police involvement in the community.[43] The evaluation was done through preprogram and postprogram interviews. Parents or guardians were also interviewed both before and after the program, and court records were collected for each participant. A total of 98% of the participants completed the intake interview, 77% completed the outtake interview and 76% the 1-year follow-up interview. A year after program completion, the results showed:

- Less drug use: 52% of the treatment group used drugs in the preceding month, compared with 67% of the control group.
- Less use of "strong drugs" (cocaine, heroin, crack): 5% of the treatment group, compared with 9% of the control group.
- Less use of marijuana: 51% of the treatment group, compared with 65% of the control group.
- Decreased involvement in drug sales: 14% of the treatment group, compared with 24% of the control group, had sold drugs in the preceding month.
- Decreased lifetime drug sales: 37% of the treatment group, compared with 46% of the control group, had sold drugs at some point in their lives.

The program also had an impact on violent crime activity: 27% of the control group committed violent crimes during the year following completion of the program, compared with 22% of the treatment group. In addition, households that participated in CASASTART accessed more resources, such as counseling and substance abuse treatment (3.4 services), than control households (2.5 services).[44] It is important to note that the program had no impact on the following: feelings of alienation, number of personal problems (including home conflict, feeling sad or anxious, and neglecting schoolwork), academic achievement, truancy, school misbehavior, property crimes, or lifetime drug use.

CASASTART is a comprehensive approach, including social support, family services, educational services, after-school and summer activities, and mentoring. The program is coordinated by a case manager who works with high-risk young people and their families.

CONCLUSION: WHAT WORKS?

Summary of Programs

The five examples of programs that had an impact on smoking and substance abuse varied significantly in the timing of intervention and the complexity of the approaches. In several of the programs, parents were the key target, building up their capacities to communicate with their offspring and deal with behavioral problems. Early intervention appears to be important, as it is in every domain of prevention work. For "middle aged" children, heavy infusions of social and resistance skills training over extended periods of time appears to be an effective approach. Peer leaders may be more successful at imparting these skills than teachers. As in many exemplary programs, innovation and imagination make a difference; an example is having students create their own culturally relevant videos about prevention. Finally, for high-risk adolescents, "intensity" is essential. Case managers are used to coordinate needed services for children and their families.

Comment

In reviewing the issues surrounding drug and alcohol abuse, one has the feeling of "déjà vu all over again." Adults continue to worry about their children's behavior in regard to cigarettes and alcohol, but at the same time, adults are the major consumers of both. In some instances, kids have begun to wise up—they are clearly turning against smoking cigarettes and are vowing at early ages never to get involved with that stuff.

Alcohol abuse is a different story; a sizable number of young people get drunk frequently and, all too often, drive in that condition and end up killing themselves or their passengers or other people. Children who are exposed at early ages to these facts about the consequences of abuse are much more likely to forgo such high-risk behaviors. They learn not to get into cars with drivers who have been drinking.

It is hard to explain why the use of marijuana continues to be on the rise. Perhaps it is the most pleasurable of these risky experiences with the least serious consequences; the evidence that it does damage to the body or the psyche is slim. But kids still go to jail for possession, which is reason enough not to get caught with large quantities.

What should be cause for concern is the increase in teenagers' "recreational" use of prescription drugs, such as painkillers OxyContin and Vicodin, depressants Valium and Xanax, and stimulants Ritalin and Adderall.[45] It would seem a good idea for pharmacies to tighten controls over cold and cough remedies and for parents to make sure that their children are not raiding their medicine cabinets.

Like all the other high-risk behaviors, drug and alcohol abuse prevention calls for early intervention, strong communication with parents and other adults, correct knowledge about consequences, and keeping kids busy with their "work" in school and at play. In addition, society has to be ready to restrict access to dangerous substances and to enforce laws that protect children.

NOTES

1. "How to Talk to Your Kids About Marijuana," http://www.changetheclimate.org/kids (accessed January 23, 2005).

2. Centers for Disease Control and Prevention, "Youth Risk Behavior Surveillance: United States, 2003," *Morbidity and Mortality Weekly Report* 53, no. SS-2, May 21, 2004, http://www.cdc.gov/mmwr/PDF/SS/SS5362.pdf (accessed February 28, 2006).

3. *Boston Globe,* March 15, 2005.

4. National Institute on Drug Abuse, *Monitoring the Future: National Results on Adolescent Drug Use,* http://www.monitoringthefuture.org/pubs/monographs/overview 2004.pdf (accessed June 27, 2005).

5. The Partnership for a Drug-Free America, "Generation Rx: National Study Reveals New Category of Substance Abuse Emerging," news release, April 21, 2005.

6. Peter Cohen and Arjan Sas, "Cannabis Use, a Stepping Stone to Other Drugs? The Case of Amsterdam," http://www.cedro-uva.org/lib/cohen.cannabis.html (accessed July 27, 2005).

7. Institute of Medicine, *Marijuana and Medicine: Assessing the Science Base* (Executive Summary), ed. Janet E. Joy, Stanley J. Watson, Jr., and John A. Benson, Jr., http://www.nap.edu/readingroom/books/marimed/es.html (accessed July 27, 2005).

8. The National Center on Addiction and Substance Abuse at Columbia University, CASA 2004 Teen Survey, press release, http://www.casacolumbia.org/absolutenm/anmviewer.asp?

9. Multicultural Advocates for Social Change on Tobacco, "Smoking Prevention and Control Strategies for Youth," http://www.mascotcoalition.org/education/youth_ smoking.html (accessed April 4, 2005).

10. Mothers Against Drunk Driving, "MADD Guide to Congress: Your Online Advocacy Center," http://www.madd.org/take action (accessed September 8, 2005).

11. D. F. Preusser, S. Ferguson, A. Williams, and C. Farmer, "Underage Access to Alcohol: Sources of Alcohol and Use of False Identification," *Proceedings of the 14th International Conference on Alcohol, Drugs, and Traffic Safety*, ed. C. Mercier-Guyon (Annecy, France, 1997), 3:1017–1025.

12. The Center on Alcohol Marketing and Youth, Georgetown University, Fact Sheets, http://www.camy.org (accessed October 12, 2004).

13. Drew Edwards and Mark Gold, "Facts About Marijuana Use," http://psych central.com.library.sa_factsm.htm (accessed November 11, 2004).

14. "Hazelden Survey on Parental Attitudes Toward Marijuana Use—1999," http://www.hazelden.org/servlet/hazelden/search.html (accessed February 2, 2006).

15. J. Kalata, "Medical Uses of Marijuana: Opinions of U.S. Residents 45+," December 2004, http:// www.aarpmagazine.org/research/reference (accessed February 2, 2006).

16. Joetta L. Sack, "School Drug Prevention Programs Found to Come up Short," *Education Week,* March 5, 1997.

17. M. Pankratz and D. Hallfors, "Implementing Evidence-Based Substance Use Prevention Curricula in North Carolina Public School Districts," *Journal of School Health* 01.74, no. 9 (November 2004): 353–358.

18. Ibid.

19. Substance Abuse and Mental Health Services Administration, "SAMHSA Model Programs," http://www.modelprograms.samhsa.gov/template.cfm?CFID=350679&CFTOKEN=18202098 (accessed March 28, 2005).

20. U.S. Department of Education, "Safe, Disciplined, and Drug-Free Schools Expert Panel," http://www.ed.gov/offices/OERI/ORAD/KAD/expert_panel/drug-free.html (accessed March 28, 2005).

21. Promising Practices Network, "Programs That Work," http://www.promising practices.net/ (accessed March 28, 2005).

22. Substance Abuse and Mental Health Services Administration, "DARE to Be You," http://modelprograms.samhsa.gov/template_cf.cfm?page=model&pkProgramID=5&section=background (accessed March 28, 2005).

23. Promising Practices Network, "Programs That Work."

24. Colorado State University, "DARE to Be You," http://www.colostate.edu/Depts/CoopExt/DTBY/ (accessed March 29, 2005).

25. Promising Practices Network, "Programs That Work."

26. Ibid.

27. J. Miller-Heyl, D. MacPhee, and J. Fritz, "DARE to Be You: A Family-Support, Early Prevention Program," *Journal of Primary Prevention* 18 (1998): 257–285, 1998.

28. Promising Practices Network, "Guiding Good Choices," http://www.promising practices.net/program.asp?programid=91 (accessed March 2, 2005).

29. Ibid.

30. Ibid.

31. R. L. Spoth, M. Guyll, and S. X. Day, "Universal Family-Focused Interventions in Alcohol-Use Disorder Prevention: Cost Effectiveness and Cost-Benefit Analyses of Two Interventions," *Journal of Studies on Alcohol* 63, no. 2 (2002): 219–228.

32. J. Park, R. Kosterman, J. D. Hawkins, K. P. Haggerty, T. E. Duncan, S. C. Duncan, and R. Spoth, "Effects of the 'Preparing for the Drug Free Years" Curriculum on Growth in Alcohol Use and Risk for Alcohol Use in Early Adolescence," *Prevention Science* 1, no. 3 (2000): 125–138.

33. Promising Practices Network, "Guiding Good Choices."

34. Substance Abuse and Mental Health Services Administration, "LifeSkills Training," http://modelprograms.samhsa.gov/template_cf.cfm?page=model&pkProgramID=9&section=bio (accessed February 22, 2005).

35. Promising Practices Network, "LifeSkills Training," http://www.promisingpractices.net/program.asp?programid=48&benchmarkid=4#top (accessed March 25, 2005).

36. Keepin' It R.E.A.L., "Development," http://keepinitreal.asu.edu/DetOverview.htm (accessed March 25, 2005).

37. M. L. Hecht, F. F. Marsiglia, E. Elek, D. A. Wagstaff, S. Kulis, and P. Dustman, "Culturally-Grounded Substance Use Prevention: An Evaluation of the Keepin' It R.E.A.L. Curriculum," *Prevention Science* 4, no. 4 (2003): 233–248.

38. Promising Practices Network, "CASASTART," http://www.promisingpractices.net/program.asp?programid=107&benchmarkid=4#benchmarksaffected (accessed February 21, 2005).

39. National Center on Addiction and Substance Abuse at Columbia University, "Program Demonstration," http://www.casacolumbia.org/absolutenm/templates/article.asp?articleid=203&zoneid=26(accessed February 21, 2005).

40. Substance Abuse and Mental Health Services Administration, "CASASTART," http://modelprograms.samhsa.gov/template_cf.cfm?page=model&pkProgramID=37&section=bio (accessed February 21, 2005).

41. Substance Abuse and Mental Health Services Administration, "CASASTART."

42. Ibid.

43. Promising Practices Network, "CASASTART."

44. Ibid.

45. Mary Pat Flaherty, "Prescription Drug Abuse Called 'Epidemic,'" *Boston Globe,* July 8, 2005.

CHAPTER SIX

HEALTH AND MENTAL HEALTH

The World Health Organization's definition of health has become a standard in the field of public health. Health is defined as more than just the "absence of disease," but rather a state of "complete physical, mental and social well-being." This broad definition has particular relevance to adolescent health. Adolescent health encompasses not only the prevention of disease and disability, but also behavioral and social issues. . . . [S]afety, social relationships, self-esteem, education and skill development all figure into adolescent development. Thus to make progress in improving adolescent health, a combination of perspectives and approaches are needed.[1]

MAJOR TRENDS

- Teens are generally in good health.
- Most have some kind of access to the medical care system.
- One in five teens use emergency room services every year.
- Teenagers' most significant health problems are depression and stress-related issues.
- Asthma and obesity are the most prevalent physical symptoms.
- Health insurance coverage is fairly widespread, but teens are loath to talk to family physicians about their high-risk behaviors.

WHAT ARE THE FACTS?

Health

Much of our information about teenagers' health comes from the annual Health Interview Survey, which reports for the age range 12–17. Adolescents are generally pretty healthy specimens. However, certain subgroups report high rates of asthma, chronic diseases, obesity, and other health problems. And, as we have seen in Chapter 3, problems related to unprotected sexual behavior—sexually transmitted diseases, unwanted pregnancy, and sexual "acting out"—are also of concern.

Most teenagers acknowledge that they feel pretty good: 53% say they are in excellent health, 28% say their health is very good, 16% say good, and only 2% report that their health is fair or poor.[2] However, as many as 15% of 12- to 17-year-olds in 2002 had been diagnosed with asthma, and 6% had experienced an attack within the past year.

Use of the Medical Care System

Most teenagers (93%) reported in 2002 that they had a usual place of medical care: 80% in doctor's offices, 17% in clinics, and the rest in emergency rooms or other places. Doctor's offices were most frequently used by higher-income families; clinics were used more frequently by Hispanic and black families.

About two-thirds (69%) of teens had visited a health care professional within the preceding 6 months, 18% had seen someone within the year, but more than 13% had not seen anyone for more than a year.

Emergency Room Visits

The National Health Interview Survey reports on emergency room (ER) use only for children ages 6–17.[3] In 2001, almost 19% of all children in that age group made at least one visit to an ER. Rates did not differ significantly by race/ethnicity, but poor children were more likely than nonpoor children to use ERs (24% versus 18%). Medicaid recipients were most likely to use ERs (26%).

Health Insurance

In 2002, 88% of 10- to 18-year-olds were covered by some form of health insurance, and 12% were not.[4] Hispanic adolescents were much more likely to lack health coverage (28%) compared to blacks (12%) and whites (8%). About 20% of low-income adolescents had no coverage, as did 6% of higher-income young people. Some 20% of all 10- to 18-year-olds had government coverage (mostly Medicaid), and black and Hispanic adolescents were much more likely to use Medicaid. Having health insurance is an important factor in health status and health care. As would be expected, those with health insurance are much more likely to seek medical care when they need it.

Healthy Eating

The Department of Agriculture has devised a Healthy Eating Index. In 2000, only 4% of teenagers were eating good diets, 77% were in need of improvement, and 19% were adjudged to have poor diets. The Youth Risk Behavior Survey asked whether the students had eaten five or more portions of fruits and vegetables every day during the preceding week. Not surprisingly, given that high standard, only 22% had done so, and only 17% had drunk at least three glasses of milk daily.

Obesity

The latest health problem to be highlighted is obesity.[5] Data from the National Health and Nutrition Examination shows that the rates for 12- to 19-year-olds have risen from 11% around 1990 to 16% in 2002. Nonwhite teenagers are much more likely to be obese: 21% of black, 23% of Hispanic, and 14% of white adolescents are seriously overweight, putting them at high risk for chronic diseases, including heart trouble and, increasingly, Type 2 diabetes.

Mental Health

In the *National Action Agenda for Children's Mental Health,* the Surgeon General warned that the nation was facing a public crisis in caring for children and adolescents with behavioral, psychological, and emotional problems. The estimate at the time of the report (2001) was that at least 1 in 10 young people suffered from mental illness, yet fewer than 20% of those in need received treatment in any given year. Estimates from the National Health Interview Survey were that three-fourths of troubled young people did not get the care they needed (69% of white, 78% of black, and 86% of Hispanic adolescents).[6]

The National Institute of Mental Health (NIMH) has recently supported research to show that half of all lifetime cases of mental illness begin by age 14. Anxiety disorders often begin in late childhood, mood disorders in adolescence, and substance abuse in the early 20s. Early onset disorders left untreated are associated with school failure, teen childbearing, unstable employment, early marriage, marital instability, and violence. Thomas Insel, NIMH Director, commenting on the importance of this finding, said it must lead to "the recognition that mental disorders are the chronic disorders of young people."[7]

According to the Youth Risk Behavior Survey, almost 29% of all high school students feel sad or hopeless, 17% have considered suicide, and 9% have attempted to kill themselves. Females are more likely than males to report feeling depressed or suicidal, and Hispanic youngsters are much more likely to report these feelings (Table 6.1). Among Hispanic females, almost half felt sad or hopeless, almost one-fourth had considered suicide, and 15% reported that they had actually attempted suicide.

An earlier study, in 1996, showed the prevalence of mental disorders among 9- to 17-year-olds during a 6-month period:

- Anxiety disorders (phobias): 13%
- Disruptive disorders (attention-deficit, etc.): 10%
- Mood disorders (depression): 6%
- Substance abuse disorders: 2%

Table 6.1 Percentage of High School Youths Feeling Sad, Considering Suicide, or Attempting Suicide, 2003

Factor	Female	Male	White	Black	Hispanic
Felt sad or hopeless	36	22	26	26	35
Considered suicide	21	13	17	13	18
Attempted suicide	12	5	7	8	11

Source: Centers for Disease Control and Prevention, "Youth Risk Behavior Surveillance, United States, 2003," *Morbidity and Mortality Weekly Report* 53, no. SS-2 (May 21, 2004): Tables 16, 18.

Other disorders in that age group include eating problems such as anorexia, learning and communication problems, schizophrenia, and Tourette's disorder. These young people are at risk of dropping out of school and into the juvenile justice system by getting arrested. Some years ago, among young people entering juvenile corrections facilities, 73% had mental health disorders and 57% had had prior mental health treatment or hospitalization.

Depression

A special study of young teens in grades 6, 8, and 10, conducted in 1996, found that one in six (18%) had depressive symptoms.[8] To determine their mental health status, the following question was used:

> When you felt sad, blue, down, or depressed for 2 weeks or more, which of the following was true about you? Mark yes or no for each statement.

- I was irritable or grouchy all the time.
- I wasn't interested in doing much of anything.
- I gained weight.
- I lost weight.
- I couldn't concentrate as well as usual.
- I couldn't sleep and was awake at night.
- I slept nearly every minute I could.
- I felt I was a really rotten person.
- I thought about hurting myself.
- I thought about death a lot.

For the purposes of analysis, the two items dealing with sleep and the two dealing with weight were collapsed so that there were eight answers. Those individuals who marked five or more statements true were classified as reporting depressive symptoms.

Prevalence of depressive symptoms was higher among females and increased with grade level. For males, the scale went from 7% in 6th grade to 14% in 10th grade, whereas for females it went from 13% in 6th to 34% in 10th grade (an epidemic!). American Indians (29%) and Hispanics (22%) had the highest rates, and African Americans (15%) and Asians (17%) the lowest, with non-Hispanic whites in the middle range (18%).

This study looked at the relationship between bullying and depressive symptoms. Both being bullied and bullying others increased among those who were depressed (or those who were depressed were more likely to be involved in bullying). Using substances was significantly related to depressive symptoms; for example, 50% of females who reported marijuana use also reported such symptoms, compared with 20% of nonusers. For males, the rates were 18% for users versus 8% for nonusers. Depressive symptoms were also associated with frequent absenteeism and complaints of headache and stomachache.

This study highlights the need for early intervention. Careful screening can identify those at risk of depression, and treatment can be implemented before the illness becomes seriously embedded into the life of the child.

Attention-Deficit/Hyperactivity Disorder

The CDC defines attention-deficit/hyperactivity disorder (ADHD) as "a neuro-behavioral disorder characterized by pervasive inattention and hyperactivity-impulsivity."[9] In 2003, an estimated 4.4 million 4- to 17-year-olds had been diagnosed with ADHD; and 2.5 million were reported to be taking medication for its treatment. The diagnosis was reported 2.5 times more frequently among males than among females; and the rate was higher in children age 9 and older than among those younger than 9.

ADHD is most commonly treated with stimulants, including Ritalin, Adderall, and similar medications. In addition to concern about adolescents' use of these drugs to get high, questions have been raised periodically about whether long-term use is safe for those for whom the drugs are prescribed.[10] Some observers wonder whether the condition and treatment are over-diagnosed and over-prescribed and whether other kinds of treatment could be effectively substituted for the medications.

Eating Disorders

Anorexia nervosa involves an unrealistic and intense fear of weight gain, which leads to eating patterns that produce malnutrition and severe weight loss. Bulimia involves compulsive eating or bingeing, usually followed by purging behavior such as self-induced vomiting or use of laxatives, diuretics, or enemas. Eating disorders are often correlated with a history of childhood sexual abuse, depression, or dissociative symptoms. Anorexics sometimes come from families with weight problems, alcoholism, or physical illnesses.

As many as 3–5% of adolescent girls have eating disorders, and many more are dieting even though they are not overweight. Among teenagers diagnosed, boys make up 10% of the patients.

Cutting

Self-mutilation—intentionally harming one's body for emotional relief—typically takes the form of cutting the skin with a razor or broken glass. It is estimated that 1–2% of female teenagers (and a few males) engage in this behavior. Cutting is often associated with other psychological problems, as well as with eating disorders. A very high percentage of "cutters" have been abused physically, sexually, or emotionally as children. The most famous "cutter" was the late Princess Diana, who told the BBC, "You have so much pain inside you that you try and hurt yourself on the outside because you want help."[11]

Mortality

The death rate for adolescents was 68 deaths per 100,000 in 2002;[12] more than 4,000 ten- to fourteen-year-olds and 13,500 fifteen- to nineteen-year-olds died within a year. The rate has declined since the 1980s, although there were upward blips in 1986 and 1991. Injury, mostly from firearms and motor vehicles, accounts for three out of four deaths.[13] Among 15- to 19-year-olds, the mortality rate for males was more than twice the female rate. Black teens had the highest rate (82 per 100,000). The rate for both white and Hispanic teens was 65, and the Asian rate was the lowest at 37 per 100,000.

Motor vehicle and firearm injury deaths are much more likely to occur

Table 6.2 Number of Firearm Deaths by Age, Manner, Race, and Hispanic Origin, 2002

Age/Race	Accident	Suicide	Homicide	Total*
10–14 white	31	73	72	180
10–14 black	6	13	45	64
10–14 Hispanic	3	5	25	34
15–19 white	79	714	593	1,386
15–19 black	26	88	902	1,023
15–19 Hispanic	19	67	371	451

*includes undetermined manner

Source: U.S. Children's Defense Fund, *Protect Children Instead of Guns* 2004 (Washington, DC: Children's Defense Fund, 2004).

among males. Black males are more than twice as likely to die from a firearm injury as from a motor vehicle injury.

Differences in the manner of firearm deaths tell some of the story. White teenagers are much more likely to kill themselves with guns; black teens are much more likely to be killed by someone else with a gun (Table 6.2).

It is important to note that 40% of all teen deaths are the result of motor vehicle crashes.[14] In 2000, more than 5,000 fifteen- to nineteen-year-olds were killed and about 348,000 were injured in motor vehicle crashes. Teenage drivers have much higher crash rates per mile driven than drivers older than 25. The higher rates, which peak at age 16, are attributed to lack of driving experience, driving too fast, not obeying traffic signs, presence of other teenage passengers, and the use of alcohol. Some 23% of fatal crashes occur among teens who have been drinking. Teens are less likely to wear seat belts than others. More than half of motor vehicle deaths among young drivers occur on weekends, and 40% after 9 P.M.

WHAT CAN BE DONE?

Policies

Although teenagers are basically healthy and seem to have some access to health care, an unacceptable number are dying from preventable auto accidents, homicide, and suicide. The policy implications are obvious, calling for regulation, enforcement, and treatment.

Prevention of Motor Vehicle Accidents

States can adopt graduated licensing programs that include a learner's period of supervised driving, then a license that limits unsupervised nighttime driving, and finally a license with full privileges. States can also enforce seat belt laws. They could ban driving while talking on cell phones. Driver education that teaches young people how to drive safely and how to protect themselves from alcohol-related accidents could be available in all schools.

If laws against drinking while driving were strictly enforced, accident rates would be lowered. Mothers Against Drunk Driving (MADD) reports that enforcement of a 21-year-old minimum drinking age has reduced traffic fatalities among 18- to 20-year-olds by 13% and saved almost 22,000 lives since 1975.[15]

Prevention of Firearm Mortality

Children should learn at an early age that guns are very dangerous. Families should not store guns or ammunition in accessible places. Looking at data by state, Murman, Drake, and Price found that firearm prevalence predicted 47% of the state-to-state variation in child and adolescent firearm mortality.[16] The more guns in a state, the more they were used by teenagers.

States can create and enforce weapon laws, limit or tax the sale of ammunition, and require safety features on firearms to prevent accidental shootings.

Implementation of Health and Mental Health Services

It is not my intention to explore here the policy implications of reforming the U.S. health care system. It is enough to say that at this point in time (the first decade of the twenty-first century), we have a very fragmented and inefficient system of health care that is badly in need of change. Because most adolescents are quite healthy, and because more and more of them are gaining access to school-based health and mental health services, their need for a reformed health system is not as great as my own. (Just this week my primary care physician closed his local practice and my local hospital showed signs of serious management problems.) But for teenagers, some changes in the delivery of services would be helpful.

The National Adolescent Health Information Center at the University of California in San Francisco, under the leadership of Claire Brindis and Charles Irwin, has produced many useful documents that give direction to policy development in the field of adolescent health.[17] The authors believe that to improve adolescent health and well-being, it is important to:

- Develop state-level coordination agencies.
- Involve youths in the policy process.
- Expand use of strategies such as case management, "one-stop shopping," family resource centers, and school-based health centers.
- Improve the capacity of schools to address student health needs by increasing funding for school nurses, social workers, counselors, health educators, and school-based health centers.
- Expand the use of data to support responsive programs and policy.

According to a Rand Corporation report, efforts are under way to improve mental health care for children and youths, including parity laws that govern private insurance and the organization of public health services that mandate equal coverage for mental health and physical health.[18] The current estimate for the cost of mental health services for children ages 1–17 is $12 billion a year. Adolescents are the biggest users of services, accounting for 60% of the total costs ($7 billion) while making up 35% of the youth population. Outpatient care accounts for 53% of the expenditure, much of it for school-based programs; 38% goes to inpatient care; and 8% pays for medications (typically antidepressants).

In addition to Medicaid, Congress created in 1997 Title XXI, the State Children's Health Insurance Program (SCHIP), to address the growing problem of children without health insurance.[19] SCHIP was designed as a federal/state partnership, similar to Medicaid, with the goal of expanding health insurance to children whose families earn too much money to be eligible for Medicaid but not enough money to purchase private insurance. SCHIP is the single largest expansion of health insurance coverage for children since the initiation of Medicaid in the mid-1960s.

SCHIP is designed to provide coverage to "targeted low-income children." A "targeted low-income child" is one who resides in a family with income below 200% of the federal poverty level (FPL) or whose family has an income 50% higher than the state's Medicaid eligibility threshold. Some states have expanded SCHIP eligibility beyond the 200% FPL limit, and others are covering entire families and not just children. The amount of the federal funds available for Title XXI programs is limited for each fiscal year both nationally and on a state-specific basis. In 2005, about $4 billion was appropriated for state use.

Prevention of Suicide: Antidepressants

In 2004, the U.S. Food and Drug Administration ordered that the manufacturers of 32 antidepressant drugs add a stern "black box" warning that says the drugs put children and adolescents at greater risk of suicidal thinking and behavior. The decision was triggered by clinical trials in which 4% of children on antidepressants showed suicidal behavior, compared to 2% on a placebo.[20]

Programs

Health is a broad subject, encompassing not only access to specific health services but also considerations of how people live, the quality of their housing, their employment situations, and how they relate to other people. As discussed earlier, health policies involve regulation and law enforcement, as well as services and education. And these broad dimensions apply to teenagers as well. In order to be "healthy," they need access to medical care, but they also need to learn a lot about their bodies and their minds in order to lead healthy and constructive lives. So programs in this area extend from clinical services to case management to various health education and prevention interventions.

In presenting an overview of health programs for adolescents, we start with school-based clinics, reflecting our view that that is the best option. Then we present a brief overview of health education, suicide prevention, and mental health services.

School-Based Clinics

I (JD) have a strong bias toward locating primary health clinics in school buildings. As I mentioned in Chapter 1, the first such clinic I encountered was in Jackson, Mississippi, in the 1980s. This clinic was supported by the State

Health Department as part of a pregnancy prevention initiative. The Rocke-feller Foundation encouraged me to find and visit other such clinics to deter-mine their effectiveness; I identified 10 clinics in those early years, and it seemed as though they would be excellent sites from which to launch a com-prehensive prevention program. The Center for Population Options (now Ad-vocates for Youth) picked up the concept and organized a center for encourag-ing the development of school-based clinics.

As the number grew, it became clear that most clinics could not take on the controversy that went with distributing contraception on school property, but they could serve to provide health care, monitoring, and treatment to children who would otherwise not have access to these services. The National Assembly on School-Based Health Care (NASBHC) was organized in the early 1990s, and today there are about 1,500 school-based clinics in the United States.[21] A review of the 2005 annual meeting program reveals how far this field has come in few years. Many workshops were offered on such topics as clinic skills; men-tal health programming; evaluation and quality; policy, advocacy and finance; and interdisciplinary issues.

The National Assembly conducts a semiannual census from which we can learn about the clinics and what they do. Most are located in urban areas, but at least 25% are in rural areas. About 46% serve students in high schools, 50% in middle schools, and 45% in elementary schools (some clinics serve several schools). In aggregate, the school-based clinics' caseload is 32% white, 33% black, 29% Hispanic, and 6% other. Some 39% of students who are served in clinics have no other medical home (that is, they do not have a private physi-cian or usual place of care). The sponsors of the clinics include hospitals, health departments, community health centers, school districts, and nonprofit agencies.

Most school-based clinics collect revenue for health visits: from Medicaid (68%), SCHIP (43%), and private insurance (45%). Fees are collected from families or students by 23% of the clinics.

Almost all of the clinics treat acute illnesses, do screenings, treat asthma, prescribe and administer medications, and perform comprehensive health as-sessments, sports physicals, immunizations, and lab tests. About half do dental screenings, and 12% have dental sealant programs. Mental health professionals are on the staff of 56% of the clinics, where they provide assessment, screen-ing, crisis intervention, and therapy.

In regard to reproductive health care, 76% offer pregnancy testing, and two-thirds provide counseling for birth control and screening for STDs. About half perform gynecological exams on site. Only one-fourth of centers serving middle and high school students are allowed to dispense contraception on site. Prohibitions are enforced by health center policy, school district policy, or state law.

Seattle's School-Based Clinics The Youth Health Services division of the Seattle and King County Public Health Department collaborates with seven community agencies to administer 14 school-based health centers in Seattle and two school-linked health centers in South King County, Washington.[22] Partners include major hospitals, health centers, children's and family services, and the University of Washington Department of Child and Adolescent Psychiatry. Clinics are funded in part by a Families and Education levy on local taxes, as well as by foundation grants and insurance payments.

These clinics all provide medical care, mental health counseling, health education, and preventive services. They offer services in familiar and "teen-friendly" settings on or near the school grounds. All of them are staffed by health professionals trained to work with adolescents. The clinics are designed to overcome barriers that ordinarily discourage adolescents from using health services; they offer confidentiality, convenient hours, no costs, and staff members who are skilled in discussing personal problems. Each site has a nurse practitioner, mental health counselor, receptionist/patient care coordinator, and either a school nurse or a public health nurse. The public health nurse also does outreach in the community and serves as a liaison between schools, young people, other service providers, and the clinic. In addition to health and mental health services, health centers provide group discussions on stopping tobacco use, health education in the classroom, health fairs, nutrition education, and parent involvement.

The Seattle school-based health centers enrolled more than 9,500 adolescents in the 2000–2001 school year. At that time, 23% of the visits in high schools and 55% of the visits in middle schools involved mental health.[23] In 2002, the public health department received a grant of $220,621 from the Robert Wood Johnson Foundation to fund psychiatric evaluations and consultation in seven of the school-based clinics.

According to Joseph Olchefske, superintendent of Seattle's schools, "Student health has a direct impact on academic achievement. Through partner-ships . . . we can provide the support and resources necessary to improve the health of our children and to ensure that every student will meet the high academic standards set for them."[24] Some 90% of the students who used the clinics reported that the service helped them be more attentive in class. In 2003, the public health department announced a dramatic decline in teen pregnancies, births, and abortions. These developments were attributed to the reproductive health education and services that teens were receiving at Seattle's school-based health centers.

Health Education

Schools provide a wide array of health education classes that address many of the topics covered in the chapters on sex, drugs, and violence. Unfortunately, the material provided in some of these classes is outdated and irrelevant to contemporary lifestyles, and students often complain about how boring and useless health education is. Curricula such as Life Skills Training (see Chapter 5) attempt to engage students in appropriate decision making and present accurate and timely health information.

The Institute of Medicine convened a Committee on School Health in the late 1990s (on which I [JD] sat) that made a number of recommendations:

- All students should receive sequential, age-appropriate health education every year during the elementary and middle grades.
- In high schools, a one-semester health education course with an up-to-date curriculum should be a minimum requirement for graduation.
- All elementary teachers should receive preparation in health education content and methodology during their preservice college training.[25]

As with many of the interventions we have looked at, there was some dis-agreement on what the outcomes of comprehensive school health education programs should be. The committee recognized that although influencing health behavior and health status should be the ultimate goal, the school shouldn't be stuck with the entire responsibility. For example, the trends in drug abuse and teen pregnancy are influenced by many factors that rest out-side the school's control. And of course, like all such committees, this one recommended further research.

Suicide Prevention

Few suicide prevention programs have been proven effective. We rely on the Suicide Prevention Resources Center, a SAMHSA-funded effort located at the Education Development Center (EDC), for information about those they recommend for teenagers.[26] Like other prevention programs, most target high-risk youths, use case management for intensive care, address social skills, and are concerned about parent involvement.

Case Management and Social Skills Training C-Care/CAST is a "hands-on" school-based intervention for high-risk students that combines one-on-one counseling with small group sessions. C-Care (Counselors Care) provides an interactive assessment and a brief motivational counseling intervention. CAST (Coping and Support Training) is spread over 12 hour-long sessions that target mood management, drug use, and school performance. An evaluation found significant declines in suicidal ideation, reductions in anxiety and anger, and improvements in problem-solving and coping skills.

Parent Involvement The goal of the Emergency Department Means Restriction Education is to teach parents of high-risk youths how to limit access to means for suicide. This instruction takes place in the emergency room and is offered by the emergency room staff to parents whose children have been seen for mental health assessments of any kind. Lethal measures addressed include firearms, medications, and alcohol.

An evaluation found that the trained parents were much more likely than untrained parents to restrict access to lethal means.

Curriculum for All Students Lifelines is a school-based package that includes four 45-minute sessions. The sessions provide information on suicide, help seeking, and resources; information and warning signs with role-playing exer-cises; and videos about responses to suicidal peers. Lifelines was developed by John Kalafat at Rutgers University. An evaluation showed greater knowledge about suicide and more positive attitudes toward seeking help among those who had been in the class.

Resiliency Building Reconnecting Youth (RY) targets high-risk students and teaches them skills to build resiliency and prevent substance abuse and depression/aggression. The one-semester RY class integrates small group work and life-skills training. Social activities are organized to improve the quality of life, and parent involvement is fostered through at-home support. Evaluation showed a reduction in behaviors associated with suicide and depression and an improvement in school achievement.

Mental Health Services

All of the suicide prevention programs—in fact, almost all prevention programs—could also fit under the rubric of mental health services. One of the important trends in adolescent health care has been the growth of a movement to build strong school-based mental health interventions. Two centers for mental health services in schools, one headed by Howard Adelman and Linda Taylor at UCLA[27] and the other by Mark Weist at the University of Maryland, are supported by the Maternal and Child Health Bureau of the Health Resources and Services Administration and SAMHSA.

Mark Weist and his colleagues attribute this new effort to the advent of school-based health centers.[28] As they began to develop, they were flooded with demands for mental health services, which led to expanding the scope of school mental health. "In this framework, education systems join with community programs such as community mental health centers, health departments, hospitals and universities to broaden mental health promotion and intervention activities and services." Services may include individual, group, and family therapy, assessment, and treatment.

Adelman and Taylor, in their work on creating "enabling" schools, have proposed a "continuum of interventions" conceived as overlapping systems:[29]

- Systems for positive development and prevention of problems, including preschool support
- Systems of early intervention to address problems as soon after onset as feasible

- Systems of care for those with chronic and severe problems, providing access to treatments

They call for major changes in the way young people are treated both in school and out:

> The marginalized status and associated fragmentation of efforts to address student problems are longstanding and ongoing. The situation is unlikely to change as long as [education] reforms continue to ignore the need to rethink the work of student support professionals. Most school improvement plans currently do not focus on using such staff to develop a comprehensive, multifaceted, and integrated approach for addressing the overlapping barriers to learning, development, and teaching.[30]

A recent study compiling the works of 150 mental health specialists concluded that teens are more likely to suffer from mental health problems than ever before but that the need for diagnosis and care is not being met. According to Dwight Evans, lead author of the report, "Teenagers are being neglected by our society, both medically and emotionally. Without more research that targets this very malleable age group—and without early detection and prevention services to get them the help they need—this mental health crisis will only get worse."[31]

These experts recommend:

- Improved school-based services for assessment, treatment, and prevention
- Better diagnosis and referral among primary care physicians
- Better insurance coverage for mental health treatments
- Enhanced public awareness to reduce stigma
- More research

Federal Programs and Initiatives

The federal government supports two major mechanisms that are resources for health education and mental health programs. The Safe Schools/Healthy Students initiative involves the Departments of Education, Health and Human

Services, and Justice in awarding grants for drug and violence prevention, healthy child development, and resiliency. About $158 million funds sites (mostly school districts) in 150 communities. In order to apply for a grant, applicants have to have partners and show how a comprehensive network of services will be made available. The plan has to address six elements:

- Safe school environment
- Alcohol and other drugs and violence prevention and early intervention
- School and community mental health preventive and treatment intervention services
- Early childhood psychosocial and emotional development
- Supporting and connecting schools and communities
- Safe school policies

A second initiative, the Healthy Schools, Healthy Communities (HSHC) program of the Health Resources and Services Administration (of the Department of Health and Human Services), was started in 1994 to encourage the development of school-based health centers that offer primary health care to high-risk children and adolescents.[32] The appropriation is relatively small; about $19 million is spread among 76 grantees who provide counseling, mental and dental health services, and nutrition and health education. Using a multidisciplinary staff and a family-centered approach, HSHC delivers services to more than 160,000 at-risk school-age children. Among the different approaches supported are violence prevention, fitness, home visits, wellness promotion, and parenting groups.

In addition, a National Initiative to Improve Adolescent Health by the Year 2010 is cofacilitated by two federal agencies, DASH (Division of Adolescent and School Health of the Centers for Disease Control and Prevention [CDC] National Center for Chronic Disease Prevention and Health Promotion) and OAH (Office of Adolescent Health of the Health Resources and Services Administration's Maternal and Child Health Bureau).[33] These agencies are expected to partner with state adolescent health coordinators, along with seven academic medical centers that provide interdisciplinary training for adolescent health professionals.

This initiative has identified 21 critical health objectives that represent the most serious health and safety issues facing adolescents: mortality, unintentional injury, violence, substance abuse and mental health, reproductive health, and the prevention of chronic disease during adulthood. For example, they expect to reduce the mortality rate for 15- to 19-year-olds from 70 per 100,000 in 1999 to 40 per 100,000 by 2010 and to reduce the rate of tobacco use by adolescents from 40% to 21%.

How do they expect to accomplish these reductions in negative outcomes? They recognize that "the traditional focus on categorical health problems and antecedent behaviors is complemented by concepts of healthy adolescent development and health-promoting environments."[34] They call on an array of societal institutions to work across systems to address these issues, including parents and families, schools, health care providers, community agencies, faith-based organizations, media, postsecondary institutions, employers, and government agencies. Communities are encouraged to develop coalitions, conduct needs assessments, and take action, using resources at the federal and state levels.

CONCLUSION: WHAT WORKS?

We have touched upon an array of programs that address the health and mental health needs of adolescents. All of these programs provide access either to the appropriate information and education or to the appropriate services. Effective health education addresses behavioral change and includes such components as social skills and resistance skills, delivered by knowledgeable teachers, case managers, counselors, or peers. Actual access to services appears to be enhanced by placing clinics in locations where "the kids are at."

The number of school-based primary health clinics has grown rapidly, cutting down on the use of emergency rooms and improving attendance at school by treating asthma, colds, headaches, and other minor illnesses. At the same time, the presence of the health clinics has made evident the growing demand for mental health services among young people. Almost all clinics are staffed by professionals with competence in dealing with psychological problems such as depression and anxiety.

Comment

Lower-class children, on average, have poorer vision than middle-class children, partly because of prenatal conditions, partly because of how their eyes are trained as infants. They have poorer oral hygiene, higher levels of lead poisoning and asthma, poorer nutrition, less adequate pediatric care, greater exposure to smoke, and a host of other problems.[35]

In the long run, health policy for adolescents is not really very different from health policy for all. The questions are the same: how to organize services so that they are accessible; how to finance health care so access is equitable; how to assure a high enough quality of care. In the United States, the picture is very uneven. Some people have wonderful doctors who put them in well-run hospitals if need be. Other people do not have private physicians and rely on emergency rooms for sporadic care. The quality of health care is highly related to economic status, although the availability of Medicaid has helped equalize access to some extent.

The one area in which health policies may be different when applied to teens is in screening for high-risk behaviors and counseling on behavioral issues (sex, drugs, violence, mental health). Physicians and other practitioners who deal with adolescents need to be specifically trained in the best practices in adolescent medicine. They have to be willing to protect their young patients' confidentiality. They have to be skilled in talking to teens and not "turning them off." They also need skills in communicating with the parents of adolescents, some of whom are overly protective and others of whom are very insecure about their parenting abilities.

I would like to see the establishment of a personal health record that could track each individual from birth. We would then be able to determine whether their individual needs were being met, and early intervention could be ensured. The record would include the identification of the adult(s) responsible for the child so that parent contact could be implemented throughout the school years. Home visiting is clearly an effective method of family contact. The record would pick up significant items about needs and problems through continuing care.

Teens are basically healthy, but they rely on their families, schools, and communities to keep them that way. It remains to be seen whether the proposed initiatives to address health problems of adolescents will really be launched or if they remain only on paper. The call for comprehensive, integrated, noncategorical initiatives seems to be universal. It is in the interest of our society to make sure that every young person has access to quality care to ensure that he or she can grow into a well-functioning, healthy adult.

NOTES

1. Serena Clayton, Claire Brindis, Jill Hamor, Hannah Raiden-Wright, and Claire Fong, *Investing in Adolescent Health: A Social Imperative for California's Future* (San Francisco: University of California, National Adolescent Health Information Center, 2000), 3.

2. Centers for Disease Control, *Summary Health Statistics for the U.S. Population: National Health Interview Survey, 2003,* http://www.cdc.gov/nchs/data/series/sr_10/sr10_224.pdf (accessed September 14, 2005).

3. National Center for Health Statistics, *Health, United States, 2003* (Washington, DC: U.S. Government Printing Office, 2004), Table 75.

4. P. W. Newacheck, M. J. Park, C. D. Brindis, M. Biehl, and C. E. Irwin, "Trends in Private and Public Health Insurance for Adolescents," *Journal of the American Medical Association* 29, no. 10 (2004): a1231–a1237.

5. Ibid., Table 69.

6. U.S. Public Health Service, *Report of the Surgeon General's Conference on Children's Mental Health: A National Action Agenda* (Washington, DC: U.S. Department of Health and Human Services, 2000).

7. "Mental Illness Exacts Heavy Toll, Beginning in Youth," *National Institutes of Health News,* June 6, 2005.

8. G. Saluja, R. Iachan, P. C. Scheidt, M. D. Overpeck, W. Sun, and J. Gledd, "Prevalence of and Risk Factors for Depressive Symptoms Among Young Adolescents," *Archive of Pediatric and Adolescent Medicine* 158 (August 2004): 761–765.

9. Centers for Disease Control, "Mental Health in the United States: Prevalence of Diagnosis and Medication Treatment for Attention-Deficit/Hyperactivity Disorder," *Morbidity and Mortality Weekly Report* 54, no. 34, September 2, 2005, http://www.cdc.gov/mmwr/preview/mmwrhtml/mm5434a2.htm.

10. Gardiner Harris, "Warning Urged on Stimulants Like Ritalin," *New York Times,* February 10, 2006, p. A1.

11. Brian Donnelly, "Scarred Soul Scarred Body," *Catholic Parent,* March 1, 2005.

12. Child Trends Data Bank, "Demographics, Death, Infant, Child, and Teen Mortality," Table 1, http://www.childtrendsdatabank.org/indicators/63ChildMortality.cfm (accessed December 22, 2004).

13. Federal Interagency Forum on Child and Family Statistics, *America's Children: Key National Indicators of Well-Being 2003* (Washington, DC: U.S. Government Printing Office, 2003).

14. Child Trends Data Bank, "Demographics, Death, Motor Vehicle Deaths," http://

www.childtrendsdatabank.org/indicators/77VehicleDeaths.cfm (accessed December 18, 2004).

15. Mothers Against Drunk Driving, "MADD Guide to Congress: Your Online Advocacy Center," http://www.madd.org/news/takeaction (accessed September 8, 2005).

16. Judy Murman, Joseph Drake, and James Price, "Association of Selected Risk Factors with Variation in Child and Adolescent Firearm Mortality by State," *Journal of School Health* 74, no. 8 (2004): 335–340.

17. Clayton et al., *Investing in Adolescent Health*.

18. RAND Corporation, *Research Highlights: Mental Health Care for Youth,* http://www.rand.org/publications/RB/RB4541 (accessed July 30, 2005).

19. Centers for Medicare and Medicaid Services, "State Children's Health Insurance Program," http://www.cms.hhs.gov/schip/ (accessed September 15, 2005).

20. C. Johnson, "Suicide Warning Ordered on Drugs," *Boston Globe,* October 16, 2004.

21. National Assembly on School-Based Health Care, http://www.nasbhc.org (accessed July 15, 2005).

22. "Seattle's School-Based Health Centers," http://www.metrokc.gov/health/yhs/sbhc-brochure.pdf (accessed July 30, 2005).

23. King County, "Seattle's School-Based Clinics Receive Robert Wood Johnson Grant to Address Rising Problems in Mental Health," February 6, 2002, http://www.metrokc.gov/health/news/02020601.htm (accessed July 30, 2005).

24. Ibid.

25. Institute of Medicine, *Schools and Health: Our Nation's Investment* (Washington, DC: National Academy Press, 1997).

26. Suicide Prevention Resource Center, "Evidence Based Practices, Lifelines," http://www.sprc.org/featured_resources/ebpp/ebpp_factsheets.asp (accessed June 11, 2005).

27. UCLA School Mental Health Project, Center for Mental Health in Schools, http://smhp.psych.ucla.edu (accessed August 3, 2005).

28. M. Weist, J. Goldstein, S. W. Evans, N. A. Lever, J. Axelrod, R. Schreters, and D. Pruitt, "Funding a Full Continuum of Mental Health Promotion and Intervention Programs in the Schools," *Journal of Adolescent Health* (June 2003): 70–78.

29. H. Adelman and L. Taylor, "The Policy Problem Related to Advancing an Agenda for Mental Health in Schools," http://smhp.psych.ucla.edu/aboutmh/earlierrec.htm (accessed February 2, 2006).

30. "Complex Problems, Limited Solutions," School Mental Health Project newsletter, *Addressing Barriers to Learning* 10, no. 3 (2005): 7.

31. Commission Chairs of the Annenberg Foundation at Sunnyland's Adolescent Mental Health Initiative, eds., *Treating and Preventing Adolescent Mental Health Disorders: What We Know and What We Don't Know—A Research Agenda for Improving the Mental Health of Our Youth* (New York: Oxford University Press, 2005).

32. Department of Health and Human Services, Health Resources and Services Administration, *Healthy Schools, Healthy Communities* (Washington, DC: Bureau of Primary Health Care, 2001).

33. Centers for Disease Control and Prevention, Division of Adolescent Health, *Executive Summary: Improving the Health of Adolescents and Young Adults: A Guide for States and Communities* (Atlanta, GA: Centers for Disease Control and Prevention, 2004).

34. Ibid., p. 5.

35. Richard Rothstein, *Class and Schools* (New York: Teachers College Press, 2004), 3.

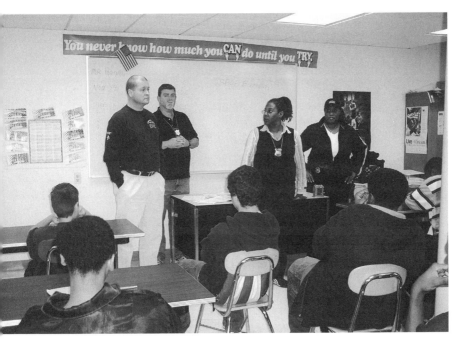

CHAPTER SEVEN

EDUCATION

It is hard to find a critical social or economic issue that does not ultimately intersect with the American High School. [The goal of] equal educational opportunity for all [must be met]. . . . It is the missing cornerstone of central city renewal and a potentially powerful tool in reducing crime and promoting youth development. . . . Yet in many places, close to half of all high school students do not graduate, let alone leave high school prepared to participate in civic life. It is no coincidence that these locales are gripped with high rates of unemployment, crime, ill health, and chronic despair. For many in these and other areas, the only real and lasting pipeline out of poverty in modern America, a solid high school education followed by postsecondary school or training, is cracked and broken.[1]

MAJOR TRENDS

- 14 million teenagers are currently enrolled in 22,000 high schools.
- Enrollment is still going up but will decrease beginning in about 2010.
- Achievement levels are mixed.
- About one-fourth of 8th and 12th graders can barely read.
- About one-third of 8th and 12th graders can barely do math.
- The "achievement gap"—white versus black and Hispanic—has widened.
- The official dropout rate, 10%, is lower than in the past.
- The unofficial rate of 9th graders completing high school is 68% (32% noncompletion).

We have reviewed the facts on teenage life to try to portray the current scene. Clearly, the story is a mixed bag. Most teens are doing quite well. You just have to visit the halls of a well-functioning high school to see hordes of attractive young people with their book bags slung over their shoulders, deep in conversation with their peers, hurrying into stimulating classrooms where they will find committed teachers. In the auditorium, the drama club is staging *West Side Story,* putting on a performance that seems very professional for a high school group. The gym is always busy with the many teams. The guidance office has a full schedule of juniors who want to figure out a strategy for getting into the best colleges. Many of the students have jobs after school, and others are involved in community service.

Then there are the other teens. Even in that school, some young people are out of the mainstream. They are failing in class and in a lot of trouble at home. They tend to be the drug users and binge drinkers; they often have health problems and frequently feel depressed and lonely. They have been left back and are edging out of school to take to the streets. If they are lucky, the school has alternative classes that try to adapt the curriculum and the schedule to the needs of these more complicated and difficult young people, and mental health workers are available to help them and work with their families.

At the same time in this complex country, there are the motivated kids attending poorly functioning schools, often in the inner cities. They would like to obtain a quality education, but it is hard to do it in oppressive, zero-tolerance environments. The classrooms are overcrowded, the cafeteria is chaotic, the halls are monitored by security guards who turn you in if you act out or don't obey all the orders. This jail-like atmosphere pervades the school, right from the 8 A.M. bell when students must pass through monitors and are even frisked to disarm them.

Here's a report from the front lines of an urban high school whose students are almost all poor and African American or Hispanic and whose principal left at the end of the previous year. It was written from one teacher to another just before the school year began. (Names have been changed to protect confidentiality.)

Hi there! I'll see you on Thursday. Be prepared for the chaos you will encounter!

As of today, schedules were still being created. Teaching vacancies still exist. The third floor will be moving to Able School. Able School will be moving to the "transition school" on Baker Street. Crane School, which was to be renovated, will not be. We have no contract. The principal will not be in until the end of September. Dave and Ellen are running the ninth grade. Fred (former social studies teacher and Continuing Ed coordinator) will be the social studies supervisor for the district and still be in charge of Continuing Ed, which is being severely cut back. George (science supervisor) is leaving for a job elsewhere. The ninth grade will be moving to somewhere in the old building, but not by the start of school. Lockers are not ready. Classrooms will have to be moved during the school year and all of the schedules will be adjusted, so be prepared to move again. The lunch period for the ninth grade will be fashionably early (starting around 10:30)—just about the time most of the kids are getting to school. There is still no director of guidance.

When we open up, there will be excitement as always, but also a lot of frustration. Just be prepared to roll with it. Since we don't make the decisions and our input is not appreciated, don't be upset when you see what is still not done.

The principal has skeletons in his closet, from what I hear. I don't think he will be that "presence of authority" we are looking for. He will be challenged as soon as he walks in. He comes to us with no regrets from his other district(s). What does that say?

Maybe by the time the kids show up, this will start to look better. Right now, everyone's running around like chickens with their heads cut off.

Expectations are low in schools like this—both expectations of the students' abilities and expectations of the administration's competence. Many of the teachers have been around a long time and remember better days. They believe that when the school was all white and middle class, the children behaved better, and the administration paid more attention to the school's needs. As poor minority children replaced the better-off white children, standards went down, and so did the morale.

The whole picture of schools in the United States is a very divided one. The achievement gap is dramatic, and so is the gap in the quality of life. Social and economic disadvantage are hard to overcome, and schools cannot take on the entire responsibility for the nation's social and economic troubles.

Public education is a huge enterprise that touches the lives of most teenagers and their families. Everyone has a view on what's wrong with the schools.

WHAT ARE THE FACTS?

Enrollment

The school system in the United States is organized by 14,559 public school districts that support about 94,000 public schools.[2] More than 22,000 are secondary schools, and 65,000 are elementary schools (others are combined in various configurations). In addition, there are an estimated 3,300 charter schools, 27,000 private schools, and 8,000 Catholic schools. In 2002, almost 14 million adolescents were enrolled in public high schools, more than 2.5 million more than the 1990 figure of 11.4 million. Another 1.4 million were enrolled in private or parochial high schools, a small increase from 1.2 million in 1990. Elementary public schools enrolled almost 34 million children, and more than 2 million went to other kinds of schools.

According to the Department of Education, rising immigration and the baby boom echo are boosting school enrollment.[3] Projections are for 14.7 million high schoolers in 2010, and after that a slowly declining number. Almost

40% of public school students are minorities, up from 28% in 1980 and 32% in 1990. Some 17% of white children are enrolled in city schools, compared with 47% of minority children; 39% of white children are enrolled in rural schools, compared with 16% of minority children.

Achievement

Test Scores

When the issue of school comes up, the focus shifts rapidly to test scores. The effects of the 2001 No Child Left Behind (NCLB) legislation on accountability have been dramatic. But the resulting picture is mixed and confusing. We start with three age groups in our target population—grades 4, 8, and 12 (or approximately ages 9–10, 13–14, and 17–18)—and two points in time, 1992 and 2002–2003 (see Table 7.1). The National Assessment of Educational Progress (NAEP) reports results in terms of basic, proficient, and advanced.[4] *Basic* denotes partial mastery of the knowledge and skills that are necessary for proficient work at each grade level; *proficient* represents solid academic performance; and *advanced* indicates superior performance.

Reading levels are based on what students should know and should be able to do in each grade. About 37% of 4th graders and 26% of 8th graders were performing below basic levels in reading, and 63% of 4th graders and 74% of 8th graders were performing at or above basic levels in 2003, slightly higher than in 1992. About one-third of both groups were at or above proficient lev-

Table 7.1 Reading Performance by Achievement Level (percentages)

Level	Grade 4		Grade 8		Grade 12	
	1992	2003	1992	2003	1992	2002*
Below basic	38	37	31	26	20	26
At or above basic	62	63	69	74	80	74
At or above proficient	29	31	29	32	40	36
At advanced	6	8	3	3	4	5

*Data were not available for 2003.

Source: Barbara Kridl, *The Condition of Education 2004* (Washington, DC: U.S. Department of Education, Office of Education Research and Improvement, National Center for Education Statistics, 2004), Tables 1, 2, 9-1.

Table 7.2 Math Performance by Achievement Level (percentages)

Level	Grade 4		Grade 8		Grade 12	
	1992	2003	1992	2003	1992	2002*
Below basic	41	23	42	32	36	36
At or above basic	59	77	58	68	64	64
At or above proficient	28	32	21	29	15	16
At advanced	2	4	3	5	2	2

*Data were not available for 2003.

Source: Barbara Kridl, *The Condition of Education 2004* (Washington, DC: U.S. Department of Education, Office of Education Research and Improvement, National Center for Education Statistics, 2004), Tables 1, 2, 9-1.

els, and 6% of 4th graders and 3% of 8th graders were at advanced levels. Certain subgroups performed better than others: females, whites, and Asians had higher scores. The number of books in the home was positively associated with student achievement, as was parents' education. The level of poverty in the school was negatively associated with scores.

The 1992–2002 trends were different for 12th graders' reading levels. Over these 10 years, the percentage at or above basic levels decreased from 80 to 74%, the percentage at or above proficient levels decreased from 40 to 36%, and the percentage of those reading below basic levels increased from 20 to 26%. This suggests that more than one-fourth of the graduating class could barely read!

The same patterns were shown for math levels, with 4th and 8th graders showing significant improvement, but not 12th graders. Some 36% of 12th graders were below basic levels in both years shown in Table 7.2.

Advanced Placement

Advanced placement (AP) courses are offered at about 60% of U.S. high schools. In 2003, more than 1 million students took 1.7 million AP tests in 34 different subjects. Although the proportion of the population taking advanced placement tests has gone up for all groups, there remains a significant disparity between white and minority students. In 2000, about 16% of white 11th- and

12th-grade students took advanced placement exams, up from 10% in 1990. In the same time period, the rate for Hispanic students went from 6 to about 11% and the rate for black students, from 2 to almost 6%.[5]

SAT Scores

SAT scores follow the same patterns as all the other indicators of the achievement gap. In 2002, white students scored an average of 527 on the verbal and 533 on the mathematical test, compared with 430 and 427, respectively, among black students and 458 and 464, respectively, among Hispanics.[6]

Educational Expectations

By 2002, most 10th graders expected to go to college. Of these, 11% expected some college, 40% expected to obtain bachelor's degrees, and 40% expected to get graduate degrees[7] (see Table 7.3). Females had much higher expectations than males, with a dramatic rise in the percentage who aspired to graduate school from 31% in 1990 to 47% in 2002. For males, the proportion went up, but only to 33% in 2002. Almost half of Asian 10th graders expected to go to graduate school, compared with 41% of whites, 36% of blacks, and 32% of Hispanics. High socioeconomic status and high test scores predicted graduate education. Only 38% of public school students aspired to graduate degrees, compared with 54% of Catholic school and 56% of private school students.

Table 7.3 Percentage of 10th Graders by Expected Attainment

	High School Diploma or Less		Some College		Bachelor's Degree		Graduate Degree	
	1990	2002	1990	2002	1990	2002	1990	2002
Total	10	9	30	11	32	40	27	40
Male	11	13	32	13	33	42	24	33
Female	9	6	28	10	31	38	31	47

Source: Barbara Kridl, *The Condition of Education 2004* (Washington, DC: U.S. Department of Education, Office of Education Research and Improvement, National Center for Education Statistics, 2004), Table 15.1.

Table 7.4 Percentage of Kindergartners' Educational Attainment Levels by Race and Hispanic Origin, 2001

	Graduate From High School	Complete at Least Some College	Obtain at Least a Bachelor's Degree
Of every 100 white kindergartners	93	65	33
Of every 100 black kindergartners	87	50	18
Of every 100 Hispanic kindergartners	63	32	11

Source: U.S. Department of Commerce, Bureau of the Census, "March Current Population Survey, 1971–2001," *The Condition of Education 2002.*

According to a Power Point slide show prepared by the Education Trust, the differential in educational status is enormous at every level (Table 7.4). Hispanics are clearly at a great disadvantage, with 63% completing high school, 32% making it to college, and 11% of those who started in kindergarten obtaining bachelor's degrees. Only half of black students make it to college, and 18% earn bachelor's degrees, compared with one-third of white students.

Students Behind Modal Grade

Being left back can become a marker of high-risk status that lasts throughout a child's life. Much has been made in recent years of "social promotion," the practice of moving students ahead even if they are not up to the standards of the class.

It is interesting to note that the percentage of students ages 10–17 who were in their modal grade (the grade considered appropriate for their age) did not change over the 16-year span from 1986 to 2002. Based on the 2002 Current Population Survey, just about two-thirds were in their modal grade, 24% were 1 year behind, and almost 4% were 2 or more years behind (about 5% were ahead). We don't know whether the 7.9 million young people who are 1 year behind their age cohort simply have birthdays late in the school year, were intentionally held back by their parents, or have been left back. But it is quite likely that the 1.3 million 10- to 17-year-olds who are 2 or more years older than their classmates were held back and are therefore in great jeopardy in terms of school completion.

Table 7.5 Percentage of 15- to 17-Year-Olds Below Modal Grade by Gender and Race and Hispanic origin, 2002

Gender, Race, and Hispanic Origin	Percent Below Modal Grade
Total	30
Male	34
Female	25
White Non-Hispanic	28
Black	36
Asian	21
Hispanic (of any race)	35

Source: U.S. Bureau of the Census, "School Enrollment: Social and Economic Characteristics of Students, October 2002," Table 2, http://www.census.gov/population/www/socdemo/school/cps2002html (accessed February 18, 2006).

Table 7.5 shows the percentage of 15- to 17-year-olds below their modal grade. Boys are much more likely to have been left back than girls. More than one-third of black and Hispanic students in that age group are behind.

According to a special tabulation of the Survey of Income and Program Participation, about 11% of all 12- to 17-year-olds had repeated a grade. Males were more likely to repeat (13%), as were black children (17%). Repeaters were more likely to have single parents with low education and low income. About the same proportions of these groups had ever been suspended.

Dropout Rates

"Official" dropout rates provided by educational authorities are much lower than the true proportion of teenagers who do not finish high school. Table 7.6 shows a census-based measure of the percentage of 16- to 19-year-olds who were not in school and not high school graduates in 1990 and 2000. About 1 in 10 fell into this category in 2000, not a significant decrease over the decade. Here the achievement gap is well documented. Fully 21% of young Hispanics are not in school and have not graduated, a much higher rate than that of non-Hispanic whites (8%). American Indians also have a very high rate (16%), followed by blacks (12%). Asian teens rarely drop out (4%). Despite all the con-

Table 7.6 Percentage of Population Ages 16–19 Not Enrolled in High School and Not High School Graduates, 1990 and 2000

Year	Total	White Non-Hispanic	Black	American Indian	Asian	Hispanic
1990	11	10	14	18	5	22
2000	10	7	12	16	4	21

Source: U. S. Bureau of the Census, Current Population Survey 1990 and 2000.

cern about noncompletion of high school, only small decreases in the rate occurred between 1990 and 2000.

In another view of dropouts,[8] Christopher Swanson projected the number of students who would graduate from public high schools at the end of the school year 2004. He estimated a graduation rate of 68%. Applying that ratio to actual numbers of enrollees in the ninth grade (3.9 million) 4 years previously, about 2.7 million graduated, and 1.3 million did not. Graduation rates differed by race, gender, and locality: for whites, 75%; Asians, 77%; blacks, 50%; Hispanics, 53%; American Indians, 51%; for females, 72%; males, 64%; high-poverty districts, 57%; low-poverty districts, 76%.

In the United States there are currently 900–1,000 high schools with low promoting power.[9] The senior class is half or less the size of the freshman class 4 years earlier. The number of these schools has grown significantly since 1993. They are predominantly minority schools. It is sobering to learn that nearly half of all black students, 40% of Hispanic students, and 11% of white students attend high schools in which graduation is not the norm.

Poverty appears to be the key correlate of high schools with high dropout rates. High schools with high minority enrollments *and* more resources (selective programs, higher per-pupil expenditure, suburban location) successfully promote students at the same rate as white majority schools.

According to a study in 2005, half of the students in Philadelphia who will eventually drop out can be identified as early as 6th grade.[10] Those with low attendance rates, poor behavior, or failing grades in reading or math have little chance of graduating from high school. If these issues are not addressed, only 10% of students with these markers will graduate on time, and only 20% will graduate a year later than expected.

Dropping out of school bodes ill for the future. Once out the schoolhouse door without a diploma, students find it very difficult to enter the labor force and equally difficult to find their way back to school. School failure is clearly associated with low socioeconomic status, compounded by race and ethnicity.

Suspensions

Racial and ethnic differences emerge in suspension and expulsion rates. Some 35% of black students in 7th–12th grades had been suspended or expelled, higher than the rates for Hispanics (20%) and whites (15%).

Summer Learning Loss

The widening of the achievement gap does not let up during summer vacation. It has been observed that disadvantaged students fall further behind, and middle-class privileged students gain. This reflects the kinds of informal educational opportunities that money can buy: stimulating summer camps, family trips, computer access, and other benefits not available to poor families.

Mobility

Students in disadvantaged communities are much more likely to move during the school year. One earlier study found that 34% of the students in high-poverty schools had transferred in a year, compared with 14% in affluent schools.[11]

Other Factors

In 1996, a special census survey asked a number of questions that were described as indicators of child well-being.[12] These data were not released until 2003, and though almost a decade old, they provide interesting insights into school experience. For example, of 12- to 17-year-olds currently enrolled in school, about 22% were in gifted classes. The rate varied significantly by social and economic characteristics: Those most likely to be enrolled were children in two-parent families, with parents with higher educational levels in professional positions. The rate for non-Hispanic white students was 24%, compared with 18% for black and 13% for Hispanic students.

At that time, the same patterns prevailed for the percentage who had ever repeated a grade. The rate for non-Hispanic whites was 9%, just over half the rate of 17% for black 12- to 17-year-olds; for Hispanic students, the rate was 11%. Those who had ever been suspended had similar rates. Children in "broken" families (divorced or separated) were most likely to have changed schools.

On all variables, teenage Asian children reported the most favorable indicators of well-being; they had heavy enrollment in gifted classes, and few had repeated a grade or been suspended. This survey also showed the percentage of children ages 12–17 who were ever in child-care arrangements: Asian children were not even half as likely to have ever been in child care as everyone else (16% compared with about 35%).

Ediberto Sanchez, 19, is like many high school dropouts: He simply faded away. In middle school he was deemed an English-as-a-Second-Language student because of his last name and put into special classes. "I was embarrassed and didn't want the other kids to know, so I didn't go to the classes," he explains. In high school he struggled with reading, and in his freshman year, he got his girlfriend pregnant. By the 10th grade, he was working and going to school, "so slowly, but surely, I started missing classes" and eventually stopped going altogether. When he went back, 2 years later, to reenroll, Sanchez says he was told that between regular classes, after-school programs, and summer school, he would have to be in school 14 hours a day to make up for lost time. When he asked about getting a GED, Sanchez says the school told him it would be too hard. In the end, he felt that the school didn't offer him much help, and once again, he walked away.

—Lucy Hood, *High School Students at Risk: The Challenge of Dropouts and Pushouts* (New York: Carnegie Corporation, 2004), 1.

School-Related Variables

Expenditures per Student

In 2001, the total public expenditure per elementary and secondary student for the United States was $8,700, an increase of about 25% over a ten-year period.[13] This figure includes interest on the school debt and capital outlay. Large cities reported the highest cost ($9,542) and large towns the lowest ($6,888), with rural areas in between ($8,423).

Current expenditures per student, which include only goods and services used within the current year, are lower than total expenditures. The U.S. average in 2001 was $7,268. The range across the country in expenditures per pupil is huge. In Hastings-on-Hudson, New York, where I lived for many years, it is about $15,000 per student. In Boston, the cost is about $11,000 per child, and in nearby Worcester, it is less than $8,000. In Alabama, the cost per student is just over $5,500, compared with Massachusetts's $8,273. One study showed that in affluent middle-class districts, the average cost was $7,510, compared with $6,254 in high-poverty districts.[14]

Teacher Quality

The characteristics and qualifications of teachers obviously have a huge impact on student achievement.[15] Various studies show that many teachers lack the necessary academic skills, do not have expertise in the subject they teach, and lack certification or advanced degrees. These less qualified teachers are concentrated in high-poverty schools.

School Size

The movement toward small high schools is the newest reform model, although not much evidence has been reported that school size makes a difference in achievement. The answer seems to be that it all depends. For students who are having a hard time, small schools appear to be related to academic growth. For students who are academically advanced, larger schools are linked to academic growth.

Class Size

Most people believe that smaller class sizes promote student achievement. Research shows that, at least in early grades and at least for disadvantaged students, it can make a difference.[16] A report by the American Educational Research Association concluded that class size reduction should start in kindergarten or first grade, include 13–17 students in a class, target at-risk students first, be con-

sistent (all day, every day), and continue over time.[17] The National Education
Association points out that reducing class size in itself doesn't guarantee that
qualified teachers and appropriate classrooms are available.[18]

The most comprehensive research on the subject took place in Tennessee.
The Student-Teacher Achievement Ratio (STAR) project showed that those enrolled in small classes as youngsters in the early grades were more likely to
graduate on time, complete advanced math and English courses, complete
high school, and graduate with honors. The achievement gap between blacks
and whites was lowered by 38%.

A consensus among educators seems to be emerging for a student-teacher
ratio of 15 to 1. This is an expensive proposition, and it remains to be seen
whether support will be found to implement this recommendation.

Uniforms

Another controversial policy requires all students to wear school uniforms.
The assumption is that when this policy is carried out, student conduct improves: Many people believe that "in an egalitarian environment—created by
uniform dress codes—a sense of kinship and cooperation is fostered . . .
which should contribute to the improvement of student behavior."[19] However,
a follow-up study of 28 Houston middle schools, which looked at average in-
school and out-of-school suspension rates before and after the uniform policy
was put into effect, did not bear this out. In-school suspension rates had decreased before the uniform requirements were implemented, from 40% two
years prior to 30% the year implemented. Two years after the uniforms were
brought in, the in-school rate went up to 49%. The out-of-school suspension
rate also went up, from 30 to 43%. (These suspension rates are shockingly
high!)

Brunsma and Rockquemore also investigated the claims that mandatory
uniform policies were resulting in massive decreases in crime and disciplinary
problems.[20] Using data from the National Educational Longitudinal Study of
1988 and three follow-up studies, they concluded, "Student uniform use was
not significantly correlated with any of the school commitment variables such
as absenteeism, behavior, or substance use. In addition, students wearing uniforms did not appear to have any significantly different academic preparedness
or proschool attitudes."

Other School Variables

After-School Programs

After-school programs have come into their own fairly recently, stimulated by a billion-dollar federal Department of Education initiative, the 21st Century Community Learning Centers (CCLC) program. In 2005, this grant program supported programs in 6,800 schools in 1,597 communities, serving 1.2 million children and 400,000 adults.[21] In addition to these federally funded programs, many schools offer private fee-for-service after-school programs, mostly in elementary schools. Additional funding is available in 21 states. The Charles Stewart Mott Foundation has committed more than $100 million for training, evaluation, and public awareness.

CCLCs are currently being tracked and evaluated, building on many studies of exemplary programs. CCLCs offer students access to art and music enrichment, homework help, computers, summer school, and weekend programs. Almost all CCLCs report partnering with community-based agencies, one-third of which are faith-based organizations.

Thomas Kane has summarized the results of four recent evaluations of after-school programs.[22] Many children attended the after-school programs only sporadically, reducing the impact. Few of the participants would have been home alone without the program. None of the evaluations found a significant impact on test scores after 1 year of participation. However, the after-school programs did promote greater parent involvement in the schools (such as attendance at school events and helping with homework), greater student engagement, and greater commitment to homework.

Gottfredson and colleagues found that participation in after-school programs reduced delinquent behavior among middle-school children, especially in those programs that incorporated an emphasis on social skills and character development instruction and practice.[23]

Sports

According to the High School Participation Survey of 2001, almost 4 million male students and 2.8 million female students reported that they had played some sport during the year. Males were most likely to play football, followed by basketball, track and field, baseball, and soccer. Girls played basketball, track and field, volleyball, softball, and soccer. Smaller numbers from both groups reported tennis, cross country, golf, and swimming.

Home Schooling

Home schooling takes many forms, from a daily formal routine that follows a scheduled curriculum to informal child-led learning in which parents supervise and help. Approximately 1.7 million children are currently being home schooled. All states allow home schooling. Parents must notify a state or local education agency of their intent, and some states test parents and require a review of curricula. Michigan requires that certified teachers be involved.

The National PTA opposes the practice, as do the National Education Association and the National Association of Elementary School Principals. However, the American Civil Liberties Union maintains that parents have a constitutional right to educate their children at home, and a majority of Americans support that view.

The effectiveness of home schooling is difficult to evaluate in terms of achievement and psychological adjustment. The problem of isolation is often overcome by home-school support groups, Scouting, and church activities.

Predictors

Paul Barton has written compellingly about the achievement gap, a relatively new phenomenon in American education.[24] According to the National Assessment of Educational Progress in 2004, the average 8th-grade minority student performs at about the level of the average 4th-grade white student. Barton looked for explanations in current research and identified significant factors that correlated with student achievement. He concluded that these gaps mirrored the inequalities in school, early life, home, and community. His findings are summarized in the following section, with some additional comments.[25]

Factors Related to School Failure

Family Factors

- *Poverty*: On almost every measure of achievement, children from poor families (those who are eligible for free lunches) do not do as well as children from nonpoor families. Schools with high proportions of poor children have higher rates of absenteeism, a lower percentage of children with positive attitudes toward school, less parent involvement, and high turnover rates among teachers.

- *Birth Weight*: Low-birth-weight infants have impaired development and are more likely to repeat grades. In 2000, 13% of black infants were born at low birth weights, compared with 7% of white and 6% of Hispanic infants.
- *Lead Poisoning*: Some 22% of black children under 6 are living with high levels of lead, compared with 13% of Hispanic and 6% of white children.
- *Hunger and Nutrition*: Black and Hispanic children under 18 are about three times more likely to be hungry and to have a limited food supply than white children.
- *Early Development*: White children and those not in poor families are read to much more often than poor minority children. One study found that 3-year-old children in professional families had vocabularies as large as those of parents who were on welfare! Richard Rothstein reported on a study by Hart and Risley: "On average, professional parents spoke more than 2,000 words per hour to their children, working-class parents spoke about 1,300, and welfare mothers spoke about 600. At 4 years old, children of professionals had vocabularies that were nearly 50% larger than those of working-class children and twice as large as those of welfare children."[26]
- *Parent Availability*: Black children are much more likely to live with one parent (usually the mother), placing a large burden on her to help educate the child. Students whose parents are involved in their school perform at higher levels. Parents of poor minority children are much less likely to volunteer in school or serve on committees.
- *Student Mobility*: Changing schools frequently is a factor in low achievement. Poor minority families are on the move much more than wealthier nonminority families.

School Factors

- *Rigor of Curriculum*: White and Asian students are much more likely to receive 4 years of education in English, 3 years in math and social studies, and 2 years in a foreign language (white, 46%; Asian, 56%; black, 40%; and Hispanic, 32%).

- *Teacher Preparation*: Students in disadvantaged schools are much more likely to have teachers who are "out of field." Among teachers of nonpoor students, 13% of 8th-grade math teachers lack certification, compared with 22% for poor students.

Barton concluded that closing the gap must be more than a "one-front" operation. Not only must steps be taken to improve schools, but governments, communities, neighborhoods, and families must also join in the effort. Some 40–60% of high school students say they feel disengaged from their schools. Students who characterized their teachers as "fair" and "supportive" were less likely to get involved in high-risk behaviors.

WHAT CAN BE DONE?

Policies

If we keep the high school system as it is, millions of children will never get a chance to fulfill their promise because of their zip code, their skin color, or the income of their parents.[27]

Educators share a nightmare known as No Child Left Behind (NCLB). Sadly, the NCLB Act is a nightmare in which everyone is naked while being pushed off a cliff because of poor performance.[28]

Rick Weissbourd describes the

steady drizzle of helplessness and hopelessness that can wear teachers down. . . . You can hardly set foot in an urban school these days without also hearing about the burden of managing students with behavior troubles. Some teachers feel physically at risk. Most teachers have brought to this work their hearts and souls, and many have lost the belief that they can make a real difference in students' lives.[29]

Too much has been written about our educational system. We have many diagnoses, and everyone has his own solution (including me). Clearly, segregation and resegregation are compelling problems. The achievement gap is worse than ever. Evidence is strong that children in high-poverty schools are much less successful than those in low-poverty schools and that minority children are stuck in those high-poverty schools.

In recent years, critics have centered on the No Child Left Behind (NCLB) legislation, but our schools, or at least those located in inner cities or disadvantaged rural areas, have been in trouble for a long time.

Legislation

The Elementary and Secondary Education Act (Title 1), created in 1965, was the biggest federal program to aid disadvantaged children and their schools. The money was used to improve academic achievement and engage families in their children's education. In 2002, No Child Left Behind became the law. This controversial piece of legislation was introduced by President George W. Bush while he was reauthorizing Title 1. It calls for accountability at the state and local levels; identification of low-performing schools; greater choice for parents, including use of vouchers for transferring to more effective schools; emphasis on Reading First; certified teachers; and allowing 20% of Title 1 funds to be used for transfers or supplemental services. By 2005, testing was required in grades 3–8 and one high school grade; by 2014, all students must achieve proficiency in reading, language arts, math, and science. In schools that lack progress, low-income students have access to supplementary services, including tutoring after school.

Critics have come from all corners. No one likes universal testing and the stress that comes with it. No one wants mandates without the resources to permit fulfilling them. The National Coalition for Public Education opposed the tax subsidy for private and religious school tuition and the voucher demonstration project because these elements of the legislation would "do nothing for education."[30] They claimed that where vouchers had been used to move children, no positive effects could be demonstrated. They were also concerned that private schools would not have to be accountable and could refuse to admit high-risk children.

Paul Houston, executive director of the American Association of School Directors, believes that NCLB has become a "nightmare" because it doesn't distinguish between "highly qualified" and "certified" teachers, because it includes special education students and those with limited English in the testing standards requirements, and because it is coercive. He objects to the "hard bigotry of high expectations without adequate resources" and points out that most of the children left behind are clustered in poor schools in poor neighborhoods. Houston suggests that if this nation were serious about NCLB, we would ensure all children and families adequate pre- and postnatal health care, parenting programs, preschool, caring as well as qualified teachers, excellent technology and learning materials, extended time in school, and access to adults who know them well and care about them.

Margaret Spellings, appointed Secretary of Education in 2005, attempted to address some of the burning issues concerning NCLB, which she calls a "new equation."[31] A revised policy was promulgated, designed to help states better assist students with disabilities. It reflects recent research findings that students with disabilities (about 2% of all students) can make progress toward grade-level standards when they receive high-quality instruction and are assessed using modified standards (not surprising!). Under this new policy, eligible states can implement adjustments to their adequate yearly progress reports to reflect alternate assessments of students with significant disabilities.

At the national level, the Department of Education has become a major player in what happens at the local level. Although lip service is given to the concept of local control of schools, financing of education is partly controlled by the federal government, even though the total federal contribution is only 7%. NCLB has imposed rigid rules regarding accountability on the states. Failing schools are identified, and if they continue to fail, parents are encouraged to obtain vouchers to remove their children to more successful schools. At the same time, the federal government supports charter schools as a kind of competition to public schools that can skim off both the more highly motivated families and the piece of the public funding that follows the departing students.

Public school systems operate under stressful conditions as they try to recruit and pay teachers who are qualified, make sure that buildings are safe and modern, and keep up-to-date on curricular developments.

Financing Education

Most people believe that federal dollars support public education, but this is a significant misperception. As pointed out earlier, only 7% of the support for public schools comes from the federal government; of the remainder, 50%

comes from states and 43% from localities. In dollar amounts, revenues for public elementary and secondary schools in 2001 reached more than $401 billion: $29 billion from federal sources, $199 billion from state sources, and $173 billion from local sources.[32]

Safety in Schools

Schools throughout the country have adopted various security measures.[33] Almost all schools require visitors to sign in. Metal detectors have been installed for random checks in 8% of schools, and a small number require daily checks as students enter schools, particularly large urban high schools. One in four schools has a daily presence of police or security guards, one in five allows drug sweeps, and 15% have video surveillance.

School Size

Bill Gates has "put his money where his mouth is." The Gates Foundation, with its $28.8 billion endowment, is almost three times the size of the next largest foundation. Its focus is on creating small high schools and helping disadvantaged students gain access to higher education. Grants have been given to start more than 1,500 high schools (half new and half conversions of existing schools) with a maximum of 100 students per grade level.[34]

Deborah Meier, one of the nation's leading school reformers, is concerned that "Gates has not asked many questions about what will sustain small schools, and whether without other systemic reforms, they can be sustained with quality. A small school can be as horrible as a big school."[35] Others have expressed concerns about losing focus on overarching issues: the problem of racism and segregation in urban education; funding inequities and budget cuts; the shortage of experienced teachers; tracking and racial stereotyping that keeps students of color out of honors courses; the dangers of privatization; and the adverse effects of NCLB.

One of the biggest questions is where long-term support for small schools will come from. A study by the New York University Institute for Education and Social Policy found that small schools cost more per pupil, but not more per *graduate* (because the dropout rate is lower).

In any case, according to the editors of the journal *Rethinking Schools,* "The small schools train has left the station. In fact, it has jumped the tracks and no one is sure where it's headed as it picks up passengers and speeds through school districts across the country."[36] In 2005, New York City was phasing out large high schools and planning for 200 small schools over the next 5 years. Chicago was planning 100 and Los Angeles 130 small middle and high schools. The concern is that, like many educational reforms, the small-school movement may have contradictory results: Small schools may be liberating and allow change to occur, or they may skim off the best students and encourage privatization, resegregation, and union busting.

Charter Schools

I am biased against charter schools because I believe that they are aimed in exactly the wrong direction; rather than strengthening public education, they draw strength away from the public domain. Yet I have to admit that if I lived in some of the cities in this country and wanted my child educated nearby, I would be first in line to start a charter school.

The Department of Education operates a grant program for charter schools that continues to grow; the latest count of charter schools is 3,200. In the 2005 budget, the appropriation was $218 million, with an additional $37 million for acquiring facilities. Every state has a different set of laws governing these schools.

There is no agreement on the success of charter schools after 12 years of experimentation. My reading of the research convinces me that, as one reporter put it, "Charter schools would have a hard time making it onto the honor roll."[37] A report of the Progressive Policy Institute that focused on Ohio found an array of problems that hurt student performance. That state has more than 240 charter schools serving an estimated 60,000 students, but only 112 of the schools were rated because the others lacked data. Of those that were rated, 58% were in the lowest categories.

Programs

What is the fundamental mission of preschool through high school education in the twenty-first century? Under what school ecology and climate conditions will students benefit maximally and teachers instruct

most effectively? Successful schools ensure that all students master reading, writing, math, and science. They also foster a good understanding of
history, literature, foreign languages, and diverse cultures. However,
most educators, parents, students, and public support a broader educational agenda that also involves enhancing students' social-emotional
competence, character, health, and civic engagement. . . . [E]ducation
should teach young people to interact in socially skilled and respectful
ways; to practice positive, safe, and healthy behaviors; to contribute ethi-
cally and responsibly to their peer group, family, school and community;
and to possess basic competencies, work habits, and values as a foundation for meaningful employment and engaged citizenship.[38]

In this society, schools tend to get blamed for all of children's problems and
also to get stuck with the responsibility for "fixing" them. If there is one thing
perfectly clear, it is that *schools cannot do it alone.* They cannot heal all the
wounds, equalize all the inequities, make up for the absent parents, and at
the same time create a learning environment that will both challenge and hold
the interest of young people today.

In this chapter, we look at various programs and approaches that may have
a long-term impact on educational outcomes, beginning with community
schools. Next, we look at one among the hundreds, perhaps thousands, of exemplary and successful schools in many parts of the country—University Park
Campus School in Massachusetts. And we present portraits of several significant school-based initiatives that may make a difference in how young people
grow and develop: social and emotional development, service learning, Facing
History, character education, and After School Matters.

Community Schools

My own bias has led me (JD) to become a strong advocate for what I call
full-service community schools.[39] Community schools are those that have
been intentionally transformed into neighborhood hubs, that are open all the
time to children and their families, and that are providing strong support
services to help overcome the many barriers schools face in producing successful students. What makes these schools different is that they are operated
through partnership agreements between public schools and community
agencies. They are not to be confused with charter schools; they are regular

public schools that are undergoing transformation within the public school system.

Advocates for full-service community schools believe that today's schools cannot possibly take on all the problems of today's children and their parents. They need other agencies to share some of the responsibility. "Open all the time" includes before- and after-school activities, evening programs, weekend events, and summer-long programs. Comprehensive support services may include primary health clinics, dentistry, mental health counseling and treatment, family social work, parent education, enhanced learning opportunities, community development, and whatever else is needed in that school and community.

In a fully developed community school, the school building is teeming with activity. Parents are involved in the classroom, on the playground, and in the cafeteria. After-school activities are designed to extend what goes on in the classroom. Teachers, parents, and school and agency support workers confer with one another to ensure that every child can function well within the school system. Parents are encouraged to "hang out" in the parent resource room, where they have access to computers, food, and advisors, as well as support and friendship. Family members have access to trained medical personnel and social workers at the site. The students perform better under these circumstances and clearly feel better in the vastly improved school climate. The neighborhood improves as well, with such projects as a new playground designed by the students and a street clean-up campaign organized by the parents.

In successful community schools, the community agency personnel and the school-oriented parents bring a strong youth development perspective into the school environment. Teachers and administrators know that they must address children's developmental needs, and they welcome the additional hands to work with them in the hands-on approaches that are required. Personal attention takes time. So does coordination.

One key to the success of community schools is the presence of a full-time coordinator, who is in this model supplied by the lead agency and who acts as a peer to the principal. The coordinator takes on the job of organizing the support services and involving the parents. Together with the principal, the coordinator works to integrate these activities with what goes on in classrooms. The principal is thus freed to concentrate on academic achievement, which is, after all, the central purpose of the school.

The concept of community schools is not really new; these ideas of collaboration and community orientation have been around for more than a century. However, the current version is more complex than those of the past, probably because the problems and pressures are greatly heightened. No other generation has had to deal with the strong arm of the No Child Left Behind Act, which forces schools to concentrate on "teaching to the test" and makes pariahs out of failing students, failing teachers, and failing schools.

The current crop of community schools has grown out of adversity, including the decay of the inner city and the widening of the achievement gap. Around 1990, various models began to emerge around the country in a surge of spontaneous innovation. Social workers at the Children's Aid Society in New York City, faculty at the University of Pennsylvania in Philadelphia, city and county officials in Portland, Oregon, health providers in California, state officials in Florida and New Jersey, and a school principal in Evansville, Indiana, were all working independently to bring support services and outside community agencies into schools and enrich the intellectual and social environment. The leaders of these efforts came together in 1998 under the auspices of the Institute for Educational Leadership in Washington, DC. The Coalition for Community Schools was launched and now has 170 participating organizations representing the educational establishment, unions, youth development organizations, health and welfare agencies, and other interested parties.[40]

The community school concept does not yet have wide recognition in the educational world. School reformers are just beginning to acknowledge its importance and to incorporate "collaboration" into their thinking. A single activity such as an after-school program can be an avenue to the fully developed model, and such activities are rapidly proliferating. After-school programs have received the most attention, at least from the federal government. Almost 7,000 schools have received grants through the billion-dollar 21st Century Community Learning Centers program to open the schoolhouse doors in the afternoons, frequently under the auspices of community-based youth agencies such as Boys and Girls Clubs, YMCAs and YWCAs, and other nonprofits. At least 1,500 schools have primary health care clinics with services provided by local community health centers or hospitals. It has been estimated that more than 5,000 family resource centers are located in schools. These are, of course, central pieces to the whole package, but without further development they will not significantly change the climate of the school. Instead, they will remain "add-ons" dropped into the building without integration with what goes on in the classroom and therefore will not significantly affect outcomes.

The "further development" is the real challenge to both youth development workers and educators. At the moment, the potential components of community schools are generally ensconced in their own domains or silos. For example, educators come out of schools of education with little knowledge of youth development and behavioral psychology. Social workers come out of social work schools with virtually no exposure to what goes on in classrooms. Yet, for contemporary students to be served, each domain must be entered and mastered by the other.

I am convinced that the concept underlying community schools is important to the healthy development of millions of young people. They cannot succeed in schools that are failing. Schools need help from community agencies not only to provide support services but also to change the environment and climate of the school building. Innovative initiatives are under way all over the country (and in many other countries as well), but "going to scale" represents a major challenge in most cities.

Successful Schools

Schools can work. The Council of Great City Schools commissioned a study of urban districts that have raised academic performance in their districts as a whole while also reducing racial differences in achievement.[41] These districts were Charlotte-Mecklenburg, North Carolina; Houston, Texas; Sacramento, California; and the Chancellor's District in New York City (a selected group of schools).

These districts faced challenges common to most urban districts: failing students, political conflict between school board and staff, low expectations, lack of instructional coherence, high student mobility, and poor fiscal operations. They also had funding problems. The case studies show that these challenges can be overcome under certain conditions:

- A new school board focuses more on policy decisions and less on day-to-day operations.
- Everyone shares a common vision and has the capacity to solve instructional problems.
- New resources are identified to support the reform.

As the reform shaped up, the districts emphasized student achievement goals, with concrete accountability systems and a set schedule for changes. They focused heavily on the lowest performing schools and attempted to restaff them with stronger people and to use district-wide curricula along with professional development. Progress was greatest at the elementary level.

The study suggested that giving incentives for staff members to transfer to low-performing schools might be a useful policy to improve outcomes. It concluded that "doing all of these things together can have a much larger impact on the performance of a district than doing any one of them alone."[42]

University Park Campus School University Park Campus School (UPCS) is a small school in Worcester, Massachusetts, with about 200 students in grades 7–12.[43] It has ranked first among urban schools serving low-income students on English and math graduation exams. All graduates so far have gone to college. The plain old brick building is located in the poorest section of the city and serves only neighborhood students. One-third of the students are Hispanic, 19% Asian, 7% African American; many of the white students are recent arrivals from Eastern Europe, mainly Albania. Thus, 78% of the students come from non-English speaking homes, and 72% qualify for free lunches.

As part of its cooperation and development program with several community agencies, Clark University, which is just down the block, started the school as a partner with Worcester Public Schools. UPCS is a regular public school, operated at the same fiscal level as other schools in Worcester.

What's different about this school is the culture of academic success. Students are oriented on arrival to uphold the high standards of the school. Instruction is individualized. Classes are 90 minutes long, with homework sessions in the morning and evening. Entering 7th graders attend a month-long August Academy to get them ready for the intensity of their schooling. Grades 9–12 are modeled after prep school courses of study, with few electives.

The culture of UPCS is one of excitement, engagement, and support. Teachers are mentors and advisers, as well as teachers. Students support their peers and mentor younger students. The teaching staff holds weekly meetings to plan together and go over student work. Clark University has a large role in this effort. All UPCS graduates who are qualified can attend Clark for 4 years tuition free. During 11th and 12th grades, students can take classes at Clark; in the earlier grades, professors from the university work with some of the classes.

These students do very well on exams. Over a 3-year period (2003–2005), 88% of UPCS students scored at proficient and advanced levels on the 10th-grade math exam, compared with 29% of Worcester public school peers and 51% statewide; in English, UPCS students scored at 91%, compared with 28% in the district and 61% across the state. In 8 years, only one student has dropped out, and 80% of graduates have gone on to 4-year colleges.

A visit to this school confirms the description. The intensity of the students is obvious in each classroom full of engaged young people concentrating on their lessons. I sat in on an 11th-grade English class that was studying *Death of a Salesman*. Groups of four had made posters highlighting themes from the play and were presenting their findings orally before the class. They performed gracefully and showed the deep understanding of the play necessary to answer the questions they were given for the next day's homework. The classrooms were loaded with stimulating materials, and the teachers were clearly heavily involved with their students.

I conducted discussions with two groups: 7th–8th graders and 10th–11th graders. The younger students were a little reticent at first (so was I), but they indicated that they loved being at this school for many reasons. It was small, so you could get to know everyone and get more attention. The teachers were involved. There were clubs you could join (such as drama, TV studio, sports, student council). It was a good place to be, a haven in a poor, violent, drug-ridden neighborhood. Clark students act as mentors for these kids.

In the two groups (11 students), only one child came from an American-born family. All the other parents were foreign-born, and almost all of them spoke another language at home. The parents were very concerned for their kids but were happy that the school offered their children better opportunities for the future. Among the younger group's view of their futures, five wanted to do something in medicine and science and one boy wanted to be a businessman. As to what wasn't good in their lives, they responded that nothing exciting happened in Worcester; they wanted a place to hang out, such as a youth center.

The older students were very talkative, especially the three boys. They felt that drugs were everywhere, the neighborhood was full of them, and many kids sold them. None of them would take drugs because all three of their fathers had served time in jail on drug charges; one had been deported to Jamaica, leaving the boy behind. One of the boys was going to be a father in a few weeks! We talked a lot about depression; they felt it was a common problem among their peers, because they came from broken homes and they did not have parents who were supportive.

These older kids, who have been in the school for 5 years or so, think it's probably too small and too gossipy; everyone knows everyone else's business, and there's no privacy.

The school culture and code of conduct is based on "what you shouldn't do." The kids know very well what is acceptable and are careful not to violate rules too often. We discussed the impact of having parents who were brought up in different cultures: "If I swore at my parents, I'd be dead." Girls are brought up differently (more strictly) than boys in immigrant homes.

When asked whether they thought life for teenagers in 2025 would be better or worse than now, six out of seven said worse, emphatically. Their concerns: the economy, bad politics, too much materialism in society (emphasis on things), oral sex, drugs, hype by media, President Bush.

A week after my visit, UPCS was named one of the 100 best high schools in the United States by *Newsweek* magazine. It was the only school in Massachusetts selected and, of the 100, the one with the highest indicators of poverty.

Successful Components

Social and Emotional Learning The goals of social and emotional learning overlap the goals of community schools and the desired outcomes for a whole range of prevention programs.

> In addition to producing students who are culturally literate, intellectually reflective, and committed to life-long learning, high-quality education should teach young people to interact in socially skilled and respectful ways; to practice positive, safe, and healthy behaviors; to contribute ethically and responsibly to their peer group, family, school, and community; and to possess basic competencies, work habits, and values as a foundation for meaningful employment and engaged citizenship.[44]

Certain practitioners (such as the coauthors of the preceding quotation) believe that schools cannot handle the demands of addressing a multitude of diverse issues such as AIDS, alcohol, careers, character, conflict resolution, and so forth. As they see the situation, categorical prevention and promotion programs are not only uncoordinated, they are disruptive "short-term fragmented initiatives." In addition, schools rarely provide adequate staff development and support. Out of these kinds of concerns came the conceptual framework for social and emotional learning (SEL), an approach that addresses the underlying causes of problem behavior while supporting academic achievement. Much of the work in SEL is fostered by the Collaborative for Academic, Social and Emotional Learning.[45]

SEL programs focus on building children's ability to recognize and manage their emotions, appreciate the perspectives of others, establish positive goals, make responsible decisions, and handle interpersonal situations effectively. This is accomplished through classroom instruction, student engagement in positive activities in and out of the classroom, and broad student, parent, and community involvement in program planning, implementation, and evaluation, beginning in preschool and continuing through high school. A number of school-based interventions are available that create caring communities using class meetings, peer leadership, family involvement, and whole-school community-building activities.

Service Learning Service learning is a teaching method that engages students in solving problems within their schools and communities as part of their academic studies.[46] It is intended to help students master curriculum content by making meaningful connections between what they are studying and its many applications in the real world. For example:

- Language arts students may hone their writing skills by organizing a campaign to reduce bullying on their school buses.
- Math students may make calculations to help persuade local authorities to install a traffic light at a dangerous corner near their school.
- History students may research local heroes identified on plaques in their community and share this knowledge at the annual Memorial Day ceremony.
- Middle school students may tutor younger students, leading to improved literacy skill for both groups.

Service learning fits into the three-part mission of public education: preparing students for academic achievement, for civic participation, and for workforce success. A national opinion poll conducted in 2000 found that the vast majority of Americans expect schools to provide students with the academic skills they need for success in life. But Americans also believe that success requires more than mastering basic academic subjects. They think that schools should link what children study in school to the skills they will need at work and in their communities, and they believe that service learning helps build the skills that students need to be successful later in life.[47]

One-third of American public schools report offering service-learning experiences for students.[48] Most support comes from local resources. The only federal funding for service learning supports programs in a small number of schools through the Corporation for National and Community Service's Learn and Serve America program.

Various studies of service learning have shown that it can have a positive impact on academic, civic, social, personal, career, and ethical development. Service learning has an especially powerful effect on students' personal and social development, which researchers believe is a key determinant for success in school.[49] For instance, prevention programs with a service-learning component are effective at reducing teen pregnancy and risky behaviors.[50] When service learning is used as a teaching strategy, students demonstrate:

- Increased academic skills and knowledge
- Increased enthusiasm for their studies
- Increased interpersonal and problem-solving skills
- Increased sense of civic responsibility
- Increased confidence that they can make a difference

Well-implemented service learning also has a positive impact on families, schools, and communities. For instance, community-based organizations can be more effective with help from students. Community members who participate in service learning view young people as valued resources and positive contributors to their communities.

Facing History and Ourselves Facing History and Ourselves[51] is an interdisciplinary course in which middle- and high-school students learn to think about individual decision making and to exercise the faculty of making judgments.[52] By illuminating common themes of justice, law, and morality in past and present,

Facing History offers students a way to examine the meaning and responsibility of citizenship and the tools to recognize bigotry and indifference in their own worlds. Through a rigorous examination of the events that led to the Holocaust, along with other case studies from the past century, Facing History helps adolescents understand that prevention of collective violence is possible through choices made by individuals and groups. Students learn to recognize universal themes of prejudice, discrimination, and dehumanization, as well as courage, responsible participation, and steps that can be taken toward prevention.

Facing History's sequence of study begins with identity—first individual identity and then group identities and their definitions of membership. From there, the course examines the failure of democracy and the steps leading to the Holocaust—the most documented case of twentieth-century indifference, dehumanization, and racism. It goes on to explore difficult questions of judgment, memory, and legacy and the necessity for responsible participation to prevent injustice. The final section, called "Choosing to Participate," provides examples of individuals whose choices made a difference.

The Facing History program draws on the concerns and issues of adolescence, particularly the preoccupation with individual and group identity, acceptance and rejection, conformity and nonconformity, labeling, ostracism, loyalty, fairness, and peer group pressure. It speaks to the adolescent's developing ideas of subjectivity, competing truths, and differing perspectives, along with the growing capacity to think hypothetically and the inclination to find personal meaning in newly learned concepts. Building upon the increasing ability to think hypothetically and imagine options, Facing History teachers stretch the historical imagination by urging delineation of choices that could have been made and alternative scenarios that could have come about.

In a major study funded by the Carnegie Corporation of New York, Facing History classes were shown to be significantly successful in expanding adolescents' capacity for interpersonal understanding and in enhancing their ability to consider the personal meaning of issues of social justice.[53] Another evaluation studied teachers trained in Facing History institutes sponsored by the State of Tennessee Safe and Drug-Free Initiative. When those teachers used the program in their classrooms, they rated their students as having increased their knowledge of the origins of hatred and violence in history, their understanding of their roles and responsibilities in a democratic society, their ability to recognize racism, anti-Semitism, and other forms of bigotry, and their ability to generate alternative solutions to aggression.[54]

Character Education A recent entry on the educational scene is character education, which is based on the idea that if students were more "virtuous," they would do better in school. Character education is the development of knowledge, skills, and abilities that enable the learner to make informed and responsible choices; it emphasizes the obligations and rewards of productive living in a global and diverse society. Character education encourages students to think critically and then to act responsibly. Instructional materials, methods, and strategies, when developed into interdisciplinary curricular themes, help teachers create meaning while allowing students time for purposeful exploration and self-reflection.

According to Boston University's Center for the Advancement of Ethics and Character, character education—helping children "develop good dispositions that will enable them to flourish intellectually, personally, and socially"[55]—is an essential mission of schools. Virtues such as responsibility, hard work, honesty, kindness, diligence, sincerity, personal accountability, courage, and perseverance can be intentionally taught, celebrated, and continually practiced.

As Superintendent Dale Frederick of Pittsburgh, Pennsylvania, put it, "Academics is the cornerstone of education, but building character is the building block of life."[56] In selected Pittsburgh schools, a specific character-related word is highlighted each week, and classroom activities are geared toward helping students develop that character trait. Teachers spend 15 minutes each day discussing the word of the week and its implications. "Honesty" begins with a story about Abraham Lincoln, continues with the reading of one of Aesop's fables ("The Boastful Traveler "), and is incorporated in classroom lessons to reinforce behavior.

Parents are involved through training programs. They are provided with a Student-Parent Activity Book that suggests topics for family discussions. The community is involved through media and special events intended to show students that they are valued by the community.

After School Matters Most of the thousands of after-school programs are focused on young children. After School Matters (ASM) in Chicago is unique in its concentration on older youths.[57] This nonprofit organization, operating since 2000, partners with the City of Chicago, the Chicago Public Schools, the Park District, and the Public Library to expand out-of-school opportunities and revitalize neighborhoods in 35 communities throughout the city. In 2004–2005, ASM had the capacity to serve almost 22,000 teens. ASM offers hands-on, interactive programs led by skilled professionals in which teens explore career paths and develop marketable skills in the arts, sports, technology, and communication. Participants receive stipends. In addition, as members of an organization that has the feeling of a club, teens can participate in sports and fitness activities and have a good time.

CONCLUSION: WHAT WORKS?

Summary of Programs

We have only touched on the subject of successful schools. Thousands of educational institutions function very well, and millions of young people are being exposed to high-quality teaching. In this chapter, we have highlighted full-service community schools because the concept is particularly useful at this time in our history when we are beginning to recognize the importance of overcoming barriers to learning. The approach is to transform schools into new kinds of community institutions, operated by partners who can bring in health and mental health services, educational enrichment, parenting education, and whatever else is needed in that situation to improve the odds for achievement.

University Park Campus School is offered as an example of a school that shows promise; it demonstrates that very high-risk children can achieve at very high levels if they are given intense individual attention by well-qualified and dedicated teachers. The principal and the staff, backed up by Clark University, have created a climate of learning and success. Failure is not tolerated. Parents are involved.

Educators, social workers, and psychologists have joined forces to produce some excellent program components that clearly enhance learning. We have reviewed curricula that address social and emotional development, learning about oneself through the study of history, making responsible choices, contributing to community well-being, and selecting appropriate career paths. These school-based interventions are strongly rooted in an intellectual understanding of youth development. They challenge young people and help them to grow.

Although these examples of successful schools and programs are quite different in content, size, and scope, they have one common attribute: They grew out of someone's (an individual or a group of individuals) concern about the welfare of young people. Someone said "we can change the course of youth development" and then invented and refined an approach. The approaches may differ, but the commonality is the intensity of the problem solvers and their desire to develop successful programs.

Comment

Education may be the key issue in the welfare of young people. If our schools are not able to respond to the needs of twenty-first-century teenagers, our whole society will be weaker. If Christopher Swanson's projections are accurate, as many as 43% of students in schools in high-poverty communities may not finish high school. What on earth will they do? The employment situation is grim for those who lack a high school diploma. They can join the army and get a general education diploma (GED), but few take up that offer. Prisons are full of young people, especially males, who dropped out of school and never made it.

Not only is education our biggest problem, it is also probably the area that has garnered the most interest and action. Everyone is an authority on schools (after all, we all went to at least one). Solutions to the problems of teaching and learning come and go, following trends that are more or less permissive, more or less intensive. New approaches may be more difficult to teach, requiring more training and more computer orientation. I remember when the big thrust was the open school, with few walls to confine the children. The result was chaos, much too much noise, and lots of distraction. Then it was school uniforms, subsequently shown to have little impact on the situation. For a while, middle schools were the rage. Young people in grades 5–6 to 8–9 needed to have a separate building because they were in a transitional period (translation: impossible brats) and should have specialized attention. Now the thrust is to go back to K–8 and, in fact, to add preschool onto the beginning.

Apparently we are entering a period of small high schools, dividing up the 3,000-student impersonal factory-like institution into five or six small units. This makes good sense in light of the strong evidence that individual attention is a major factor in successfully teaching today's adolescents. But the size of the school or the class is only part of the story. If we are going to ensure that students have access to large quantities of individual attention, the individual who gives the attention had better be up to the job. This means intensive training for classroom teachers and plenty of other support personnel on hand to deal with the complex psychosocial issues that make it hard for many adolescents to concentrate on schoolwork.

I would like to see schools transformed into community hubs that bring together all the forces and supports that kids need in order to succeed. This means very early intervention, with home visitors recruiting parents for parenting education when the child is very young. This means excellent pre-K classes that not only prepare children for the academic demands of school but also offer them the psychosocial skills they will need in order to get along. This means highly trained teachers in the classroom, backed up by teacher aides, on-site health and mental health services, and a stimulating school climate. High schools, large or small, have to approach young people as individuals and help them find the right path to further education. Schools also have to recognize that they can play a major role in shaping the social environment of the community. They can bring together community members to celebrate their diversity, their cultures, and their customs, and, in doing so, they can become places that attract adolescents instead of repelling them or turning them off.

NOTES

1. Robert Balfanz and Nettie Legters, *Locating the Dropout Crisis* (Baltimore: Johns Hopkins University, Center for Social Organization of Schools, June 2004).

2. The Center for Education Reform, "K–12 Facts," http://www.edreform.com/index.cfm?fuseAction=section&pSectionID=15&cSectionID=97 (accessed September 11, 2005).

3. U.S. Department of Education, National Center for Educational Statistics, *The Condition of Education 2004*, Report No. NCES 2004-077 (Washington, DC: U.S. Government Printing Office, 2004), 39.

4. Ibid., 210.

5. College Board AP Central, "Advanced Placement Report to the Nation," http://

www.apcentral.collegeboard.com/article/0,3045,149–0–0–41919,00.html (accessed July 28, 2005).

6. Infoplease, "Average SAT Scores, 1972–2004," http://www.infoplease.com/ipa/a0883611.html (accessed July 16, 2005).

7. U.S. Department of Education, National Center for Educational Statistics, *The Condition of Education*, 137, Table 15-1.

8. Christopher Swanson, *Projections of 2003–04 High School Graduates* (Washington, DC: Urban Institute, Education Policy Center, 2004).

9. Balfanz and Legters, *Locating the Dropout Crisis*.

10. "Dropouts Identifiable by 6th Grade Factors," Report Roundup, *Education Week* (April 7, 2005): 13.

11. M. J. Puma, C. Jones, D. Rock, and R. Fernandez, *Prospects: The Congressionally Mandated Study of Educational Growth and Opportunity: Interim Report* (Bethesda, MD: Abt, 1993).

12. U.S. Census Bureau, *Survey of Income and Program Participation, 1996 Panel* (Washington, DC: U.S. Government Printing Office, 2003), Wave 12, Tables 70–89.

13. U.S. Department of Education, *The Condition of Education 2004* (Washington, DC: U.S. Government Printing Office, 2004), Table 35-1.

14. Kevin Carey, *The Funding Gap: Low-Income and Minority Students Still Receive Fewer Dollars in Many States* (Washington, DC: The Education Trust, Fall 2003), Tables 3, 7.

15. Jane Hannaway, "Poverty and Student Achievement: A Hopeful Review," in *Literacy Development of Students in Urban Schools*, eds. James Flood and Patricia Anders, 3–21 (Newark, DE: International Reading Association, 2005).

16. Ibid.

17. American Educational Research Association, "Class Size: Counting Students Can Count," *Research Points* 1, no. 2 (Fall 2003).

18. National Education Association, "Class Size," http://www.nea.org/classsize/index.html (accessed June 15, 2005).

19. School Uniforms Debate, Message 539, "Comment on Houston Study," http://www.groups:yahoo.com/groups/SchoolUniformsDebate/messages/502?viscount=100 (accessed February 2, 2006).

20. David Brunsma and Kerry Rockquemore, "Effects of Student Uniforms on Attendance, Behavior Problems, Substance Abuse, and Academic Achievement," *Journal of Education Research* 92, no. 1 (September-October 1998): 53–62.

21. After School Alliance, *21st Century Community Learning Centers: A Working Model* (Washington, DC: After School Alliance, 2005).

22. Thomas Kane, "The Impact of After-School Programs: Interpreting the Results of Four Recent Evaluations," (working paper, William T. Grant Foundation, University of California–Los Angeles, January 16, 2004).

23. Denise Gottfredson, Stephanie Gerstenblith, David Soule, Shannon Womer, & Shaoli Lu, "Do After School Programs Reduce Delinquency?" *Prevention Science* 5, no. 4 (December 2004): 253–266.

24. Paul E. Barton, "Why Does the Gap Persist?" *Educational Leadership* 62, no. 32 (November 2004): 9–13.

25. All data from Barton, ibid, unless otherwise noted.

26. B. Hart and T. Risley, *Meaningful Differences* (Baltimore: Brookes, 1995), quoted in Richard Rothstein, "The Achievement Gap: A Broader Picture," *Educational Leadership* 62, no. 3 (November 2004): 40–41.

27. Bill Gates, "The Gates Foundation and Small Schools," *Rethinking Schools Online* 19, no. 4 (Summer 2005).

28. Paul Houston, "NCLB: Dreams and Nightmares," *Phi Delta Kappan* (February 2005): 469–471.

29. Rick Weissbourd, "Moral Teachers, Moral Students," *The Best of Educational Leadership 2002–2003* (Alexandria, VA: Association for Supervision and Curriculum Development, 2003), 25–29.

30. The National Coalition for Public Education, Letter to U.S. Senate, February 12, 2003, http://www.ccsso.org/content/pdfs/NCPEtoSenateReVouchers021103.pdf (accessed February 3, 2006).

31. U.S. Department of Education, "Spellings Announces New Special Education Guidelines, Details Workable 'Common Sense' Policy to Help States Implement No Child Left Behind (press release), May 10, 2005.

32. National Center for Education Statistics, "Revenues and Expenditures," *Digest of Education Statistics* (Washington, DC: National Center for Education Statistics, 2003), Table 156.

33. Ibid., "Student Activities and Behavior," Table 146.

34. Gates, "The Gates Foundation and Small Schools."

35. Ibid.

36. "The Small Schools Express," editorial, *Rethinking Schools* 19, no. 4 (Summer 2005).

37. Caroline Hendrie, "Charter Studies Offer Caution on Achievement," *Education Week* (February 6, 2005).

38. Mark Greenberg, Roger Weissberg, Mary O'Brien, Joseph Zins, Linda Fredericks, Hank Resnik, and Maurice Elias, "Enhancing School-Based Prevention and Youth Development through Coordinated Social, Emotional and Academic Learning," *American Psychologist* (June/July 2003): 466.

39. Joy Dryfoos, Jane Quinn, and Carol Barkin, *Community Schools in Action* (New York: Oxford University Press, 2005).

40. Coalition for Community Schools, http://www:Communityschools.org.

41. J. Snipes, F. Doolittle, and C. Herlihy, *Foundations for Success: Case Studies of How Urban School Systems Can Improve Student Achievement* (Washington, DC: MDRC and Council of Great City Schools, September, 2002).

42. Ibid.

43. Dan Rastuccio (math teacher, University Park Campus School), in discussion with the author, April 4, 2005.

44. Greenberg et al., "Enhancing School-Based Prevention."

45. The Collaborative for Academic, Social, and Emotional Learning, http://www.CASEL.org.

46. Information provided by Elizabeth A. McGee, executive director, and Jessica Donner, director of district initiatives, National Service-Learning Partnership, Academy

for Educational Development, http://www.service-learningpartnership.org.

47. The poll was conducted by Roper Starch Worldwide for the W. K. Kellogg Foundation and the Ewing Marion Kaufman Foundation. For a summary, see National Service-Learning Partnership, "Service-Learning Delivers What Americans Want From Schools," http://www.learningindeed.org/Tools/other/sldelvrs.pdf (accessed February 3, 2006).

48. Christopher Chapman and Rebecca Skinner, *Service-Learning and Community Service in K–12 Public Schools* (Washington, DC: National Center for Education Statistics, 1999).

49. Shelley H. Billig, "Research on K–12 School-Based Service-Learning: The Evidence Builds," *Phi Delta Kappan* 81, no. 9 (2000).

50. D. Kirby, *Emerging Answers: Research Findings on Programs to Reduce Teen Pregnancy* (Washington, DC: National Campaign to Prevent Teen Pregnancy, 2001).

51. Information provided by Martin Sleeper (associate director, Facing History and Ourselves).

52. The full course sequence is elaborated in the Facing History and Ourselves resource book by Margo S. Strom, *Holocaust and Human Behavior* (Brookline, MA: Facing History and Ourselves, 1994). Further information is available in Margot Stern Strom, Martin Sleeper, and Mary Johnson, "Facing History and Ourselves: A Synthesis of History and Ethics in Effective History Education" in ed. Andrew Garrod, *Learning for Life: Moral Education Theory and Practice* (Westport, CT: Praeger, 1992).

53. Lynn Hickey Schultz, Dennis J. Barr, and Robert E. Selman, "The Value of a Developmental Approach to Evaluating Character Development Programs: An Outcome Study of Facing History and Ourselves," *Journal of Moral Education* 30, no. 1 (2001), 3–27.

54. Lynn Hickey Schultz and Dennis J. Barr, "An Outcome Study of Facing History and Ourselves in Tennessee" (unpublished manuscript, 2002).

55. Center for Advancement of Ethics and Character, Boston University School of Education, "What is Character Education? Frequently asked questions," 2002, http://www.bu.edu/sed/caec/files/FAQ.htm (accessed February 3, 2006).

56. "One Character Education Program That Works," *Education World* (accessed June 6, 2005).

57. After School Matters, http://wwwafterschoolmatters.org (accessed July 30, 2005).

CHAPTER EIGHT

QUALITY OF LIFE

Adolescence: You thought it was over at 18. Not so fast. For those who study adolescence as a stage of life, treat it as a disease, sell to it as a market, entertain it with songs and shows that make it seem the greatest time of life, it is growing and growing, providing ever new opportunities for grants, fees, jobs and changing how we think about kids.[1]

Quality of life for teenagers is a multifaceted subject. We have covered some of the more traditional parts of teenagers' lives: how they deal with sex, drugs, and violence, what kinds of health and mental health problems they experience, and, most important, what happens in school. But there is more to teen life than that. A number of other factors that influence the growth and development of young people are lumped together here as "quality of life."

One big area might be called "electronic"—computers (Internet and games), TV, and cell phones. Another we might call "cultural"—reading for pleasure, music, movies, and theater. A third area is "relationships"—parents, peers, and others—and a fourth is "work"—teenagers in the labor force. Finally, "attitudes"—views of the world, political expressions, community service, among many other topics.

Of course, a full discussion of quality of life extends beyond the subjects addressed here. It would be interesting to include an analysis of how teenagers are portrayed in film and how they respond to films about teenagers. The same could be said about novels, past and present. The whole subject of the influence of religion on behavior is barely touched upon. These subjects are important, but time and energy limit the dimensions of this discussion.

We have used a number of sources of data for this chapter, but we have also relied on our own experiences both as teenagers and mothers of teenagers. Everyone remembers his or her teen years. Despite my advanced age, I (JD) remember mine in great detail. Maybe it's because I have spent more time thinking and writing about adolescents than most people, but I seem to have total recall about many experiences in my early life. Most of my recollections of my high school years are troubling, and those feelings were exacerbated in 2004 when I spent a lot of time at my old high school with the intention of writing a book about then and now.

What I remember most about high school is the clique. My first 2 years of high school were governed by the mores of the "Fourteen," surely the best-looking, highest-class girls in the school. We wore hand-knit sweaters, Peter Pan collars, pleated skirts, saddle shoes, and bobby socks. Every afternoon we met on a certain piece of sidewalk (our turf) in front of the school and went to the Park Avenue Drug Store, where we drank Cokes, smoked cigarettes, and passed judgment on everyone else. On weekends we had parties in houses where parents seemed to be out. Some kids got drunk and other kids made out; I pretended to be part of it, but I hated beer and no one asked me to make out.

When I was almost 16, I suddenly grew out of that group. I realized how superficial these relationships were and how distant from the real-life world of 1941 and Pearl Harbor. I threw myself into the war effort and got to know a few other outsiders. It was with a great sense of relief that I went to Antioch College in 1943 and met a whole bunch of people who felt the same way about the world as I did and who were looking for new and mind-opening experiences.

Of course, cliques and outsiders are part of today's teenagers' lives—in that sense, little has changed.

ELECTRONIC

The most significant change in the lives of young people since my day derives from the availability of television, computers, and electronic devices such as iPods. Movies have been around for a long time, and they continue to exert an influence over the minds of teenagers. A study of 8- to 13-year-olds in 1999 found that in their own bedrooms, 65% had TV sets, 34% VCRs, 74% tape players, and 64% CD players.[2] That's quite a lot of equipment for very young people.

The Internet as a Learning Tool

Not all teenagers use computers just for fun. A study by the Pew Internet and American Life Project showed that 94% of 12- to 17-year-olds who had Internet access used it for school research, and 78% said they thought it was helpful with their schoolwork.[3] Most of their parents agreed: 55% said that the Internet was a good thing for their children, 6% thought it was bad, and 38% thought it had little effect.

Video Games

Researchers have found plenty of evidence to show a negative association between time spent playing video games and school performance at every school level.[4] Those who use computers for schoolwork perform better in school than those who use computers only for play. In general, playing games can increase aggressive behavior and decrease prosocial behavior. In Gentile, Lynch, Linder, and Walsh's study of 8th and 9th graders, the average amount of time spent on the computer was 9 hours per week, with males spending 13 hours and females 5 hours. Parents were rarely in the picture. Only 13% of the respondents said their parents frequently put limits on the amount of time, and 43% said they were never limited. The amount of violence experienced through video games seemed to predict hostility, including physical fights and arguments with teachers.

Only 6% of these students never played, and 59% reported playing at least once a week. On average, in addition to video games, these young people watched 25 hours of TV and spent 21 hours listening to music and 3 hours reading for pleasure. This all adds up to 58 hours a week, or more than 8 hours a day! When do they play with their friends, go shopping, eat meals, and talk to their parents?

Control of Internet Use

In another poll of 5th–12th graders and their parents, a third of the students said they did not have any rules at home for Internet use, yet 92% of the parents said they do. Obviously there is a disconnection in perceptions about what is going on. One observer said that adults go online to get information and children go online to socialize. Instant messaging is the most popular activity, and it has bred its own form of cyberbullying, in which Internet communication is used to embarrass, humiliate, or harass other kids. Chat room predators are also a danger.

One set of rules that parents can apply to their children, promulgated by an Internet safety organization called cyberangels.org, suggests: no chat rooms, no X-rated sites, no instant messaging with strangers, no personal information to strangers.[5] Parental control software is sold as a method of protecting youngsters from pornography, but it is not sufficient. Parents are urged by CyberPatrol (a marketer of the software) to pay close attention to what their children are doing on the Internet.

Access to Pornography

Most young people have viewed pornographic materials unintentionally while doing homework on the Internet. According to a poll by the Kaiser Family Foundation, 70% of teens ages 15–17 had come across porn—not surprising, since 12% of all websites are porn sites. Controls can be placed on computers to limit access,[6] but it is difficult to keep up with fast-evolving technology, as the discovery in 2005 of hidden pornography in a popular video game showed.

Table 8.1 Percentage of Children Ages 3–17 With Computer Access at Home and Percentage of Those Using Computers at Home, 2003

	Children With Computer Access	Children Using Computers
Total, 15–17 year olds	79	65
By race for all children 3–17		
White non-Hispanic	87	52
Black	54	25
Asian	84	52
Hispanic	55	24
By family income		
Under $15,000	43	17
$75,000 and over	96	63

Source: Child Trends Data Bank, Table 1, http://www.childtrendsdatabank.org/tables/69_Table_1.htm (accessed February 13, 2006).

Computer Availability

In 2003, 79% of teenagers 15–17 had computers at home; 42% actually used them (see Table 8.1). Computer access is much higher among white and Asian families and is significantly related to family income. Only 43% of children from low-income families had access to computers, compared with 96% in high-income families.

Television

It has been estimated that the average child watches 23–28 hours of TV a week and that by age 18, a child will have witnessed 200,000 acts of TV violence, including 40,000 murders. According to the Youth Risk Behavior Survey (YRBS) in 2003, 38% of all high school students watched more than 3 hours of TV every school day, with marked differences by race/ethnicity (29% of white, 46% of black, and 67% of Hispanic students).[7]

One international study of 15-year-olds found that 18% of girls and 27% of boys in the United States watched 4 hours or more of TV each day. But this was a lower rate than in many other countries; for example, well over 40% of Lithuanian, Slovakian, Israeli, and Welsh young people watch TV for 4 hours a day or more.

Cell Phones

In 2005, more than 56% of 13- to 17-year-olds had cell phones, a huge increase from 2000, when only 5% had them.[8] According to *Wired News,* the cell phone has become the primary means of socializing for teens. They reported on a study that found that teenagers saw little difference between meeting face to face and talking on the phone. "A common scene . . . was a group of teenagers sitting together—all with ears glued to cell phones—talking with faraway friends rather than to each other."[9] Teens without cell phones run the risk of being isolated by a kind of "digital divide."

The cost of cell phones is typically underwritten by the family. Parents have been persuaded to support their children's phones because of safety issues; they can always stay in touch. Most schools discourage phone use on school premises, but more than a third of teens use their phones during school hours for messaging or video games. New York State and a few other places ban the use of hand-held cell phones while driving.

CULTURAL

Reading

The more people watch TV and play with computers, the less they read for pleasure. Although teenagers were not included in a study of reading habits, the findings about 18- to 24-year-olds are indicative of a pattern that seems to be emerging.[10] Asked whether they had read any novels, short stories, plays, or poetry during a 12-month period, only 42% said yes—the lowest of all age groups except those over 75. The average for all ages was 47%, less than half.

Not surprisingly, reading was highly related to income and education. The study pointed out that the average child lives with 2.9 TV sets, 1.8 VCRs, 3.1 radios, 2.1 CD players, 1.4 video game players, and 1 computer. (Makes you want to go into the electronics supply business!) With all those other sources of entertainment in a household, it's hard to imagine when anyone finds time to read.

Yet some teenagers do read, both books assigned for classes and books chosen for pleasure. Carol Schoen, a retired professor of English in New York City, looked at the changes in literature for teens.

Many of the works currently assigned in the classroom were originally published for the adult market and, largely because they deal with youthful characters, have drifted into the young adult group. Classics from the past such as *Tom Sawyer* tend to honor family, honesty, honor, even as they provide a place for youthful rebellion and ingenuity. A more modern work in this category, popular with a wide range of schools, is *To Kill a Mockingbird* by Harper Lee. From its first page the story presents a world very much controlled by a sense of family. There is a clear sense of adult control over children's behavior, yet they have sufficient freedom for readers to feel that they are independent actors with sufficient support from each other to constitute a kind of peer group all young people yearn to belong to. At the same time, the world of the school provides the bewildering rules and procedures that jibe with many a teenager's experience. Despite its rather gentle atmosphere, the novel does not shirk from presenting the reality of evil and suggests that there are no immutable rules to make the world more comprehensible.

A substantial group of books appeared after the end of World War II for what was then considered the adult market and became a major source of assigned reading for teenage classrooms. These writings began a serious challenge to the certitudes that underlined the world painted by Mark Twain and Harper Lee. *The Diary of Anne Frank* expanded the horror of racial prejudice to the point where caring parents with all the vestiges of authority could no longer protect their children. *The Catcher in the Rye* by J. D. Salinger added the concept that parents themselves are not always helpful or concerned with their children. *Go Tell It on the Mountain* by James Baldwin presented parental figures who are openly hostile to their child's own wishes, as did *The Bluest Eye* by Toni Morrison and *The Color Purple* by Alice Walker. While these works overtly seem to set forth a consistent pattern of values, intent on condemning intolerance and showing the dangers of discrimination, they begin to bring into question the frailty of adult leadership.

Set against these works are books created after 1967 directly for teenage readers. The major difference was the focus on teenage characters and the treatment of problems that these young people faced. The first item published under this rubric, *The Outsiders* by S. J. Hinton, is still a part of many teachers' reading lists. It explored a world in which teenagers, forced to cope with parental absence or indifference, searched for something that could substitute for the family unit. The novel reflected ideas from such films as *Rebel Without a Cause* and *West Side Story,* but it differed from them in its concentration on a world where economic distinctions had serious social consequences.

In another direction, Judy Blume's *Are You There God? It's Me, Margaret,* published in 1970, treated a problem overlooked in most literature at that time—a young girl's effort to deal with the emotional and physical demands of puberty. Much of what Judy Blume wrote was condemned by parents and teachers who claimed it encouraged girls to experiment with sex, but it is also true that young girls at that time were already involved in sexual activity and many of them were worried and confused. Other books dealt with the problems of divorce, of male sexuality, of dominating parents, of teenage cruelty to one another. While the characters in her novels are generally from white, middle-class families, the books are read by young people from all levels of society.

Many of the works from that time to the present deal with what are perceived as the day-to-day problems young people face. This concern with realism has been countered by an increased attention to fantasy. And rather than avoiding the problems that troubled the characters in realistic fiction, the characters and situations in fantasy literature in fact mirror those presented in fact-based books. They may actually tackle them more piercingly because the air of imagination provides a shield behind which to hide the seriousness with which those issues are considered. For example, the parent surrogates in the Harry Potter series capture, if in an exaggerated form, the sense that adults create stupid rules, make unreasonable demands, have not the slightest clue as to what their children need or want. As subversive of adult authority as any piece of realistic fiction, the Harry Potter series emphasizes the failure of the real world to admit the uniqueness of each and every young person and the importance of the search for a sense of one's own identity.

The works discussed so far have, for the most part, been selected for teenagers by adults. But teenagers make their own choices. The literary merit may sometimes be questioned, but series such as the Gossip Girls or the Princess Diaries, biographies of sport stars, and collections of horror tales make the rounds today in the same way Nancy Drew and the Hardy Boys did ages ago. The Gossip Girls presents a strange amalgam of surface knowledge of the upper-class world of New York private schools and dreamlike exaggerations of the actual facts of that world. The girls in the stories seem to spend most of the time drinking, smoking, minor drug taking, planning to meet with or meeting with boys, and behaving with overt cruelty toward one another. Yet they also have time to do all the things necessary to gain admission to top-level colleges. Parents are generally too busy with their own activities to pay much attention to their children, who are left almost always unsupervised. Parties involve lots of alcohol, hot tubs, and king-size beds, but actual intercourse is rare. Appealing mostly to 10- to 13-year-olds, these tales again bemoan the failure of parenthood and adults in general and focus on the importance of friendship.

In the wildly diverse world of teenage literature, the most obvious pattern seems to me to be that the adult world, once protective even when overly authoritarian, is no longer to be trusted, and therefore home is no longer the safe haven other generations experienced. The only adult figures with any respect seem to be grandparents. Instead of home and parents, the characters in teenage fiction look to friends for leadership and/or comfort. Such reliance may lead to what we see as uncommonly strong peer pressure, but counteracting that is an almost universal agreement that the individual is unique and is responsible for and capable of undertaking responsibility for his or her own actions. Such values should not be underestimated, and this generation should be honored for its dedication to such a high moral tone.[11]

Teen Magazines

I had never heard of *Twist* or *J-14* ("just for teens") magazines, but my granddaughter buys them monthly, along with *Cosmo for Girls* and *Teen People*. The formula for these publications seems to be lots of pictures of young media stars, fashions, makeup, exercises, discussions and advice about boy-girl relationships, all squeezed in between the ads. Occasional articles are on serious subjects, such as "Don't Be Too Thin." One popular feature appears to be "most embarrassing moments" that focuses on gross subjects such as nose snots, farts, peeing in one's pants, and "poo." *Cosmo* asked, "What do boys do when they are alone?" and received answers that also featured farts, biting and eating toenails. *Cosmo* also asked readers "Who's the hottest guy you know?" and then presented pictures of boys with their pants pulled down to just above their private parts—"guys so yummy you'll want a piece of them."

It is interesting that *Faze*, the leading Canadian magazine for teens, is in excellent taste (from an adult point of view) and geared toward teaching about health, education, equality, and prevention. A recent copy addresses world issues, graffiti, and peace, as well as entertainment, beauty, sports, and book reviews.

Music

Observing teenagers around town, it seems to me that all of them are wearing earphones (when they are not talking into their cell phones). What are they listening to? *USA Weekend Magazine* conducted a survey of 60,000 teens' listening habits.[12] Most listened to music while doing chores (79%) or doing homework (72%). One-third did so while eating meals at home, and 18% reported that they listened to music while in class.

They were asked to select the one type of music they would listen to exclusively if so restricted. Hip-hop (27%) and rap (23%) were the main choices, with another 17% for rock/punk. Some 6% selected Christian/gospel, and only 1% selected jazz. They were most influenced in terms of music by the radio (43%) and friends (30%); only 7% were influenced by parents. About a third said their parents forbade them to listen to certain music, but almost half of these listened anyway.

RELATIONSHIPS

The most powerful influences on children are unquestionably their parents. More and more children are being brought up in nontraditional families. A third of all teens live in a single-headed household, usually with their mother. In any case, Mom is in the labor force, and kids often come home to empty houses. Takeout food is the norm.

In an international comparison of 15-year-olds, the United States had the highest proportion living with a single parent (23%) and close to the lowest rate of living with both parents (62%). Israel, Greece, and Poland topped the charts with 80–90% living with both parents. Only Denmark and Greenland had lower levels than the United States.

How parents and their teenage children get along together is a vast subject. Tons of books and articles have been devoted to the subject, as well as TV series, movies, plays, pop songs, Internet chat rooms, counseling groups, and more. Parenting an adolescent ranks high on the list of life's most difficult challenges. Few parents are so skillful or children so perfect that they don't go through periods of anguish and frustration.

I would love to write about my own experience bringing up my son, but I don't think he is eager to have his history in print. I could also write about my observations of my granddaughters' entry into adolescence, but they deserve their privacy as well. I can, however, write about my own teen years (as I have throughout this book) and recognize that bringing up children today is tougher and scarier than when I was young. We could walk to school or downtown at very early ages without fear of molestation. Our families didn't have to monitor our clothes because we were quite conventional. Radio was the entertainment medium of choice, and it was, as far as I know, totally innocent. My family listened to "One Man's Family" once a week and got our thrills from their sophisticated life.

Today there are daily skirmishes over clothes (cleavage, shoulder straps, short skirts, jeans worn around the butt, exposed belly buttons), bodies (tattoos, pierced ears, noses, lips, belly buttons), media (anything is available for everyone), safety (molesters, Internet predators, identity theft), cars (drunk drivers), and violence (especially guns). No wonder today's parents feel so overwhelmed. And on top of all that, frequent high-stakes testing in schools makes children and their parents tense and uncomfortable.

We do know that communication often breaks down. Teenagers have considerable difficulty talking to their mothers and even more difficulty talking to their fathers. Many of the successful programs we have reviewed include some form of parent training, helping them to relate to their children.

The conventional wisdom is that peer influence is dominant. However, young people are not as strongly moved by their peers as we think. In a survey of adults and 12- to 19-year-olds in 2003, the teens were asked who was most influential in their decision making: Parents (42%) won out over peers (31%), religious leaders (7%), teachers and sex educators (6%), media (4%), and other (10%). A majority looked up to their parents as role models, and younger teens, ages 12–14, in particular, were highly influenced by their parents. Parents in the same survey underestimated their potential impact. Only 32% of parents thought they were influential in their teenage children's decision making, and almost half thought their teenagers' friends were most influential. These findings are quite similar to those in previous years.[13]

It's true that teenagers, like adults, tend to "hang out" with like-minded friends, so that heavy drinkers associate with other heavy drinkers, the brainy crowd sits together in the cafeteria, and the cheerleaders are a clique; but such associations can change rapidly. And children who do not relate to their peers often experience behavioral problems as they mature. Parents should encourage their children to develop significant friendships but also help them learn to differentiate between positive and negative influences.

WORK

In the past, teenagers dug coal, stitched boots, planted corn, and picked cotton and then turned the proceeds over to their families. Today many teenagers work, either legally or illegally, at low-skill jobs and use the money to buy clothes, media equipment, and other nonessential items. The U.S. Bureau of Labor Statistics provides annual figures on 16- to 19-year-olds, although we know that many people younger than 16 work (many of them illegally). In 2001, 7.8 million 16- to 19-year-olds (almost half of the 16 million total in that age group) were in the labor force; 6.5 million (about 41% of the total) were employed, and about 1.3 million (8%) were unemployed.

Does working have a positive or negative effect on teenagers? The research is not clear; the answer is "it all depends." Working long hours appears to be related to more school absences, lower achievement, and ultimately dropping out. However, working shorter hours (low-intensity jobs) is not harmful.

The American Youth Policy Forum addressed the issue of helping low-income young people who failed to either gain high school diplomas or find employment, a group estimated at 2.4 million 16- to 24-year-olds:

> Since the 1960's, federal and state governments and philanthropic foundations have supported a variety of programs, ranging from the Job Corps, youth service and conservation corps, a variety of job training programs, and most recently, supported the Workforce Investment Act. Overall, policy makers have paid scant attention to such interventions, know little about their effectiveness, and do not accord this large segment of our population a high priority in public policy discussions.[14]

There are, however, some excellent programs, the most noted of which is YouthBuild, in which unemployed youths work toward their GEDs while learning job skills by building affordable housing for homeless low-income people. Since 1993, YouthBuild has worked with 47,000 youths in 200 programs that have produced 13,000 units of affordable housing. Program participants enter with many problems, including abuse, mental illness, family instability, and early parenting. Few have graduated from high school, and more than a third have been in the juvenile justice system.

Local YouthBuild programs are small, supportive minicommunities, usually operated by independent community-based and faith-based organizations. Dorothy Stoneman, the founder of this program, believes that several factors explain its success.[15] The participants feel empowered by being included in the design, implementation, and outreach. The staff is very caring. The package has many elements, including the resumption of education, skills training, role in the community, wages, counseling, peer support, sense of belonging, linkages and placements with colleges and employers, and continuing support after "graduation." The program costs about $20,000 per person, including the wages paid.

At least three-fourths of the graduates are employed or in school, and few are dependent on welfare. Most are involved in their communities; 70% are registered to vote, and 50% did so.

ATTITUDES

Adolescents and Advertising

At younger and younger ages, kids are being deluged with advertising messages pushing them toward a consumer's eye view of the world. Everywhere they turn, they are exhorted to purchase pricey items that range from techno-chic (iPods, camera-equipped cell phones, personal computers, video games) to just plain chic (jewelry, cashmere sweaters, designer brand jeans).[16]

This advertising campaign must be working. Teenage Research Unlimited reports that the average American teen spent more than $91 per week in 2004, which adds up to a projected figure of $169 billion, a slight decrease from the previous year (it decreased again in 2005). More than one in five teenagers has his or her own credit card or access to a parent's. Credit cards can be used 24 hours a day. About $1.3 billion of teenage spending is done online.

Thirteen-year-old Tracy Quigg has a stereo, TV and VCR in her room. Her parents buy her the latest CDs. . . . And they give her a daily allowance of $10. "If I want something or I need something, I just say, 'Can you take me shopping?' If I go to the mall with my friend, my parents give me money. They don't tell me no, really." Tracy, however, says she's not spoiled. She does not have a cell phone, for instance—unlike many of her friends.[17]

As you can see, teenagers are a marketer's dream and will probably continue to be spendthrifts throughout their lives as long as credit cards are in existence. According to sociologist Robert Manning, "Parents are deferring to corporations on how to shape a child's spending attitudes. . . . [I]t's all about immediate gratification."[18] The proliferation of commercial teen magazines, as well as direct marketing to youth, has stimulated this market mentality.

However, teenage spending patterns may be changing slightly. "Teens entered 2004 with a more value-conscious mindset. Especially in tough economic times, teens can be a little frugal with their personal spending money. . . . Though teens may have finally felt a trickle down from the tough economy, they tend to remain more optimistic than adults because of their lack of fixed expenses."[19] And it appears that looking for bargains may be the new cool, at least for some middle- and upper-class teens.

Escalating prices . . . have made some teenagers budget-conscious. Still others are tightening their purse strings in response to a shift in personal values. . . . Dr. Juliet B. Schor, who teaches a class on consumerism at Boston College, said she has noticed a new frugality in her students' diaries of their buying patterns. For many influential teenage consumers, she said, "it has become socially acceptable, indeed there is even a positive valence to going to shop at discount retailers."[20]

Priorities

What issues are most important to teens? A survey of 7th–12th graders was conducted in 2001 by an organization called Do Something. It revealed their top 10 concerns:[21]

- Drunk driving
- Depression and teen suicide

- Guns at school
- Improving schools/education
- Discrimination
- Violence in school
- Drugs
- Self-esteem
- AIDS
- Abuse at home

It is interesting to note that the children's concerns are markedly similar to the policy issues raised in this book. More than three-fourths of the teen respondents believed that they could create a positive change in their communities, and 64% thought that people their age had good ideas about how to help the community. They favored getting involved with people their own age, volunteering, doing things online, and being part of student-led groups as approaches to action. Those who already participate in community service are much more likely to do well in school than nonparticipants.

In this survey, although half of the teens thought it was important for them to get involved in the political process, only one-fourth believed that elected officials care about teens, and only 5% thought that calling, writing, or visiting an elected official can make a difference. According to Dana Markow at Harris Interactive (the survey organization), "The political disengagement teens feel is in stark contrast to their interest and participation in community service. . . . [T]hey don't see the political process as the way to make necessary changes."[22]

In 2001, a telephone survey of teens was conducted under the auspices of 4-H about attitudes and perceptions concerning community involvement.[23] Teens were asked what was most needed to improve their communities. About 20% said building respect and tolerance for others, followed by mentoring and tutoring children and teens (17%), protecting the environment (17%), and helping an older person or one who is physically or mentally handicapped (14%). Some 63% of the teens felt that the need for discussions with adults about community well-being had increased. Fully 87% were willing to volunteer, but they would be more interested if they saw that their parents and teachers were more involved and talked to them more about the possibilities.

TWO DIFFERENT VIEWS

Surveys are useful for getting a general idea of the lifestyles of young people growing up today, but they are absolutely inadequate for portraying the realities of teenagers' lives. The world in which poor minority children live is very different from that of middle-class suburban children. Here are portraits of two contrasting teenage realities.

An Alternative to Suspension

In 2005 I visited the Counseling and Intervention Center, which serves as an alternative to suspension in the Boston Public Schools.[24] When students violate rules in any of Boston's schools, they may be sent to this center for 1–5 days (elementary students) or 1–2 weeks (middle and high school students). At the Center they receive an array of intensive interventions, including violence prevention, alcohol and drug abuse prevention, general counseling in a group, and academic work. They may also meet individually with a psychologist or police officer. About 30–40 students are there at any given time, including a few elementary school children who have their own classroom and teacher.

My introduction to the school was the "lineup." The students were standing silently waiting to go through the metal detector, manned by a uniformed police officer. They had been picked up by a bus driver from all over the city, beginning at 7:00 A.M.; the school day ends at 12:45 P.M.

I spent a morning in the violence prevention room, which is staffed by Jodee Elgee, a vibrant, sympathetic teacher who has no difficulty maintaining the rigid structure required by the institution. She assigned the students to work on a list of questions that we had prepared together in order to stimulate discussion. Over the morning, we worked with three different groups. All of the students were nonwhite—mostly African American boys, with a few Hispanics and one Asian girl. I will try to summarize what they told me.

What Do You Do for Fun?

Essentially, they sounded like most young people in terms of what they like to do: sports (basketball), skateboard, listen to music, make rap music, go to movies, watch TV, sleep, hang out, "chill with people," "hang with my peoples," go to parties, get smash (sex), smoke, "chill in my 'hood," "get girls and money."

However, one large boy reported, "I don't have fun no more, I gotta take care of my 4-month-old daughter."

Do You Feel Safe at the School You Usually Attend?

Most of these students do not feel safe at school or anywhere else. "School is almost as dangerous as the street." "I am a person who never feels safe at school . . . because I go to a school with metal detectors, meaning that many students are coming around with weapons that may lead to serious injury."

The main problem is guns—"you don't know who has 'em." "It [getting shot] could happen anywhere. Someone could just look at you funny, like tell you get off the sidewalk." "If that happens to me, I ain't movin.'" One student is worried by "people I go drama with."

In one school, the fire alarm has gone off every day in recent months. Whether you feel safe in school depends on what neighborhood you are from. "I don't trust nobody except my circle [gang of 35 boys]."

Teachers are perceived as racists, mean, ignorant, sarcastic. "I went to 11 schools so far and all the teachers have been racist." Some teachers are threatening or on a power trip and take advantage of students. Teachers' attitudes were described as "go drop out. Nobody wanted to do nothing to help you. If you don't do the work, they get paid regardless of how you do, you know what I am saying?" Teachers have low expectations for these students, and the students know that. Teachers are punitive, taking their anger out on kids. "In my school you can't go to the bathroom until the end of the day."

"Police are there but they don't do anything, and there are fights every day. In my school there are no metal detectors and kids carry knives."

Gangs are important. "I feel safe because I have a lot of friends, and if I get into a fight with a lot of people, someone would help." "I don't feel safe because someone could have problems with me or some of my boys and call someone up after school and I won't know that they are coming."

How Could School Be Better?

Teachers who are supportive and not "trying to get into your business"; administrators who are fair; better food; need more art, could make murals; more hands-on activities; more supportive people. School should not be boring.

"Certain schools discriminate or treat other students less fair. Students shouldn't be favored because they are smarter or because they are a certain skin tone. Every student has the right to get the best education possible, and unfair schools or teachers are the ones to affect that."

"Remove all teachers and the crappy principal." "Remove cops from school." School could be better with less work, no MCAS (Massachusetts Comprehensive Assessment System tests), and more sports.

"The teachers would help the students a lot more, not just with schoolwork but with the problems in their personal life."

Let kids go to the bathroom; don't be so strict. Don't bother kids in the hall.

"Have kids on cigarette breaks."

"School could be better if the police would not be on everybody like we are doing bad."

School should look like a community center.

To Whom Do You Go With Problems?

God (side comment: "He ain't gonna help you"). Largely family and friends: mother (many mentions), brother, parents, aunt, grandmother. One boy "don't talk to nobody."

Who Has Hurt You the Most?

"Myself and my parents." "My mother has hurt me: she's trying to put me back in a foster home when I'm doing good now."

Police harassment, especially racial profiling: White cops are suspicious and bother some of these boys. Several students mentioned their fathers in a negative way: "He wasn't around when I needed him."

One boy recounted the experience of losing his best friend, who was shot in the head at the age of 14. "I saw him a half hour before it happened. There was something weird about that day. One dude [from another gang] said that he was gonna shoot him in his head. Two dudes shot him, one got bagged and was bailed out and the other moved to Brockton. After that, I went and got a [gun]. After all, I seen my brother get stabbed and my mother get jumped."

Another student "lost" his cousin, who was shot on the subway train. Another had a cousin murdered in his crib. However, several students said nobody had hurt them.

Why Are You Here?

Of the five students present when I asked this question, the answers were:

> I was carrying a knife for self-defense.
> They said I threatened a teacher and now I have to go to court.
> I assaulted someone.
> I brought a knife to school (everyone does) and someone snitched on me.
> I was carrying a piece of wood and a razor to protect myself.

A film strip on gunshot wounds preceded a discussion with Dr. Goldstein, a pediatrician from Children's Hospital. The images showed very gory outcomes from being shot in the stomach, liver, and near the heart. The first and last slide showed eight medics in an emergency room saving the life of one patient. Jodee emphatically pointed out to the students that they could be one of the medics rather than the person who was shot: "You could be the life saver rather than the victim if you make good choices."

Almost all the students knew someone who had been stabbed or shot, and more than half knew someone who had died. They wanted to know how much blood you could lose before you died. They were fatalistic about their chances to survive: "One person who don't like you has a gun, happens regardless, nothing to protect you." "If you hang with the wrong crowd, fights come to you."

What Will You Be Doing in 10 Years?

Most of the students were planning to go to college. Some were quite specific about career plans: police trooper, pro football (NFL), restaurant owner, lawyer, doctor, plumber, boxer. One said, "I think I would be in the studio making rappers rich from my beats." One expected to be "sipping coffee," another living in a house he had built. The answers ranged widely: "Living in an apartment with a girl and working two jobs." "Have a good family with a wife, doing good." "I will probably own a dancing club or be in the NBA or maybe be something like a cop or detective." "Hopefully in ten years I'll have a job and still be alive."

However, some were pessimistic: "Hopefully not in jail—if you got a police record, you can't do nothing."

Driscoll School

Here is a picture of a very different school, written by Amy Rodgers-Dryfoos:

Over the last 8 years, I guess you could say I haven't just *gone* to the school, I've grown up at this school. I have been educated here and have become an individual as the years have gone by. Now about to enter the eighth grade, I feel like I'll have so much to look back at when I start at the high school.

I'm not saying that everything is perfect, fun and easy 100% of the time, but then again, no *good* school is like that anyways. I've learned that there is a lot of hard work and more to come in 8th–12th grade as well, and then on through life. Homework can get stressful at times and occasionally you feel as if you need summer vacation in December. Some teachers can give you no homework one day and 2 hours of it the next. If you get "lucky," you'll stay up all night long asking yourself if the answer came out $5y + 6c + 4y = 9y + 4y$ or if "lackadaisical" was spelled right on your pretest. This isn't as terrible as it sounds, though; it's good to have work to do. If there was never any homework, it can get boring a lot of the time.

The 7th and 8th graders have rather complex schedules (we would kill for nap time). My schedule this year went as follows:

8:00–8:15	Homeroom
8:15–9:00	English
9:03–9:40	Language (I took Chinese)
9:43–10:20	Monday: PE
	Tuesday: Tech Team
	Wednesday: PE
	Thursday-Friday: English
10:25–11:03	Math
11:05–11:45	Social Studies
11:45–12:30	Lunch/Recess (at this time kids can have conferences with the teachers)
12:33–1:15	Science
1:17–1:59	Monday, Wednesday: Art/Guitar
	Tuesday, Thursday, Friday: Computers
2:00	Dismissal

We also spend a lot of time in the library, Driscoll has a really good book selection and it is a great place to go to study or do homework.

That was just my schedule; everybody has a slightly different one. There are about 36–50 kids in a grade, and two homerooms in each grade. Once a week for the 7th and 8th graders there is an activity period; in the beginning of the year everyone chooses between four activities. The first is Chorus, which performs during school assemblies. There is also Band, which also performs during some assemblies. Tech Team is a computer club that works on operating the computers throughout the school; the tech team also meets during recess. Or you can take Child Development, in which you help out in grades K–3 classrooms. All of these activities are graded in the report cards at the end of the term.

There are four report cards distributed in four terms, and four academic progress reports in the middle of each term. The term report cards have nonacademic subject grades on them, such as the activity period grades, PE grades, and also behavior and attitude numbers. The progress reports have only academic subject grades and attitude and behavior numbers. Of course every teacher has his/her own way of grading things, a B in one class could be the equivalent of an A or C in another class. Parent-teacher conferences also happen throughout the year. My belief is that grades are another part of the growing-up process and becoming an independent person, everyone is responsible for what grades they get and what they do in life.

Another part of Driscoll is the learning center, or like most people call it, SPED (special education). A lot of the black and Hispanic kids in my grade go to the learning center, but there are some white kids who go as well—some are in the METCO program [Metropolitan Council for Educational Opportunity, Inc.]. The learning center is just a place for kids to go if they need to be taught differently, not necessarily slower, just in a different way. All of the kids that go there hang out with us and are treated no differently socially at all. We just think of it as a different class that some of us have to take.

The Driscoll website says that "Brookline was one of the founding METCO communities. The program, funded by the State Department of Education, enables African American, Asian, and Hispanic students from Boston to attend Brookline schools. This urban/suburban collaboration benefits both Brookline and Boston students and their families. A part-time METCO instructional aide provides academic support for both METCO and Brookline children during the school day and after school during Homework Club." I think it's hard for many people to understand that being in either program (METCO or SPED) doesn't make them any different. All of those kids are really just like everyone else and a lot of them are really popular socially.

Outside of school I have a billion things to do. I played soccer for a while, was on the track team, and I played on the girls' basketball team at school and for the town team, though I'll admit I'm not exactly the best player. I also play the trumpet; I take lessons once a week and am in two bands, a jazz band called Blue Infinity, and another jazz band called The Little Big Band, both I enjoy playing in very much. Everyone I know does some kind of after-school activity, whether it's sports, music, singing, dancing, whatever, at school or outside of school, so finding time to have free time does get extremely hard. But the after-school activities are also what makes Driscoll and Brookline such a great community, to have kids doing something they love doing is a great thing for all of Brookline.

It's not to say that we kids don't have any free time. We couldn't live if we didn't have free time, so whenever we have any, TV, instant messaging, music, magazines, friends, cell phones, and Coolidge Corner [local downtown] will do for us. For the 7th and 8th graders, there is a dance every month; they are not usually fun, though. Basically, it's a place where you'll go deaf, sit around, occasionally dance, get mad at the stupid chaperones for not letting you dance as "close" as you want with someone, and eat candy. We all hang around with friends for most of our free time.

Cliques . . . an interesting topic. Everyone in my grade is kind of friends with each other, but there are, well, cliques, you could say. There are the "guys"—basically the boys who all sit together at lunch and all hang out together most of the time. Then there are the "girls"; the girls all sit together at lunch as well, and hang out with each other most of the time. There is also the basketball clique, the guys who play basketball all the time and are obsessed with hip-hop/rap and stuff. Then there's the not-so-social clique; both boys and girls are in this. Basically, they don't really want to hang out with the rest of the bunch, and they're happy with that. I guess you could call them not-as-popular, but that's kind of misjudging them, they are all "popular" to each other I guess. Everyone else is just friends with everyone. The so-called "cliques" aren't very strict. Occasionally there will be dating, but always, *always* there are crushes and boy-girl issues. All in all, the friendships at Driscoll are really strong.

I think, overall, my experience going to Driscoll was excellent. I've learned so much over the years and I'm excited for what comes next. I love the teachers and the friends I have. I've done so much at this school and have had so much fun. The only thing I would change is the cafeteria food, it is *naasssttyyy!!* But bad cafeteria food isn't going to change the fact that DRISCOLL IS THE BEST SCHOOL EVER AND I LOVE IT THERE!

COMMENT

The quality of life for my granddaughter stands in stark contrast to that of the students at the Counseling and Intervention Center. I believe we have a grave responsibility to figure out where young people like those I interviewed fit into our society. All the policies that we have reviewed regarding guns, sexual activity, access to drugs, educational enrichment, and health and mental health services apply most specifically to the problems faced by these adolescents. Identifying ways to deal with their problems and then making sure that successful programs are put into practice can begin to improve the quality of life for many young people.

Middle-class children in suburban schools are protected from guns and knives. Their schools are stimulating and enriching. Their parents can afford to pay for outside activities and to provide large enough allowances to purchase all kinds of media and trendy clothes. These young people don't have babies to take care of. They don't get frisked by the police, and they aren't threatened with annihilation every time they go out of their houses. And the quality of life in a school like Driscoll seems close to ideal.

But many middle-class teens are increasingly being isolated by electronics. They spend long hours in front of the TV and computer, or talking on their cell phones, or piping music into their ears . . . some do all these things simultaneously. This creates huge walls between them and the adult world and separates them from significant adults, as well as their peers. It is essential that young people learn how to relate to others and especially to have open lines of communication with their parents and/or other significant adults.

The contemporary scene, the quality of life in the twenty-first century, does not seem to encompass effective communication—there are neither the opportunities nor the time for talking and reflecting. My friends with teenage children often ask my advice, assuming that since I write books about adolescents, I can help them deal with their kids. I have to admit that I possess no special expertise. All I can really come up with is "keep talking with your kids and listening to them." Don't be rigid, but establish standards and maintain them. Continuity and consistency are important. I know that all this is easier said than done. Eventually they do grow up, and if you are lucky as I was, they turn into responsible adults.

NOTES

1. Laura Stepp, "Adolescence: Not Just for Kids," *Washington Post,* January 2, 2002.

2. V. Rideout, U. Foehr, D. Roberts, and M. Brodie, *Kids and Media, The New Millennium: A Comparative National Analysis of Children's Media Use* (Menlo Park, CA: Kaiser Family Foundation, 1999).

3. A. Lenhart, M. Madden, and P. Hitlin, "Teens and Technology," Pew Internet and American Life Project, Reports, http://www.pewinternet.org/pdf/r/162/report_display. asp (accessed February 12, 2006).

4. Douglas Gentile, Paul Lynch, Jennifer Linder, and David Walsh, "The Effects of Violent Video Game Habits on Adolescent Hostility, Aggressive Behaviors, and School Performance," *Journal of Adolescence* 27 (2004): 5–22.

5. Barbara Meltz, "Cyberbullying Is a Problem That Parents Could Be Missing," *Boston Globe,* November 18, 2004): H4.

6. Bella English, "The Secret Life of Boys," *Boston Globe,* May 12, 2005.

7. Centers for Disease Control and Prevention, *Morbidity and Mortality Weekly Report* 53, no. SS-2, May 21, 2004.

8. Elisa Batista, "She's Gotta Have It: Cell Phone," *Wired News,* May 16, 2003, http://www.wired.com/news/culture/0,1284,588611,00.html (accessed August 2, 2005).

9. Ibid.

10. Reading at Risk, "Survey of Literacy Reading in America," www: nea.gov/ pub/readingatrisk.pdf (accessed January 26, 2005).

11. Carol Schoen, "Literature for Teenagers," unpublished manuscript, 2005.

12. "Tunes & 'Tudes: Full Survey Results," *USA Weekend Magazine,* May 5, 2002, http://www.USAweekend.com/02_issues/020505/020505teenmusicresults.html.

13. The National Campaign to Prevent Teen Pregnancy, *America's Adults and Teens Sound Off About Teenage Pregnancy,* Annual Survey Report (Washington, DC: National Campaign to Prevent Teen Pregnancy, 2003).

14. American Youth Policy Forum, "Why Do Some Programs for Out-of-School Youth Succeed?" http://www.aypf.org/publications/PreparingYouthforEmployment.pdf (accessed April 14, 2005).

15. *YouthBuild Facts* (Somerville, MA: YouthBuild USA, January 2005).

16. Don Aucoin, "All-Consuming Adolescence," *Boston Globe,* December 15, 2004).

17. Cindy Rodriguez, "Teens with Wads of Cash Flex Spending Muscle," *Boston Globe,* February 20, 2002.

18. Ibid.

19. ASD/AMD Merchandise Group, "TRU Projects Teens Will Spend $169 Billion in 2004,"http://www.teenresearch.com (accessed March 26, 2005).

20. Ruth Laferla, "Teenagers Shop for Art of the Deal," *New York Times,* September 22, 2005.

21. Harris Interactive News Room, "Study Shows Teens' Top Causes, Readiness to Get Involved and Make a Difference," http://www.harrisinteractive.com/news/allnews bydate.asp?newsID=353 (accessed May 22, 2005).

22. Ibid.

23. National 4-H Council, *Public Opinion Survey on Community Service and Dialogue Between Youth and Adults,* 4-H Centennial Report (Washington, DC: National 4-H Council, 2001).

24. Visit and interviews conducted at Counseling and Intervention Center, Boston Public Schools, May 19, 2005.

CHAPTER NINE

SUMMING IT UP

ADOLESCENTS IN THE TWENTY-FIRST CENTURY

What's it like growing up in the twenty-first century? Young people live in very different circumstances because of their families' social and economic status, their race, and their luck. They live in circumstances that in some ways are very

215

different from those of my own adolescence and in some ways are much the same. The differing circumstances reflect the historical period, as well as changing mores and technology.

I "came of age" during the Second World War, a time of national unity behind a common cause. In 1944, Franklin D. Roosevelt was the first president I campaigned for, although I was not old enough to vote for him (you had to be 21). My tender teen years, 13–17, had been spent in an academically superior suburban public high school, going to advanced classes and following a classical curriculum. For the first 2 years, I hung out with *the* female clique and after that made my own way. Because I was fat (chubby) and different (Jewish), no one from the male in-group asked me out, so I suffered from rejection by the (quite dopey) boys I pined for. My high-risk behaviors were smoking and, when I got my driver's license, taking off with the family car and using purloined coupons for rationed gas to get to the beach. My parents were so involved with the war effort and the family business that they assumed I was perfect. Their main advice was to "act responsibly," and they were unaware of any risky behavior on my part. I made the great escape to Antioch College before I finished high school (you could do that during the war), where I came into my own, found my equals, and grew up.

I visited that high school recently. It was no longer academically superior.[1] Of course, a lot can happen in 62 years! The community had changed from white to black between 1960 and 1980, and by 2004, about 75% of the high school students were black and 25% Hispanic. Performance levels were poor, morale was low, academic offerings were at a marginal level, many on the staff had low expectations for the students, and the students knew that they were being cheated out of a quality education—it was a different school in every way. Uniformed guards manned the doors, examined all entrants, and monitored the halls and cafeteria. It was like being in a prison. I believe that this school typifies failing schools all over the country.

But schools don't have to be that way. Young people who are fortunate enough to live in communities that give high priority to education can have wonderful experiences in school. As we have seen, Driscoll School in Brookline, Massachusetts, which my granddaughters attend, is an example of excellence in public schools, and there are many others all over the United States.

Quantifying Risk Groups

We have looked at a wide array of behaviors among teenagers—some, like binge drinking, that have serious negative consequences, and others, such as exploring the Internet for new information and ideas, that may enhance the quality of their lives. The picture is quite mixed, somewhat confusing, and very challenging, with many factors that relate to social class, race, location, and motivation. This society clearly has a lot of work to do in the twenty-first century.

To begin that work, we need to figure out which teenagers are at risk of negative consequences and require immediate and specialized attention. Then we need to consider what policy initiatives and what program interventions are necessary to ensure that all the 33 million 10- to 17-year-olds in the United States experience a high-quality life and the opportunity to grow into responsible adults.

We start here by summarizing the antecedents of high-risk behaviors and then take a look at the overlap, or co-occurrence, in these behaviors (see Table 9.1). Antecedents are the behaviors that occurred earlier in the young person's life or in the situation of their family. They are not to be construed as causes but rather as statistically related events or predictors. The chart of antecedents is derived from a number of sources that are referenced in Chapters 3–7, such as the Youth Risk Behavior Survey and the National Longitudinal Survey of Adolescent Health (Add Health). The findings are remarkably consistent across studies and over time.

Several antecedents appear to be the most frequently mentioned:

- Early use of drugs or alcohol
- Alienation, out of the mainstream
- High-risk friends
- Poverty
- Lack of support, lack of attachment to adult
- Low achievement
- Learning disabilities

You can almost see the young person who has these characteristics: an alienated and disadvantaged adolescent caught in a downward spiral that leads to failure. It would be useful to be able to quantify the number of young people

Table 9.1 Summary of Antecedents of High-Risk Behaviors

Antecedents	Drug/ Alcohol	Sex/ Pregnancy	Violence	School Failure	Health/Mental Health Problems
Individual					
Use of drugs/alcohol		X	X	X	X
Gender male			X		
Black/Hispanic		X		X	X
Low expectations for future		X		X	
Depression	X				X
Hyperactivity			X		X
Alienation/out of mainstream	X		X		X
History of sexual abuse/child abuse		X	X		
Aggressive as young child	X		X		
Low birthweight				X	X
Lead poisoning				X	X
Hunger and nutrition				X	X
Poor early development				X	X
Peer					
High-risk friends or siblings	X	X	X		
Low religious involvement	X	X			
Involvement with gangs	X		X	X	
Rejected by peers			X		X

Family

Risk Factor					
Poverty/low socioeconomic status		X	X	X	
Low parent education		X		X	
History of substance abuse/alcohol use	X				
Parent criminality	X		X	X	
Lack of support, discipline, monitoring, supervision	X		X	X	X
Authoritarian			X		
Poor communication with parents, detached	X	X		X	
Single-parent family		X		X	X
School					
Learning disabilities		X	X	X	X
Left back			X	X	
Low commitment			X	X	
Low educational achievement	X		X	X	
Truant			X	X	
Attending school with high delinquency rates			X	X	
Quality of school			X	X	
Community					
Disorganization; gangs, poor housing, drugs			X	X	
Transiency			X		X
Lack of economic opportunity			X		
Exposure to violence and racial prejudice		X	X		X

219

like that who are in need of specific kinds of attention. Chapters 3–7 summarized data from an array of studies and reports. If the age groups covered had been the same in each study, the task would be simpler; one would merely multiply the percentage of the population at risk times the number of 10- to 17-year-olds (33 million). This was not always the case, so adjustments had to be made, primarily to use as a population base those ages 13–17 (20 million) that roughly correspond with those in 9th–12th grades. (If ages 14–18 had been used, the total still would be about 20 million.)

Table 9.2 shows the results of this exercise. We know that about 5% of 10- to 17-year-olds were arrested, which is about 1.6 million youths. From the YRBS, 17% of high school students (ages 13–17) carried a weapon, equaling 3.4 million. The age groups covered are included on the table.

These are not separate population groups, because many of the behaviors overlap. The person arrested for breaking and entering (probably a boy) may also carry a weapon, smoke, binge drink, have unprotected sex, fall behind in school, and feel sad or hopeless. Another person (probably a girl) may be 1 year behind in school, have had an unwanted pregnancy, and have suicidal thoughts.

Overlap

The overlap in high-risk behaviors is measured by the number of different behaviors reported by each individual who responds to a survey. According to Anthony Biglan and his colleagues, "The tendency for problem behaviors to co-occur is one of the most common findings in studies of adolescent development, but the extent to which it occurs is not appreciated sufficiently and the deleterious consequences of patterns of multiple problem behaviors have not been adequately documented."[2] Their book cites many examples of the co-occurrence of risky behaviors, showing that young people who are involved in multiple problem areas have more serious levels of each problem and that these findings hold true across diverse racial and ethnic groups. In an analysis of the 1999 National Household Survey of Drug Abuse among 12- to 20-year-olds, the highest-risk individuals with two or more problem behaviors made up less than 20% of the youth population, but they accounted for 70% of those with health problems associated with alcohol, 87% of those with health problems associated with drug use, 72% of total arrests, and 88% of arrests associated with violence.

Table 9.2 Summary of Percentages and Numbers of Youths in High-Risk Categories

Behavior (age group)	Percent	Number (millions)*
Arrested (10–17)	5	1.6
Carry a weapon (13–17)	17	3.4
Heavy substance abusers (13–17)		
Cigarettes	3	0.6
Alcohol	28	5.6
Marijuana	3	0.6
Hard drugs	5	1.3
Light substance users (13–17)		
Occasional smoke	19	3.8
Occasional drink	17	3.4
Occasional marijuana	19	3.8
Engaging in sexual intercourse (13–17)		
With condoms	21	4.2
Unprotected	13	2.6
Pregnant (15–19)	4	0.8
One year behind modal grade (10–17)	24	4.8
Two years behind modal grade (10–17)	4	0.8
Dropouts (16–17)	10	0.8
Suicidal thoughts (13–17)	17	3.4
Feeling sad or hopeless (13–17)	29	5.8

*Total 10- to 17-year-olds = 33 million
 Total 13- to 17-year-olds = 20 million

In 1998, the Centers for Disease Control conducted a survey of students in 1,390 alternative high schools, with a sample of 8,918.[3] Although this was some time ago, it is a unique study of high-risk adolescents. Demographically, about 43% were white, 21% African American, 25% Hispanic, and 11% other. During 30 days preceding the survey, 52% had ridden with drivers who had been drinking, 33% had carried weapons, 65% had drunk alcohol, and 53% had used marijuana. During the preceding year, 16% had attempted suicide, 88% had had sexual intercourse, and 54% had not used a condom at last intercourse. These are much higher percentages than among the larger sample of all high school students.

In another attempt to get at the co-occurrence of problem behaviors, Lindberg, Boggess, and Williams looked at 10 high-risk behaviors to determine the overlap.[4] This study, based on the 1995 Add Health survey and the 1995 National Survey of Adolescent Males, included measures of smoking, alcohol, marijuana, other illicit drugs, fighting and weapon carrying, suicide attempts, and unprotected intercourse. Although these data are more than a decade old, the analysis is important because it confirms the earlier findings, in the 1991 edition of this book (*Adolescents at Risk*), that some teens do it all and others don't do any of it. The most common behavior was fighting. Use of illicit drugs other than marijuana was the least common.

Table 9.3 shows that engaging in multiple high-risk behaviors is not typical of teenagers. Some 46% of students in grades 7–12 did not participate in any of the most prevalent risk behaviors. About one-fourth engaged in one behavior; another fourth, two to four; and a very small percent (4%), five or more.

Differences by race/ethnicity were not striking. As would be expected, high-risk behavior increases with grade level and is more prevalent among boys than girls.

Among students who are engaged in one risk behavior, just over half also engage in a second. Among students who smoke, 85% engage in another risk behavior. According to Lindberg et al., "The co-occurrence of health risk behaviors is rarely so strong that two specific behaviors always occur together."[5] When prevalences were combined, in only a few cases did the co-occurrence exceed 50%; for example, 52% of binge drinkers also report fighting, and 53% also report marijuana use. Although only 5% of youths were users of hard drugs, 76% of those users also used marijuana.

This study also looked at positive behaviors and found that almost all students engaged in at least one. The majority of students were religiously involved (72%) and involved with their families (76%), and more than half had good grades (54%) and/or were in school sports (56%). Those with the highest number of positive behaviors were younger, female, and non-Hispanic.

A unique study of American and Chinese 7th–9th graders by Richard Jessor revealed distributions of the number of problem behaviors that are very similar to the Lindberg data.[6] The five behaviors among the Americans included

Table 9.3 Number of Health Risk Behaviors Among Students in 7th–12th Grade, by Grade, Gender, and Race/Ethnicity (by percentage)

	Risk behaviors engaged in by individuals					
	0	1	2–4	5+	Total	2+
Total	46	26	24	4	100	28
7–8 grade	53	27	17	2	100	19
9–10 grade	44	25	25	5	100	30
11–12 grade	40	25	30	6	100	36
Male	39	29	26	5	99	31
Female	52	22	22	4	100	26
Non-Hispanic White	47	24	23	5	99	28
Non-Hispanic Black	39	32	26	3	100	29
Hispanic	45	27	24	4	100	28

Laura D. Lindberg, Scott Boggess, and Sean Williams, "Multiple Threats: The Co-Occurrence of Teen Health Risk Behaviors," June 1, 2000, Table 2, http://www.urban.org/url.cfm?ID=410248

drinking, smoking, marijuana use, sexual intercourse, and delinquency (see Table 9.4).

A little less than half of the American cohort reported no problem behaviors; almost 25% reported one, 20% reported two to three, and 10% reported four or more. In this survey, students were asked what kind of grades they received, and their answers were significantly related to problem behavior. Among those who got A's, 57% reported no problem behaviors, compared with 27% of those with C's and D's. Among those with A's, 6% reported four to five problem behaviors, compared with 20% of those with C's and D's.

The Chinese students were asked about only three behaviors (smoking, drinking, and minor delinquency). They showed similar patterns, although almost two-thirds reported no problem behaviors, and about 10% reported two to three. Their behavior patterns were also significantly related to their academic achievement. Among the top students, 59% of the males and 79% of the females reported no problem behaviors, whereas among the lowest level students, about 40% of both males and females reported no problem behaviors.

Based on the research, how many adolescents have multiple problem behaviors? How many young people fall into the various risk categories: no risk,

Table 9.4 Percentage of 7th Graders With Problem Behaviors

Number of Problem Behaviors	Males	Females
0	47	48
1	23	24
2–3	21	19
4–5	10	9

Source: Special tabulations from Richard Jessor, University of Colorado

low risk, moderate risk, and high risk? To determine this, a simulated estimate was produced. This is a process in which the numbers are forced into a cell based on knowledge of interrelationships, assumptions, and intuition. Here we started with the Lindberg analysis (Table 9.3) and modified it by the Jessor and other data. My estimate would be that about half are at no risk, 20% are at low risk, 20% are at moderate risk, and 10% are at high risk. Applying these rates to the total youth population of 33 million yields rough estimates for 10- to 17-year-olds in 2005 of about 16.5 million at no risk, 6.6 million at low risk, 6.6 million at moderate risk, and 3.3 million at high risk.

Description of Risk Groups

Most of these high-risk behaviors were practiced by a relatively small number of adolescents. One in 10 young people between the ages of 10 and 18 did it all, and another 20% did most of these things: They drank and used pot, they "acted out" and got into trouble in school and with the police; they had early unprotected intercourse that often led to premarital parenthood, and they were behind in school and had low grades. Thus, 30%, or close to 10 million young people in the United States, exhibited what social psychologists call "multiproblem" behavior. They were at exceptionally high risk of not maturing into responsible adults, and they and their families needed intensive and continuous help if they were ever going to "make it."

Another 20% of young people (6.6 million) engaged in high-risk behaviors some of the time. The majority of young people drank (often mirroring what they saw at home), and the majority had premarital sexual intercourse before they left their teen years. These children were less at risk, but they still needed to know the facts about the consequences of their behaviors and to acquire the social skills to deal with the demands of modern life.

Just about half of all young people, more than 16 million, were doing reasonably well. They were on what I call the "achievement train." In fact, from the time those children were born, their parents did everything possible to ensure their success. The children may have experimented a bit and got into trouble once in a while, but someone was always there to support them.

Reviewing the chart of antecedents confirms the embeddedness of these problems that confront young people. It is difficult to imagine changing the course of their lives without starting early, addressing psychological issues, working with parents, changing the school experience, dealing with racism, and improving the economic and social opportunity structure.

Changes Since 1986

Table 9.5 shows the distribution of young people by estimated risk status in 1986 and 2005. Because the population was greater in 2005, so are some of the estimates: More 10- to 17-year-olds are at high risk and more are at low risk.

The estimated number of very high-risk young people has increased by half a million, from 2.8 to 3.3, and the number at high risk has increased by 2.5 million, from 4.2 to 6.6. This suggests that almost 10 million adolescents need immediate and intensive attention from highly qualified teachers, social workers, youth workers, parents, and anyone else who will take an interest in them. The good news is that the number of low-risk youths has also grown by 2.5 million, and they are probably functioning well enough so that they do not require additional social intervention.

Many of the indicators of high-risk behaviors have gone down during the two decades between 1986 and 2005. We have seen reductions in smoking and other substance use, in alcohol use except for binge drinking, in violent behavior and gang activities, and in crime rates. One major problem area is school-related: More young people are falling behind, scoring poorly, and eventually dropping out. Another problem area is mental health, which is not unrelated to educational problems. Young people are more likely to report feeling depressed and stressed out. These numbers should give us some insight into our society.

Focusing on what happens in schools, the outcomes are very different for

Table 9.5 Estimates of the Number and Percent of 10- to 17-Year-Olds Who Fell Into Four Behavioral Risk Groups, 1986 and 2005

Risk Group	Numbers (millions)		Percent of Total	
	1986	2005	1986	2005
Total	28.0	33.0	100	100
Very high risk (do it all)	2.8	3.3	10	10
High risk (do most of it)	4.2	6.6	15	20
Moderate risk (experiment)	7.0	6.6	25	20
Low risk (not in trouble now)	14.0	16.5	50	50

middle-class white children than for poor minority children. Every measure points toward a growing gap between social classes, in writing and math achievement, grade retention, absenteeism, and discipline.

WHAT DO WE KNOW ABOUT PROGRAMS?

We have identified a number of programs and approaches that appear to be effective in preventing high-risk behaviors and/or ameliorating the problems that arise from them. But, having conducted a similar review previously in *Adolescents at Risk,* I have to admit that not much has changed in two decades. Even some of the programs that were around in the 1980s are still operating at full speed. One difference is that categorical programs, those aimed at a single behavior such as drug abuse, are less prevalent than they were, and there seem to be many more comprehensive programs that address multiple issues and encompass multiple components, such as combining social and emotional learning, community service, and academic enrichment.

Here are some observations about effective programs:

- Some of the most effective programs are the most complex. They combine several components, require highly trained personnel, and extend over a long period of time.

- The message is clear and reinforced frequently (no matter what the focus of the intervention), and the information provided is accurate.
- The young people in the program establish relationships with one or more adults, ranging from volunteer mentors to skilled therapists.
- Attention is given to involving adults, often through outreach directly to the participant's family.
- Effective programs are intense and often costly.
- The programs have been designed and implemented by well-informed "gurus"—practitioners and professors who build their interventions on theories of change.
- Modeling and practice of communication, negotiation, and refusal skills are offered.
- Programs are age-appropriate and sensitive to cultural differences.
- Some of the most positive evaluations are conducted by the same "gurus," so they are studying their own programs.
- Training is an important issue. Many of the programs require extensive orientation and supervision. They are built around curricula that must be taught by people with a deep understanding of the work.
- Schools are the sites for some of the most successful programs, but some efforts may flourish in community-based agencies, away from what teenagers may perceive as the hostile atmosphere of the school.
- Evaluation remains a problem for many youth development programs because of high turnover, sporadic attendance, and the difficulty of finding control groups.

The National Youth Employment Coalition's Promising and Effective Practices Network (PEPNet) has identified almost 100 effective youth development programs.[7] They found common themes among interventions that mirror our own conclusions: individual attention, intense collaboration, use of mentors and advocates, continuity and follow-up, and youth leadership .

Table 9.6 summarizes the components found in the programs highlighted in this book. Case management, social skills training, and parent involvement are the most frequently mentioned components of these successful interventions.

The evaluation outcomes shown in Table 9.7 follow the category of the in-

Table 9.6 Program Components

Program: Sex, violence, drugs	Case Management, Individual Therapy	Social Skills Training, Communication	Parent Component	Comprehensive Services	Specific Information	Service Learning, Community Service	Job Training	Academic Enrichment, School Climate
Teen Outreach Program		X			X	X		
Carrera Teen Pregnancy Prevention Program		X		X	X	X	X	X
Seattle Social Development Project		X	X					
Safer Choices		X	X		X			
Adolescent Sibling Pregnancy Prevention Program	X	X		X	X		X	
Incredible Years Training Series	X							
Functional Family Therapy	X		X					
Project ACHIEVE		X	X					X
Olweus Bullying Program	X	X	X					
Operation Eiger	X		X	X			X	
Dare to Be You			X					
Guiding Good Choices		X	X					
Life Skills Training		X						
Keepin' It R.E.A.L.		X						
CASASTART	X			X				

Table 9.7 Evaluation Outcomes From Selected Programs

Program	Less Sex	Fewer Pregnancies	Increased Use of Contraception	Higher Academic Achievement	Lower Dropout Rate	Less High-Risk Behavior	Improved Mental Health	Less Aggressive Behavior	Improved Social Competence	Lower Recidivism Rate
Teen Outreach		X		X	X					
Carrera Teen Pregnancy Prevention	X	X	X						X	
Seattle Social Development Project	X	X	X	X		X				
Safer Choices			X							
Adolescent Sibling Pregnancy Prevention Program	X	X								
Incredible Years Training Series						X	X		X	
Functional Family Therapy										X
Project ACHIEVE								X		
Olweus Bullying Program								X		
Operation Eiger										X
Dare to Be You						X				
Guiding Good Choices						X				
Life Skills Training						X				
Keepin It R.E.A.L.						X				
CASASTART						X				

tervention approaches. It is not surprising that the five teen pregnancy prevention programs all have outcomes that relate to that goal, that violence prevention programs prevent violence (aggressive behavior, recidivism for juvenile delinquents), and that the substance abuse programs have an impact on substance abuse.

Greenberg and colleagues reviewed meta-analyses of school-based prevention programming that targets positive youth development, mental health, drug use, antisocial behavior, and academic performance.[8] The various researchers had, in aggregate, looked at more than 900 studies, from which they extracted those with quality evaluations. In summarizing the work, they found three key strategies across domains:

- Teaching children to apply social-emotional learning skills and ethical values in daily life through interactive classroom instruction and by providing frequent opportunities for student self-direction, participation, and community service.
- Fostering respectful, supportive relationships among students, school staff, and parents.
- Supporting and rewarding positive social, health, and academic behavior through systematic school-family-community approaches (such as restructuring schools).

They found that short-term interventions were not as effective as multiyear, multicomponent programs. Finally, they recommended that prevention programs start as early as preschool, before the risk behavior "sets in."

WHAT DO WE KNOW ABOUT POLICIES?

We don't really have a "youth policy" in the United States. We have a profusion of policies that govern our very fragmented systems.

Some of the policy issues discussed in this book include:

- The need for support for broader sex education (beyond abstinence)
- Expansion of the family planning program

- Protection of the right to abortion without parental consent when necessary
- Gun control
- Restoring community police
- Keeping juveniles out of adult jails
- Decriminalizing marijuana
- Enforcing age restrictions on sale of alcohol and cigarettes
- Enforcing laws regarding drunk driving, seat belts, and cell phone use while driving
- Discouraging advertising of alcohol
- Encouraging media to clean up their act
- Expanding health insurance
- Opening primary health care clinics in schools
- Training physicians and other medical personnel about psychosocial issues among adolescents
- Supporting the training of qualified teachers
- Supporting full-service community schools
- Dividing large schools into smaller units
- Ensuring smaller class size
- Exposing young people to social and emotional learning, character education, and service learning
- Stamping out commercialization and getting kids to stop spending so much money

Current attempts to create a national youth policy are of interest here. In 2003, a White House Task Force for Disadvantaged Youth reported that about 10 million teens were at serious risk of not becoming responsible adults and that programs to address their problems spread across 12 federal departments with little communication or coordination among them. Based on these conclusions, the Federal Youth Coordination Act of 2005 was introduced with strong support from the National Collaboration for Youth, a coalition of 50 national human service organizations.[9] This act calls for establishing a Federal Youth Development Council as a forum of federal agencies and their partners in nonprofit agencies and faith-based communities; an annual assessment of the well-being of youth; recommendations for coordination; holding agencies accountable for implementing the recommendations; and encouraging states and localities to do the same. In 2005, the U.S. House of Representatives passed the act with a huge majority: 353 to 6. As of February 2006, no action had been taken in the Senate.[10]

COMMENT

One could question whether the quality of life is really of a high standard for adolescents growing up today in the United States. As we have addressed each issue (sex, drugs, violence, health, education), we have seen that the situation is complex. In each case, some young people are in terrible trouble and pain, while at the same time, some young people manage their lives with great ease and maturity. Some but not all of the differences in the quality of life and behavioral outcomes relate to socioeconomic status. Clearly, children from disadvantaged families living in crime-ridden neighborhoods have a hard time overcoming the odds. Children living in upper-class communities, mostly in the suburbs, are very privileged, with the best schools and the most available parents who drive them around to enrichment experiences that add to their educational prowess.

It is very important to recognize that some young people make it despite the odds against them. The term "resilient" has become popular in the psychological literature to describe these people. They have a kind of inner strength that helps them get through the hard times. Usually, when they grow up and write their autobiographies, they give credit to an adult, either in the family or the community, who stuck with them and supported them in times of need.

We have estimated that as many as 10 million teenagers are at risk of not growing into responsible adults unless they receive various kinds of help, depending on what their problems are. The good news is that we have a pretty good fix on "what works." We know what to do. Assuming that a high-quality intervention such as the Carrera Teen Pregnancy Prevention program were to be made available for these young people at a cost of about $5,000 per case, the bill would be approximately $50 billion a year. That sounds like a lot until you consider that in 2005 the war in Iraq had already cost a total of $204 billion and that the total military and defense budget for fiscal year 2006 is $511 billion.

The big question is what life will be like for adolescents in the future, given the patterns and situations we have reviewed here. In the final two chapters, we present two scenarios. The first is a pessimistic view of what is likely to happen if some of the current negative trends continue. The second scenario is our optimistic view of what could happen if better decisions were made about policies and programs.

NOTES

1. Joy Dryfoos, "A Tale of One City—White Flight and a Failing School System," *Education Week,* March 30, 2005.

2. Anthony Biglan, Patricia Brennan, Sharon Foster, and Harold Holder, *Helping Adolescents at Risk: Prevention of Multiple Problem Behaviors* (New York: Guilford Press, 2004), 21.

3. Centers for Disease Control and Prevention, "Youth Risk Behavior Surveillance, National Alternative High School Youth Risk Behavior Survey, United States, 1998," http://www.cdc.gov/mmwrhtml/ss480721.html (accessed February 4, 2006).

4. L. D. Lindberg, S. Boggess, and S. Williams, "Multiple Threats: The Co-Occurrence of Teen Health Risk Behaviors" (Washington, DC: Urban Institute, 2000), http://www.urban.org/urlprint.cfm?IC=7290 (accessed February 4, 2006).

5. Ibid., 7.

6. Richard Jessor, "Descriptive Findings From Analysis of Wave 1 (2000) Data: The Project on Adolescent Risk Behavior and Development in China and the U.S." (unpublished manuscript, University of Colorado, 2005). Tables made available to author.

7. National Youth Employment Coalition, "PEPNet, Promising Programs," http://www.nyec.modernsignal.net/page.cfm?pageID=21 (accessed September 19, 2005).

8. Mark Greenberg, Roger Weissberg, Mary O'Brien, Joseph Zins, Linda Fredericks, Hank Resnik, and Maurice Elias, "Enhanced School-Based Prevention and Youth Development Through Coordinated Social, Emotional and Academic Learning," *American Psychologist* (June/July 2003), 466.

9. National Collaboration for Youth, "National Collaboration for Youth Hails the Introduction of Bipartisan Legislation to Better Serve At-Risk Youth" (press release, February 16, 2005), http://www.nassembly.org.

10. H.R. 856, Federal Youth Coordination Act, 109th Congress, http://www.govtrack.us/Congress/bill.xpd?bill=h109-856 (accessed February 4, 2006).

CHAPTER TEN

WORST-CASE SCENARIO FOR THE FUTURE

We have tried to portray what life is like for teenagers at the beginning of the twenty-first century. Now we turn to questions about the future. What will life be like in America in 2025 for young people, given some of the current trends? We have created two scenarios; the first is pessimistic, the second optimistic.

In the worst-case scenario, things look pretty bad. Teenagers in the future may be deprived of life options, not because of their own high-risk behaviors but because they live in a high-risk society that does not value them as individuals and offers little in the way of support.

CHANGING DEMOGRAPHICS:
MORE SEGREGATION

It is projected that by 2025, close to 45% of all teens in the United States will be black or Hispanic. And in most urban communities, that figure will be close to 90%, with few whites and a growing number of Asians. In 2005, the Hispanic teenage population was growing very rapidly, while the white population was actually decreasing.

As the country is becoming more diverse, it is also becoming more segregated. Schools in cities are more segregated than ever. Desegregation as public policy is over and done with. Few white children remain with whom "minority" children can integrate. So within a few years, young people of different races and nationalities may be even more isolated from one another than they are now.

Immigration will begin to be regulated more strictly, even though illegal immigrants perform many jobs in agriculture and industry that citizens are unwilling to perform. In 2005, various state referenda were being promulgated to prevent these immigrants from receiving any kind of welfare, health care, or driver's licenses. Young people in these families will feel society's rejection and may respond in violent or antisocial ways, through organized gangs.

INCREASING POVERTY

It sounds obvious, but children in poor families have always had a harder time than children in rich families. Social class remains the most significant factor in shaping life courses. About 15% of all teenagers live in families that are below the poverty line now, and that percentage is likely to increase, given the growing income gap. The prices of housing, gas, consumer goods, food, education, and even cultural events are all spiraling upward, with little evidence of any downward trends. More and more families are falling behind. Middle-class families have difficulty paying their bills—many are deeply in debt and have huge credit card bills—and the Bush administration has made it very hard to go into bankruptcy.

At the same time, many middle-class and higher-income people continue to believe that if poor people would only work harder, they would no longer be poor. Of course, in order to earn a substantial living, one needs at least a college degree and, increasingly, an advanced degree, which are out of many poor families' financial reach. This negative attitude toward poor families will further isolate disadvantaged children.

Eligibility for welfare and other forms of assistance is tightening. Fewer families can get financial aid, Medicaid, and food stamps. Children are increasingly coming to school hungry. In addition, the American economy was shaky as the twenty-first century began. The national deficit had mounted to a new high–more than $650 billion, almost 6% of the total economy.

WEALTH INEQUALITY

> Race has always been a basis on which U.S. society metes out access to wealth and power. Both in times when the overall wealth gap has grown and in times when a rising tide has managed to lift both rich and poor boaters, a pernicious wealth gap between whites and nonwhite minorities has persisted.[1]

The median family income in 2002 was about $29,000 for black families and $46,000 for white families. In 2001, when the net worth in the United States was $42 trillion,

- the top 1% of households had 33% of the wealth;
- the next 4% had 25% of the wealth;
- the next 5% had 12% of the wealth;
- the next 40% had 27% of the wealth; and
- the bottom 50% had 3% of the wealth.

SEGREGATED HOUSING

The rising cost of housing will continue to keep low-income families in inadequate homes. Only the most successful families can afford the huge price of a

nice home in the suburbs; meanwhile, funds for subsidizing affordable housing are decreasing. Poor children live in decaying urban or rural areas, with little hope of moving to suburban communities.

The rapid development of exclusive senior citizen enclaves, with guarded
entrances, sends a strong message to young people: We don't care about you;
we have our swimming pools and golf courses and each other. In some communities, the older population outnumbers the young people and actively
works to keep school and recreation budgets low.

LESS ACCESS TO HEALTH CARE

Medicaid and state child health insurance plans are also being threatened with
cutbacks. It will become harder to enroll, and the reimbursement rates for doctors will be reduced below their already minimal levels. Thus, fewer doctors
will participate in such programs in the future. Poor children will increasingly
use emergency rooms as their source of care, resulting in fragmented treatment, long waits, and inadequate care.

WIDENING ACHIEVEMENT GAP

Testing has taken over education. Black and Hispanic children score lower than
white and Asian children on just about every test, and the trend is toward a
widening gap. This growing difference in test scores reinforces the low expectations of minority youths by the education establishment, and the low expectations contribute to poor performance, neatly completing this vicious cycle.
The stigma attached to the lowest echelons of ability groupings makes it even
harder for minority children to succeed.

Because of the budget crunch and the focus on testing, schools are elimi-
nating arts, sports, gym, and other "extras" in order to concentrate on literacy
skills and math. They are also having to let go of school nurses and guidance
counselors, who provide the only health and mental health monitoring many
children get. Library services are being cut back, and many schools report a
shortage of books and other materials.

DETERIORATING PUBLIC EDUCATION
SYSTEM

"No Child Left Behind," the Bush administration's major thrust to address the achievement gap and equity concerns, has placed enormous pressure on schools to raise test scores. Schools that fail to meet the standards are stigmatized, and it is predicted that thousands may close. Children from those schools will receive vouchers that can be redeemed at religious and private schools, as well as other public ones.

The concept of "choice" has been used as a rationale for beginning to dismantle the public school system. Charter schools, offered as an alternative, allow private groups to set up independent schools to compete with those that are run by school systems. Charters siphon off students from the public system, as well as the dollars that follow them.

By 2025, it is possible that we will see an even more fragmented school system in the United States.

LACK OF EARLY CHILDHOOD EDUCATION

Poor and minority children are much less likely to come to school ready to learn. Although we have known for a long time that early and sustained intervention can make a huge difference in later life, access to quality day care continues to be inequitable. Despite efforts to tack universal pre-K classes onto the K–12 school system, it has not happened. Rich people still send their youngsters to private day care while both parents are in the labor force, and poor people still rely on family baby sitters or just stay home. Head Start has made a big difference, but the most recent federal budget limits its growth.

DECLINING QUALITY OF LIFE

Media have taken over the lives of our children. Many young people watch television 4–6 hours a day, while others spend an equal amount of time on the Internet. The quality of TV programming continues to deteriorate, and viewers are exposed to a steady stream of high-risk behaviors: smoking, drinking, violence, straight sex, "queer" sex, marital disputes, and major stupidity.

Teenagers already spend billions on stuff marketed on TV and on the Internet, in movie theatres, and in teen magazines.

Fewer and fewer U.S. citizens vote. Children will grow up without role models who participate in community activities or elections.

HARSHER SENTENCING OF JUVENILE OFFENDERS

A trend toward punitiveness is reflected in the sentencing practices for juvenile offenders. Tough-on-crime laws have made it easier to try juvenile offenders as adults, resulting in thousands of young people being sent to prison for nonviolent crimes. Such incarceration practices increase the likelihood that juveniles will commit more serious crimes when released. In adult prisons, juveniles are deprived of adequate counseling, drug treatment, and education. "Three strikes and you're out" policies have led to long prison sentences for drug addicts, a poor substitute for prevention and treatment.

ENVIRONMENTAL CHAOS

Lack of action in regard to significant environmental issues could result in an increasingly poisoned atmosphere in the future. American children may suffer from the impacts of pollution, global warming, deforestation, and excessive drilling.

PRIVATIZATION OF GOVERNMENT RESPONSIBILITIES

If current trends continue, the United States will have to deal with major financial adjustments over time. The Social Security battle was begun with a strong push to privatize the system by allowing people to invest in the stock market instead of saving the monthly social security deduction until retirement.

No one seems to know what to do about health care. Every other Western country has found a way to ensure access to medical care and prescriptions for all, but there is strong resistance to the concept in the United States, despite evidence that shows it would save money and result in more equitable medical care for all.

INCREASING SUPPORT FOR FAITH-BASED ORGANIZATIONS

The government gave more than $1.17 billion to faith-based groups in 2003; this is about 12% of the $14.5 billion spent on social programs in five federal departments. The White House expects this total to grow. Civil libertarians worry that the government money will be used to pay for worship rather than social services. The administration says a group may sponsor worship and other religious activities as long as they are separated by time and location from activities paid for by the government. About half of the 2003 total went to Head Start and to the Housing and Urban Development Section 202 that builds housing for low-income people. But the door is now open for federal funds to go to religious organizations.

INCREASING LIMITS ON SEXUAL BEHAVIOR

Federal funding has been shifted from comprehensive sex education programs to those that promote only abstinence. Young people are being told that condoms are not effective and that, in any case, they should not have sex until marriage. This is unrealistic in light of the rising age of marriage, the ubiquity of sexually stimulating media, and the lusts and desires of nubile young people. Some young people will remain abstinent, but the majority will have sex without adequate contraception, and many will experience unwanted pregnancies.

The same people who are promoting abstinence are working hard to limit access to abortion. New regulations are being introduced to require waiting periods, parental consent, and other measures that will make it more difficult for young women to end a pregnancy. In addition, the continuing hostility toward homosexual relationships at all levels of government makes it difficult for young people to envision a safe and comfortable future if they decide to come out.

It has been reported that a number of very young teen females are involved in performing oral sex, often with older males ("hooking up"). Aside from the inequity of the situation, the girls are at risk of exposure to sexually transmitted diseases unless condoms are used (rarely the case).

TIGHTENING DRUG LAWS

Although an increasing number of people believe that marijuana should be legalized, especially for those who are in pain, thousands of young people are incarcerated every year for using or selling it. Once in jail, they are exposed to hardened criminals as role models.

The use of hard drugs such as heroin and cocaine appears to be on the wane, but use of over-the-counter and prescription stimulants as well as "designer drugs" such as Ecstasy is increasing.

ERODING CIVIL LIBERTIES

The latest trend is to remove information about biological evolution from textbooks and allow teachers to teach "creationism." Some recent cases that protested the display of the Ten Commandments in public buildings have been lost. The judiciary system is increasingly dominated by very conservative and often fundamentalist religious judges.

The recent passage of the Patriot Act, aimed at enhancing antiterrorism activities, allows for more government surveillance. Library and bookstore records can be obtained by government investigators, threatening the civil liberties of American citizens.

LIVING WITH TERRORISM

The threat of terrorist acts is real. There is little agreement about how to diminish that threat, yet it would be foolhardy to deny or ignore it. In the beginning of the nuclear age, kids were taught to "duck and cover"—to dive under their desks in the event of an explosion. I can't imagine how children in the future can be helped to deal with suicide bombers and other kinds of terrorist acts.

A DIVIDED SOCIETY

Every poll seems to give evidence of the great differences between Americans' views of their society. The country is split between those who feel that we as a nation are on the right track and those who fear that we are not. This division in opinions is true for most of the issues mentioned here: civil liberties, abortion, drug sentencing, legalization of marijuana, the environment, welfare, social security, and certainly war and peace. This bifurcation does not bode well for the future. It definitely is not good for children to live in a society that is so ambivalent about the major issues of the times. It is not good for anyone to live in a society in which he or she feels powerless.

Not a very pretty scene. Does it have to be like that?

NOTE

1. Meizhu Lui, "Doubly Divided: The Racial Wealth Gap," http://www.ilcaonline. org/modules.php?op=modload&name=News&file=article&sid=1729 (accessed September 16, 2005).

CHAPTER ELEVEN

POSITIVE SCENARIO FOR THE FUTURE

In the previous chapter, we presented a pessimistic view of the future for young people in the twenty-first century and asked the question: Does it have to be like that? I maintain that it does not!

ENHANCING THE LIVES OF CHILDREN

If I had the power to implement a plan to enhance the lives of adolescents and to make sure they grow up into responsible adults, what would I do? First of all, I would recognize that interventions have to start long before children are teenagers. So many problems could be avoided if we really embraced the concept of beginning at the beginning.

Parent Involvement

When babies are born, or even before, their parents should be in contact with an agency that will help them to parent. They may need assistance in many aspects of their lives (housing, employment, immigration, health); without it, they may find it difficult to focus on child rearing. Home visits by family guidance workers (or whatever they may be called) help ensure that families can be drawn into a web of support. Parent training classes would be held for families with infants to teach them how to rear babies and, eventually, how to help their children get ready for school. Books and toys would be available for enrichment activities. A major campaign would be conducted to make sure every child is read to at an early age—if not by a parent, then by someone else. A very strong case can be made for some form of universal parenting education. Few parents are completely comfortable with their child-care responsibilities, particularly when they feel stressed by the pressures of their jobs. For parents of teenagers, some kind of support is very helpful in dealing with the many kinds of high-risk behaviors we have reviewed on these pages. The bottom line seems to be "communication": Parents have to be taught how to talk to their children from infancy until they leave home (and even thereafter). In fact, an increasing number of high school graduates continue to live at home and college graduates return home, so twenty-first-century parenting seems to go on forever!

Child Record

In order to organize the necessary interventions, every child's record should be entered into a computerized tracking system and updated at least annually. The record should include basic health information, school reports, work and community service history, and family status. This record keeping could be operated by a local nonprofit "Council on Children" or a public system set up by the city or state government. Although this sounds a little like "big brother," having up-to-date data is essential for planning services and making sure they are delivered. A child's record would also be useful for establishing accountability and implementing evaluation.

Preschool

The value of preschool is undisputed. Strong research shows unequivocally that children who attend quality preschools perform better in the upper grades. The impact of early intervention is significant; the earlier the better. Every child should be ensured a place in a preschool. Preschools should be attached to elementary schools to ease the transition into kindergarten and higher grades.

Mentoring

One of my mantras is "every child must be attached to a responsible adult—if not a parent, then someone else." The need for close and consistent mentoring can change over time, but particularly in the early teen years, when communication with parents may be difficult, that someone else can play a significant role. Such a someone else can be a teacher, relative, friend, friend's parent, volunteer mentor, or youth worker, preferably with some knowledge of youth development.

Quality Schools

Quality schools, of course, are central to any positive plan for the future. Without them, not much is going to change. And we don't have to start from square one. We know how to improve the achievement levels of high-risk children. The record is replete with examples of successful schools in disadvantaged communities. Many are magnets or alternative schools; most are small and well equipped. Highly qualified and committed teachers with high expectations are essential. Effective schools offer imaginative and challenging curricula, as well as art, dance, music, physical education, recreation, links to work, and community service.

This is labor-intensive work, but we know how to do it. Young people must believe that they can "make it." And the people who touch their lives—parents, teachers, youth workers—have to believe that the children can "make it." It's clear that schools cannot do this work alone. It will require collaboration with community agencies, businesses, parents, civic leaders, and other stakeholders to build strong new institutions. Money isn't the only answer, but you can't change failing education systems without the injection of resources to pay for such essentials as teachers, buildings, mentors, support services, and after-school programs. Current efforts in some states are directed toward equalizing funding, compensating for the differences in educational expenditures per child in inner cities versus suburban communities.

Extended Hours for Schools

I believe schools in disadvantaged areas should be open for extended hours. (Suburban schools already stay open for after-school programs, sports, and community education.) Attendance should be mandatory from 8 A.M. to 6 P.M., allowing time for what is now considered "after-school programming" (sports, arts, fun), as well as for traditional academic programming. Scheduling could be open and flexible so that sports might be offered in the morning and math in the afternoon, whatever is the best "learning" time for each activity. Prevention programs (sex, drugs, violence, suicide) could be integrated into the curriculum so that they would be more effective and timely. A comprehensive approach to social and emotional learning should be incorporated into the curriculum.

Extended hours require extended staff. Responsibility for coverage of the 10-hour days could be shared through partnerships between schools and community agencies. I strongly support the concept of "full-service community schools," school buildings that become community hubs, that are open all the time, and that integrate what goes on in the classroom with what goes on in out-of-school time.

More Access to Health and Mental Health Care

We have proposed the wide-scale development of full-service community schools. If all the schools in the nation that serve needy children and their families could be transformed into community hubs with on-site comprehensive services, a number of the problems cited here could be addressed simulta-neously. Placing primary health clinics in schools would ensure access to diag-nosis, treatment, and routine health care. The array of services offered would depend on what is needed in each particular school and community. Typically, in low-income areas, asthma, obesity, dental care, headaches, and colds are at the top of the medical list. The most significant need is for mental health ser-vices because of very high rates of depression and anxiety.

Children at high risk of psychological and emotional problems, and those with chronic diseases, can be identified at very early ages. As mentioned earlier, children should be evaluated and tested routinely, from birth, to make sure that they are functioning normally. This information should be fed into a system of care to ensure that those with problems are treated as early as possible and continue to be monitored as long as necessary. The availability of twenty-first-century computerized systems makes this recommendation feasible.

Promoting Healthy and Safe Sexual Behavior

Despite all the efforts to prevent teen pregnancies and sexually transmitted diseases by promoting abstinence until marriage, some teenagers continue to "do it." Although intercourse rates are going down, oral sex is increasing. It is hard to imagine what form of sexual expression will emerge in the future. But we can be sure of one thing: Teen sex is not going to disappear. Thus it is im-portant that preteens and teenagers be well informed about sexual issues, in-cluding how to protect themselves from negative consequences. They do need to be taught how to "just say no," but they also need to understand how to use condoms and how to access family planning clinics. It is also important to pro-tect the right to abortion without parental consent when necessary.

Treating Juvenile Offenders

We need to rethink the juvenile justice system. Early intervention with aggres-sive children could have a significant impact on later behavior problems. Re-quiring community service and treatment rather than incarceration for minor offenses, particularly for drug abuse, would be sound social policy.

Viable Drug Laws

The time has come to differentiate between dangerous drugs and marijuana. Sending young people to prison because of marijuana arrests is counterproductive, because the prison experience is rarely positive.

Better Quality of Life

How do you wean millions of young people away from TV, the Internet, iPods, video games, and whatever other isolating and largely passive entertainment consumes most of their waking hours? A strong system of alternative activities can be implemented. After-school programs can play a major role in filling up those hours between 2 P.M. and 6 P.M. Sports programs are always attractive to young people. Arts and cultural enrichment can be offered in imaginative and stimulating ways.

Community service is one of the most useful approaches for young people—useful to the recipients (senior citizens, nursery school students, etc.) and useful to the young people who supply the services. They can learn about other people's lives, about the community, and about what the community needs in order to thrive.

Personnel

Trained personnel of many disciplines will be required in order to successfully implement a plan that focuses on family involvement, quality education, adequate health and mental health services, and whatever else is needed. Teachers, administrators, youth workers, and medical personnel all have to be aware of the complexity and requirements of healthy youth development. They have to enter their professions with respect for all children and high expectations that those children will succeed.

IMPROVING THE QUALITY OF LIFE FOR ALL

You cannot separate the welfare of children from the welfare of the society as a whole. Children don't make war and they don't decide social policy, but their lives are deeply affected by adult decisions, and they surely suffer from the consequences. We do not expect youth workers to solve the problems of income distribution, but their work is profoundly affected by the inequities of our economic system.

Changing Demographics: Less Segregation

Segregation and racial discrimination grow out of a value system. In societies in which everyone is respected regardless of race or class, integration can occur. Young people usually inherit those values from their families. They may also be exposed to ethical principles through religious, educational, or community experiences. Concerned educators and psychologists have begun producing curricula that address "character education." I have learned to value the concept of "intentionality." To me, this means working to shape a future society with certain dimensions rather than just letting things happen. Thus, to live in equity, meaning that all children and families have access to the same opportunities, the society would have to specifically embrace and work toward this ideal. The social structures would have to be designed to further this cause:

- Children would be born wanted and cared for. Early intervention would identify problems and treat them.
- Schools would be child-centered and effective.
- Housing would be adequate for families' needs.
- Neighborhoods would be made up of all kinds of families, of different economic classes, races, and ethnic backgrounds.
- Communities would be rich in arts and culture, with high value placed on participation.
- Streets would be safe.

Gary Orfield, director of the Civil Rights Project at Harvard University, addressed the question "What will it take for Boston to become less segregated?" His response is applicable to any city:

Minority families prefer integrated areas, and the vast majority of new jobs and strong schools are outside the segregated ghettos and barrios, so integration is vitally important. We need serious fair-housing enforcement and real sanctions, since research shows violations are common and the fear of minority families is deep. We also need integration of the staffs of suburban realtors, counseling for minority families, fairness in mortgage lending, and a welcoming of newcomers into suburban communities and white families back into the city.[1]

Desegregated and Affordable Housing

Programs that encourage more integrated housing patterns can be launched. They must be intentional. In a county with a central city, subsidized affordable housing can be created in the suburban ring for poor minorities

Decreasing Poverty and Increasing Wealth Equality

It is not within our area of competence to make predictions about the economic system and what it might look like in 2025. At best, measures would be passed to equalize the distribution of income. This can be accomplished through tax policies that result in taxing the rich rather than the poor. One simple mechanism for increasing wealth at the bottom is to increase the minimum wage.

The society has to embrace a value system in which there is greater equity in income distribution. This will take new leadership with the courage to publicly support these ideas.

FINAL WORDS

How can we help adolescents grow into responsible adults? I believe the key is attachment. It has been said so often that it seems trite now, but I have never forgotten Urie Bronfenbrenner's important but simple statement, "Someone has to be crazy about the child." I don't know when this was first discovered—probably at the beginning of time. I am more convinced than ever that (1) every child has to be nurtured by an adult, and (2) if a society set that idea up as a goal, it would be attainable.

This book is replete with descriptions of programs of all kinds, and they are only a small segment of what's out there. At one time it was estimated that at least 17,000 youth agencies were operating in the United States. Currently more than 2 million social service workers, including youth workers, work with children and families, and more than 6 million teachers and administrators are employed in K-12 education. So we start with a huge number of people who could act as special persons for the millions of children who need that individual attention (we know that many children are already well looked after by their parents). In addition are countless national advocacy and research organizations, many of which have been referenced in this book, such as Advocates for Youth, Campaign to Prevent Adolescent Pregnancy, Coalition for Community Schools, Forum for Youth Investment, Public Education Network, and Search Institute. These groups and hundreds of other organizations stand ready to join in the struggle to make a better life for America's children and youth.

The future of teenagers in the twenty-first century is deeply imbedded in the future of our nation and the world. The quality of life for everyone is dependent on many factors, but the one that seems to surface most strongly from this analysis is the "value system." The American people must decide that they want a higher standard of social structures and of quality of life. I don't mean more "things," but I do mean more intentional caring about equity.

We need to pull ourselves together, if not for our own welfare, then for the good of our children. We cannot be relaxed about what our kids are being exposed to. Everywhere they turn, they are being seduced by "entertainment" machines, things to listen to or to stare at, and "come ons" to buy the latest fashions and emulate unstable rock stars.

The majority of the country must be convinced that the social landscape can change, that it would be better for our children to live in a country that was more equitable, caring, and democratic (small "d") and less punitive.

It will take a mighty force of action to get America back on the track of ensuring that every young person has access to the means of obtaining an excellent education. It will take enormous energy to make sure that every child is fed, housed, and nurtured. But these are not impossible tasks or pipe dreams. Schools cannot do it alone, but schools that accept help from the outside can serve as a major locus for these actions. Youth workers cannot do it alone, but they can play a major role in meeting this giant challenge, especially if they are recognized as important and paid accordingly. Parents cannot do it alone, but they will do whatever is necessary, if they receive the kind of support and direction they need to do their jobs as guardians of their children.

I suppose the greatest gift we could bestow on future generations is to ensure a peaceful world. Young people would not have to grow up with the threat of war and terrorism.

This book will come out shortly after my 80th birthday. I don't expect to make it to 2025 to find out what life is like for adolescents at that time. I hope that the material and ideas contained here will inspire thought and action. We do know what to do, and we know why we have to do it. Children deserve a better future.

NOTE

1. Gary Orfield, "What Will It Take for Boston to Become Less Segregated?" *Boston Globe Magazine*, April 17, 2005.

INDEX